The Body Electric

JONATHAN BENTHALL

The Body Electric
Patterns of Western Industrial
Culture

THAMES AND HUDSON · LONDON

To Bibi Winkelhorn

Printed in Great Britain by
Latimer Trend & Company Ltd Plymouth

Contents

Preface   6

1   Introductory   7

2   The Romance of Technology – with a note on the City   21

3   The Recoil to the Body   67
The Recoil to the Body in Literature
The Recoil to the Body: Away from the Word

4   Towards a Theory of Technology   140
The Evidence of Marx
The Evidence of Rousseau
The Evidence of Mauss

5   Towards a Human Technology – and a Human City   162

Notes on the text   206

Bibliography   214

Index   222

Preface

I wish to thank the following for the benefit of stimulus or criticism, without wishing to implicate them in any of the book's shortcomings: George Banu, Alan Beattie, Jean-Marie Benoist, David Dickson, Vilém Flusser, John O'Neill, Ted Polhemus, Alan Sheridan, Caroline Tisdall, Paul Willis, and especially my publishers. Like many other writers, I have been greatly helped by the resources of the London Library.

TEXT ACKNOWLEDGMENTS: Max Horkheimer and Theodor W. Adorno: *Dialectic of Enlightenment*, translated by John Cumming (Allen Lane, 1973), pp. 231, 232, 232–3, 233–4; translation copyright (C) 1972 by Herder & Herder Inc. Original (C) 1969 S. Fischer Verlag GmbH, Frankfurt am Main. Reprinted by permission of the publishers, The Seabury Press, New York, and Penguin Books Ltd, London.

'The Dawn', 'The Spur', eight lines from 'Leda and the Swan', and four lines from 'A Prayer for Old Age', from *The Collected Poems of W. B. Yeats*. By permission of M. B. Yeats, Miss Anne Yeats and Macmillan of London and Basingstoke.

Twelve lines from 'Masters', from *A Case of Samples* by Kingsley Amis. By permission of Victor Gollancz Ltd.

Saul Bellow: extracts from *The Adventures of Augie March*. By permission of Saul Bellow and A. M. Heath & Co. Ltd.

ILLUSTRATION ACKNOWLEDGMENTS: IPC Ltd and British Newspaper Library, 1–4; Derby Museums and Art Gallery: 5; Galleria Civica d'Arte Moderna, Milan: 15; International Museum of Photography at George Eastman House, Rochester: 22, 23, 24; Louvre, Paris: 17, 18; Collection of Mr and Mrs Paul Mellon: 6; Musée Rodin, Paris: 19; Museum of English Rural Life, University of Reading: 9; National Gallery, London: 7; National Gallery of Art, Washington, gift of Mrs Huttleston Rogers: 8; Philadelphia Museum of Art, Louise and Walter Arensberg Collection: 20; Tate Gallery, London: 16; Victoria and Albert Museum, London: 25

PHOTOGRAPHIC CREDITS: Photographie Giraudon: 17, 18; Douglas H. Jeffery: 27; Hans Namuth, New York: 21; Edwin Smith: 10; Eileen Tweedy: 1, 2, 3, 4; United States Information Service, London: 26; John Webb: 19

Chapter One

Introductory

Thousands of British boys of my generation – and no doubt many girls – must have been entranced by the first issue of the *Eagle* comic which appeared on 14 April 1950, when I was eight. With its superior full-colour printing, it raised itself well above the underground press of *Beano* and *Radio Fun* without belonging to the official culture. The contents included: PC49 (a policeman); Cortez, Conqueror of Mexico; Jeff Arnold in 'Riders of the Range'; Harris Tweed, Extra Special Investigator; Tommy Walls the Wonder Boy (advertising Walls ice cream); and the Great Adventurer (St Paul). But the show was stolen by Dan Dare, who occupied the first two pages. Later I learnt that the *Eagle* was a conscious attempt by its publishers, and an editor in holy orders, to promote a morally serious children's comic. The parson subsequently became managing editor of two commercial magazines, *She* and *Cosmopolitan*. We were being manipulated when we thought ourselves most free – a dilemma to which I shall return later in the book. Yet the glamour of those early issues was real enough to children used to the austerities of the post-war period; the *Eagle*'s pages seemed to carry the smell of the future. The first Dan Dare adventure ended in late 1951 and was succeeded at once by a sequel; but by then the artist, Frank Hampson, and his writing team seemed to me to have lost their touch. When I checked on this recently in the British Museum Newspaper Library, my earlier critical judgment was confirmed.

The *Eagle* appeared every week and the artist made sure that the suspense was kept up, running several branches of his complicated narrative in parallel. We were switched from a world cabinet meeting on Earth, to an underground river on Venus, and then to a spacecraft between the two planets. Most issues of the comic ended with an intriguing enigma that was resolved in the next. In summarizing the bare bones of the narrative and abstracting from it the moral that the artist succeeded in conveying, we can also tease out its *unexamined assumptions*, which are just as interesting and which point to a major dilemma that faces any 'humanist' view of technology.

It is the 1990s and there is world government. Doctors 'have nearly every disease taped' and poverty is conquered – but food supplies are running out. Everyone is tired of synthetic vitamin tablets and there are food riots in China. The scientists want to send an expedition to Venus to grow crops there, 'compress' them and bring them back to Earth; they guess that the climate of Venus, unlike that of the moon and Mars which have already been explored, will make agriculture possible. The chief characters are members of the international space fleet, whose two leaders – Sir Hubert Guest, controller, and Dan Dare, chief pilot – are reassuringly British. Comic relief is supplied by Dare's batman, Digby, a native of Wigan in Lancashire, and by Pierre (French) and Hank (American). Professor Peabody is a brilliant woman scientist who joins the expedition, and whose cool behaviour in a crisis eventually wins over the misogynist Sir Hubert.

The trip to Venus involves some problems with defensive shields round the planet which have destroyed previous spacecraft by blocking their 'impulse waves'. Eventually the party arrives scattered in pairs over the planet – rather as in the shipwreck in Shakespeare's *The Tempest* – and the social structure of the planet is gradually revealed. The natural ecology is spectacular: dragons, treacly water, rocks, quicksands, a domesticated boar with spiked tusks (called a 'zom' and used as a bloodhound), trees with green wood. The intelligent beings fall into three races, two in the Northern Hemisphere and one in the Southern. The Northern Hemisphere is inhabited by the Treens and the Atlantines.

The Treens are green humanoids wearing a kind of copper-wire suiting and are slightly reminiscent of the Ancient Egyptians. Their main interest is scientific research; Dare explains to Sir Hubert that they are 'Boffins run wild, sir – and quite inhuman – they seem to have no emotions at all'. When Sondar, a Treen who defects to the Earthmen, shows fear, he says that the Treens will want to analyse him to trace the fault. (Later, the Treens show total panic in an emergency and they learn that they were mistaken to repress their emotions.)

The Lord of the Treens – one of the great mythic figures of our age – is the Mekon, who has a huge green brain and tiny atrophied body. He has been specially reared with injections from childhood – no doubt similar to the *encéphale isolé* preparation used by some experimenters in animal psychology – and travels on a throne hovering in the air. At one point Dare puts the throne out of action with a special gadget and carries the Mekon off under one arm; but the Mekon escapes.

The Treens use as serfs a race called the Atlantines, who were brought back from the Earth after a spaceship survey 15,000 years before. They are divided into three castes – soldiers, priests and peasants – surviving from their earthly culture. They have turned blue, a change in pigmentation due to a difference in the sun's rays. They have also grown a lump on their foreheads, providing them with extra tear-ducts and a time-adjuster to cope with the Venusian day, which is twenty times longer than on Earth. The Atlantines have a myth that Kargaz, the only one of them who successfully defied the Treens, will return to liberate them. Kargaz will be identified by the fact that he has no lump on his forehead (the Atlantines believe that their race, with the exception of Kargaz, have always possessed this lump). Dare in due course has his skin turned artificially blue in order to pass as an Atlantine serf, and is equipped with a false lump and a wig containing a device permitting him to speak their language. When the false lump and the wig fall off in a skirmish, he is taken for Kargaz and eventually leads the Atlantines to liberation, thus reasserting a spirit that has been crushed for many generations by the Treen yoke.

The Southern Hemisphere is separated from the north by a flame-belt. It is inhabited by the Therons, ruled over by a benevolent president, Kalon. The Therons are like beautiful human beings, with long hair. Aeons ago, their science was more advanced than the Earth's, and in the north was a 'barbarous, brutal and reptilian' culture. The Therons once tried to explore the north and though attached by giant reptiles, they were successful. Their reward for teaching science to the Treens, however, was a Treen rebellion.

The Therons had once explored the Earth too, but for 'friendship' not for slaves. Now they lead a 'balanced life', devoted to the arts, especially music and poetry, and the beauties of nature. They wear exquisite clothes. 'Machines here work for us', says the president; 'we are not their slaves. They leave us free to care for things that matter.' The Therons have fully automated their cities, so they do not have to live in them. They have had no contact with the Treens for centuries, thanks to the flame-belt; but the visit of the Earthmen accidentally precipitates a war.

Eventually, by a stroke of narrative brilliance, the machines of both sides are incapacitated by jamming each other. Meanwhile, the Treens land on Earth and attempt to deceive the Earth government into co-operation, but they are foiled by means of a private message passed by Digby to his Aunt Anastasia in Wigan. Dare persuades the Earth government to help the Therons – for two reasons: first, moral obligation, and second, Earth needs food from Venus. Dare now delivers a memorable soliloquy:

It is true that the Treens have gone ahead of us scientifically but on the way they've lost a lot of qualities we value. Our illogical human love of things for their own sake, and not their practical value – the impulse that makes a man sail a yacht in a world of diesel engines, or ride a horse in a world of motor-cars – the love of silent, soaring flight that makes a pilot fly a glider when he could have a jet; our 'waste of time' – indulging in sports for the sheer fun of it – these are our trump cards now!

So the Earth sends cowboys, archers, Canadian Mounties and London horse-guards to Venus; and the Treens are quickly defeated, though the Mekon escapes to rear his ugly head in a sequel. Instead of colonizing Venus the Earthmen request the Treens' collaboration in supplying Earth with food, since Venus is luxuriant and not fully exploited agriculturally. The Treens agree to supply Earth with all the food they can. The narrative ends with an exhortation by Dare on the importance of disarmament.

Looking back after almost a quarter of a century it is easy to criticize the *Eagle*'s ethnocentricity – a kind of happy scenario for the new British Commonwealth that was just coming into being after the partition of India – and its naive, if humorous, glorification of 'officer qualities'. For instance, the Atlantine revolt is led by their blue sergeant-major, who has huge moustaches and a stentorian voice; when he ends his life heroically, Dan Dare thinks, 'Thanks, Handlebars, old timer – your planet won't forget'; and Sir Hubert describes him as 'a very gallant gentleman'.

I see much to admire and nothing to sneer at here. The real trouble is that the Treens and the Mekon are more vivid than anything else in the story. Like Milton's Satan in *Paradise Lost*, the Mekon becomes the true hero. At least, this is how he worked on me, because I could remember very little about the Therons and the Atlantines when I read the *Eagle* a second time in 1973, but many of the frames concerning the Treens had made an indelible impact. The Therons recall what used to be a particularly American characteristic: the belief that you can easily have *both* the power and convenience of advanced industrial technology, *and* an uncontaminated idyll of rural life. Well, if you *can* do that, so much the better, and the moral lessons that the Therons have to teach the Earth culture are very acceptable. It was Marx's vision of life under communism that man would be able to fish in the day and be an art critic in the evening. But the implicit distinction between 'work' (mainly delegated to machines) and 'leisure' (recreation, entertainment and the arts) is surely questionable, and the Theron way of life is really a culmination of suburbia – though commuting to the unpleasant city is cut down magically to zero.

The structure of Treen society, with its race of Atlantine serfs to act as 'bodies' to the Treen minds, which have evolved their own bodies virtually out of existence, is highly convincing. (After all, modern industrial Europe depends economically on the labour of ethnically distinct castes of workers, and modern Brazil on that of a vast pool of poor people from the north.) By contrast, we are told little of how the Therons build and service their sophisticated transport systems, their weaponry and their electronic gadgets; nor of how President Kalon avoids being deposed by his generals and technocrats. This would not seem such a gap if their technology were different in principle from Earth technology – but their cities and aircraft seem simply more advanced than Earth technology; they carry the same principles to a logical conclusion. Since the early days of the *Eagle*, we have come to learn that much of our technology *itself* has power relationships built into it – a point appreciated by some perceptive poets and artists long ago. If I had a Theron friend to tell me about the bits of their social structure which the *Eagle* left out, he might be able to satisfy me that my objections were unjustified. For instance, it might be that technological knowledge is diffused right through the population rather than being confined to elite specialist groups; or alternatively that safeguards are built into the constitution so that technological competence can never develop into political power. But one has doubts, too, about the quality of the Therons' leisure and art. How do they keep themselves amused? How do they distract their pampered adolescents from the temptations of drugs and delinquency? Again, my native informant from southern

Venus might be able to put me wise on these matters. As it is, they point to a serious gap in the *Eagle*'s otherwise very sound parable – or anti-parable, since this is a heavenly story with an earthly meaning.

Though the Therons teach the Earthmen how to relax and enjoy life, they are as helpless as the Treens when their machinery is jammed. The Earthmen have a reciprocal lesson to teach the Therons: not to lose touch with their bodies. The picture of an Earth where the space age has not wiped out village cricket – the Treens land on a village green in England in high summer – and where the Canadian Mounties can be shipped to win a battle on Venus against the crippled Treen robots, is both engaging and profound. Yet we have the advantage of hindsight over the *Eagle* in 1950. We know that the sturdy qualities of loyalty, discipline and magnanimity, tempered by humour, which saw Britain through the Second World War, are not in themselves sufficient to cope with the problems of a world dominated by what Marcuse calls 'technological rationality'; for those are naive virtues, too easily manipulated. (Guest, the fleet controller's surname, is the same word as 'ghost'.) And some of the world's most repressive regimes attach great importance to sport and 'physical culture', as did the Nazis. The human body, it will be argued in this book, possesses a kind of inalienable honesty, and even a subversive potential; but these can be defused when the body is supplied with all facilities for exertion and enjoyment, linked with competition and national prestige, so that it is reduced to the protected margin of a technocratic society – just as golf-links and show-jumping stadiums belong to the margins of industrial towns, carefully simulating the countryside with sandy bunkers or rustically carpentered jumps.

The Earthmen, the Therons and the Atlantines are all psychologically castrated. Among the Treens it is only the Mekon who allows his desires free play, and the dice are loaded against him by his creator since he is given only an atrophied mauve body. But when this wriggles under Dare's arm (a climax of the narrative which must have etched itself on many a young reader's mind, for it is at such moments that the characters seem to pop up from the page) the Mekon's torso becomes an object of forbidden eroticism, like the penis of an animal.

The only scientist from Earth whom we get to know well is Professor Peabody. She too lives by her intellect (as her name confirms), but here again we can recognize a ruse of her creator's.

How was the artist to depict a 'good' scientist from Earth, as convincing as the other Earth characters, to contrast with the perverted Treens and the idealized Therons? Any male scientist from Earth would either come across as uncomfortably like the Treens (representing mind cut off from body), or his spiritual distinction would make the lesson of the Therons unnecessary. Or – a third possibility – he might have been made a comic or minor character like Digby or Hank; but this would have been to injure the dignity of science. So the scientist presented to us is a woman, and the issue that she raises is the side-issue of women's emancipation.

The *Eagle* clearly succeeded in articulating a critical, humanistic approach to technocracy. I doubt that I was alone in suffering from an antipathy towards science and scientists which lasted, in my own case, until I was about twenty-three, and no doubt the bogey of the Mekon had something to do with it. Nevertheless, the Mekon survived – not only in the narrative to keep the Dan Dare series going, but also in the minds of the strip's readers as its most potent symbol. The technological rationality which he represented has survived too. And we still have no 'counter-culture' of any comparable potency to set up against it, any more than the creator of Dan Dare had in the Therons.

Yet what Dare says to the friendly Treen, Sondar, on the occasion of the revolt of the Atlantine serfs, is quite right:

Your Mekons should have studied the history of our world more carefully, Sondar – if they had, they'd realize that, despite all logic and reason, you can never quite kill the last spark of spirit and hope in a human being.

More than that, you can never kill that fresh, unpremeditated, visceral experience of the world and other people which renews itself in every child – the sum total of which experience we may call, for convenience, 'the body'.

In this book, I attempt to analyse how the *Eagle*'s vision of a human technology might be achieved in reality.

My title is stolen from Walt Whitman's poem *I Sing the Body Electric*. It is meant to bring out the contradiction which is this book's subject-matter and riddle.

Modern technology is largely made possible by our ordering of the world through grids of analysis and measurement. Man romanticizes his technological capacity because this summons him to create his own future. His body, however, reminds him inescapably of two truths: first, that his brain cannot operate on, or communicate with, or be changed by, the world directly; and second, that he has also a long history as a sexed being, a species, a mammal, a form of life in a universe older than life. It could be argued that these are two *separate* truths we can learn from the body, but I shall treat them in this book as two aspects of a single field of meaning.

The contradiction between 'technology' and 'the body' has been faced by man ever since he first began to reflect on his situation in myth, art and philosophy. The experiences and perceptions of the body are to a great extent immune to the objective, analytic description that technology prefers; they can be hinted at in poetry and art, but they always constitute a real and inexhaustible resource against narrow rationality – if often a dangerous, even 'diabolic' resource, for the body is easily sentimentalized. Man's body has also always been seen as binding him with the non-human natural world, even though an evolutionary interpretation of this relationship was not available till modern times; and from this point of view, it is the proliferation of technology that is dangerous and sometimes 'diabolic', because it seems to violate the natural order.

The contradiction I have just set out could be made the subject of a purely philosophical analysis, but this would have to be very abstract and theoretical. I shall pursue the contradiction in the context of the present cultural situation of the 'advanced' industrial nations today; it has become ever more intense since the industrial revolution of the eighteenth century, and demands analysis primarily in the terms that have arisen from our own industrialized society. This book, then, will adopt the discipline of confining itself almost exclusively to Western cultural sources from 1750 to the present day. The year 1750 is an arbitrary cut-off point, since it can be argued that the 'modern world' really began in the seventeenth century or even with the technological innovations of the Middle Ages; but it has obvious conveniences. I might have gained some historical depth by going back to Plato or Greek mythology, but only at the risk of diluting the book's effect with generalizations about the human condition. I might have gained some breadth and detachment by introducing evidence and insights from non-Western cultures, but only at the risk of producing a jackdaw's nest of glittering, exotic ideas and facts, with no methodical relationship. In many ways the edifice of Western civilization has been seriously undermined by its critics in recent decades, yet I believe that there remains a great wealth of resources within that edifice available for reconstruction. Scraps of Pygmy lore or Tantra or Maoism can serve only as stimuli or challenges to us, not as direct solutions. One of the most valuable lessons we can learn from the discipline of social anthropology is that our own society is much richer and more diverse than is commonly realized.

I have borrowed some of the analytical tools of historical materialism without accepting the Marxist creed. This borrowing will seem deplorably eclectic to those who are committed to Marxism; but I make no apologies for it. Other readers may be put off for opposite reasons: by the emphasis placed on Marxian theories at some points in the book. The interpretation of Marx is important because no theory of technology can be satisfactory which does not adopt a clear position with regard to some ambiguities in his texts. Similarly, the outlines of a general theory of technology are a prerequisite for a review of the urgent practical problems that technology poses. Some may find these passages irksome, partly because Anglo-Saxons as a rule avoid thinking from first principles (and we are usually wise to do so) and partly because it might seem indecent to use Marxian social theory as an analytical tool when this has led historically to a perversion of Marx's original intentions. My position is that Stalinism is dreadful, and leftist projections of a Messianic future are unconvincing, but none the less nobody has yet prepared better analytical tools than Marx's to help us understand the problems here under review.

I do not claim to have solved any of the dilemmas that a reading of Marxian theory imposes on a bourgeois English liberal whose sympathies are tugged in the opposite direction by the claims of individual excellence, tradition, moderation and the 'decent drapery' that Burke, in *Reflections on the Revolution in France*, saw as clothing naked power relations; and whose revolutionary ardour is damped by the manifest absence in the world of an international proletarian consciousness without which no revolution that would have satisfied Marx is possible. But the conceptual framework I have chosen does flatly exclude some apparently over-simple solutions which have won quite a following in the modern world, such as a recourse to private mysticism and cultivation of the individual ego. I have chosen not to enter a dispute with their advocates, with whose position it is often impossible to argue. Rather, I think it more honest to state at the outset that this book will give a high priority to the social and political dimension. The cultural phenomena under survey are interpreted here as pervaded by political and economic relations, though not as necessarily reducible to any political or economic 'base'. Clearly, it is in keeping with an historical–materialist conceptual framework (albeit an impure one) to study 'mystical' and 'spiritual' expression as forms of linguistic play or private mythology, rather than as introducing us to some extra-terrestrial sphere of being or to some spiritual or 'interior' level of consciousness. The value of staying within the confines of an historical–materialist framework as much as possible stems from the valuable tools for analysis and demystification thereby provided. The framework adopted does not by any means deny that there may, for instance, be forms of valuable human relationship which are not given a chance to develop in Western society as we know it. It does, however, assert that currently fashionable flirtations with mysticism and spiritualism demand to be studied as social phenomena.

I have chosen *The Body Electric* as an oxymoron to bring out the contradiction exposed in this book, and to force into collision the strong partisanship that has been felt on behalf of two opposite currents of Western cultural life during the last two centuries. The two opposed aspects of the contradiction I will call the Romance of Technology (which logically comes first) and the Recoil to the Body.

Many distinguished individual minds have opted for one or other of these 'sides', and I will, among other things, attempt to analyse the history of some of the most significant of these individual commitments. I shall take examples from the arts, and particularly from literature, since it happens that during the last few centuries, until very recently, many of the most clairvoyant insights into social and cultural issues have been expressed in poetry and fiction.

Some specialist readers may be perturbed by my decision to take examples from a wide range of different media – from academic painting to comics. I am well aware of the importance of understanding both the specific physical constraints that every technical medium imposes, and also the history of changing styles and conventions. No disciplined analysis of media and art-forms will be found in this book, but there is, perhaps, a discipline of another kind present. My discipline is to weave a coherent argument through the examples covered, all of which come from the last two and a quarter centuries. I should add that this book is committed to the value of 'close reading' – of a detailed study of the thing under review, be it philosophical text or a painting. I have preferred to go into some detail in teasing out the meaning for our theme of some carefully-chosen illustrations, rather than attempting to mention by name every single writer or artist that could be considered relevant to the subject. I have also found it useful to summarize, and comment on, conflicting opinions between different authorities on a subject. This seems more honest than to claim a special competence in many different fields.

One further word about how I have selected the examples to be studied: the critical study of one's own culture is more difficult than first appears. This book swings between two modes of approach. One is a 'critical' mode, where the distinction of certain great men, perpetuated in their work, serves as a touchstone in a process of unremitting discrimination: 'Discrimination is life, indiscrimination is death', writes F. R. Leavis.[1] The other is an 'ethnographic' mode where an attempt is made, necessarily incomplete, to adopt the perspective of an alien anthropologist. The limitation of the 'critical' approach is that it is blinkered by ethnocentricity, unable and unwilling to step out of its own categories and assumptions. The limitation of the 'ethnographic' approach is that, while it can deal very well with such phenomena as (for instance) the economic systems whereby art and literature are produced, or the social organization of sub-cultures, it disqualifies itself from distinguishing between the run-of-the-mill and the eminent, between the routine and the creative, since this would be to endorse the values of the society under observation. The ethnographer must refrain, for example, from going further than noting that Blake and Rimbaud are among the culture-heroes of literate Westerners; he must beware of responding to their call himself. He can note the ethnomusicological features of contemporary pop music, but should not judge whether it offers genuine human fulfilment to the working-class or, on the contrary, is merely spreading garlands of flowers (in Rousseau's phrase) on their iron chains. We shall see later in this book an apparent disagreement between John Berger's writings on the nude as an art-form and those of Kenneth Clark and Adrian Stokes; this is really a difference between Berger's 'ethnographic' analysis and Clark's and Stokes's selective concentration on this art-form's highest manifestations. I cannot reconcile the 'critical' and the 'ethnographic' mode; but if the reader considers the problems of adequately studying one's own culture, I hope he will agree that my solution of switching explicitly from one mode to another is a useful *ad hoc* solution to the dilemma.

The analysis gets rather complicated when we come to the Recoil to the Body. This is because, as I shall argue, the society in which Western technology has developed tended, and still tends, to repress the body. Until recently, only a few outstandingly clear-sighted minds were able to face directly the challenge of the human body. The more usual response of those objecting to industrialization was to avoid bringing the body itself to consciousness, and to replace it by notions of 'nature', the 'primitive' and so forth, which were more easily dealt with and not censored out. Or some singled out the genital-erotic aspects of bodily experience, for which there were already accepted conventions; but this was to impoverish the body's total resources, to exalt that very fragmentation and mechanization of experience which the 'whole body' is able to defy. This sense of the 'whole body' had often been articulated before the eighteenth century, both in love poetry, and in painting and sculpture depicting the human figure. After the late eighteenth century these particular conventions became so academic as to be rarely congenial to the kind of imaginative commitment I am tracing here, though always available for reclamation by an original artist or poet.

The Romance of Technology and the Recoil to the Body are two possible attitudes or options today. There are three other types of response, which I shall outline here briefly:

1. Sidestep the issue altogether, or find a compromise whereby the force of both options is mutually diluted. Most people's daily lives fall into this category. One of the legends on the Paris Métro walls in May 1968 read as follows: 'Métro, Boulot, Dodo' (subway, work, sleep). The occasional novel or visit to an exhibition or cinema does not disturb the pattern. This lack of reflection is not confined only to commuters and organization men; it is shared by many literary and artistic coteries.

2. Accept the force of each option, since both are valid and valuable aspects of human experience; but gloss over their fundamental incompatibility. A classic example – impressive and typically American – is Walt Whitman, whose poetry I shall discuss in Chapter 5. Also adopting this response is, say, an enthusiastic

computer systems analyst who sails or rides a horse at weekends –
quite a common life-pattern today.

3. Accept the full force of each option so that a *fundamental
conflict in the development of our culture is exposed*. In this book I shall
argue that this *seizing* of the contradiction is the only adequate
solution for today, the only valid starting-point for genuinely
advancing the debate and clarifying the cultural crisis in which we
find ourselves. It is, however, rare. The reason why Marx's theory
of technology is the most useful to date is that no other systematic
thinker has seized the contradiction so finely, though one or two
modern interpreters of Marx (such as Herbert Marcuse) have
enlarged on him imaginatively.

My central purpose is to offer a new framework for understanding
the interactions between Western technology and Western
civilization since about 1750. Chapter 2 will cover the Romance of
Technology and Chapter 3 the Recoil to the Body. Both the
Romance of Technology and the Recoil to the Body can be
imaginatively limiting or socially and politically regressive;
neither is necessarily so. In Chapter 4 I focus on the theoretical
relationship between technology and the body because this is
necessary in order to advance the discussion further. I try to tie up
the relevant ideas of Rousseau and Marx with the writings of
Marcel Mauss and some other authorities.

This book does not pretend to deal with the question of cities
thoroughly, but suggests that an adequate theory of cities can only
be constructed when the social relations of technology have been
better clarified. The city is regarded as sharing with technology
one essential characteristic: both are products of an increase in the
permutability of resources.

This book purposely leaves unexamined the relationship
between its theme and the position of women in society. Anthropologists have argued that cultures all over the world emphasize
the primary role of women as wives and mothers, since societies
must regenerate themselves; and that women often come to be
seen in closer relationship to the uncontrollable forces of nature
than are men. In our own society, the domain of technology and
machinery has become particularly identified with men, for many
reasons. The issues in question are important and closely related
to my theme; but no simple alignment of technology with men,
and 'the body' with women, can usefully be made within the
context of this book. Such an alignment would mean abandoning

the assumption – surely a productive one – that human beings are bisexual.

The Romance of Technology and the Recoil to the Body are sharply opposed; yet they constitute a unity in that each sustains the other's existence. In Chapter 5, the book finally focuses on various possible ways of seizing the contradiction and escaping from this impasse. The notions of 'deconstructing' and 'reclaiming' technology are considered. The central contradiction would only be completely resoluble in a perfect society. However, it is a fundamental property of man that he is always, if he wishes, able to elude determinism, and it is this which enables us to face the future with reasonable hope. Artists, planners, intellectuals and other members of 'elite' groups have special responsibilities and opportunities for subverting technology into more humane channels. Nevertheless, it may be that certain relatively disadvantaged and unselfconscious people are achieving this with equal success.

We live in a world shaped more by the nuclear bomb and the Yalta Agreement than by the screeds of theoreticians, major and minor. Much needs to be done towards reasserting man's ability to reshape his future through reshaping his technology and institutions; and the hierarchies of great-power politics may seem scandalous when subjected to theoretical analysis. Yet one effect of the nuclear bomb seems to have been to justify the continuation of the power structures that developed it. Are these not relatively benign when compared to the risks of any attempt to unscramble them?

Problems such as the world's food and energy crises should not be regarded as insoluble. It may be, however, that we have created in the nuclear bomb the first technology that has imposed itself on man as a fixed determinant whose presence must hereafter govern and limit all responsible social and political debate. Faced with this situation, the individual's primary concern should surely be to find spaces of activity where he is not totally determined himself. It is in such a project that men are really equal, and that clerks should know when to be silent.

Chapter Two

The Romance of Technology
with a note on the City

There is one major complication in the Romance of Technology: the world inhabited by those who submit *uncritically* to it – including some, but by no means all, of the figures discussed in the chapter – is one-dimensional, a kind of Flatland. It can be elating for a time because it ignores so much that is difficult. Soon, however, one becomes desperate to get away. A common mistake is then to over-compensate, to try and make the Romance of Technology disappear, ignoring its legitimate claims. This is to replace Flatland by a suffocating cupboard of primitivism or nostalgia.

A simple thread runs through this chapter, but it also reveals a variety and energy in our culture's appreciation of technology over the last two centuries which has not always been noticed.

First, let me make clear that when the word 'technology' is used in this book, it may be understood to include 'applied science'. The distinction between 'pure science' and technology, though useful in many contexts, will not be stressed. In fact, 'pure science' and technology are two forms of social practice which have the closest interrelations with each other.

Why do we get excited or inspired by technology? Because it opens new possibilities for human action, and in turn these technical possibilities can lead to an enrichment of moral, cultural and social life. In some cases, we can pin down a direct relationship between a given technological innovation and social benefits that are considered to have ensued from it. One such case is the agricultural tractor. This, together with the electric power-station, has duly become a supreme official symbol in communist countries for technological-*cum*-political progress, appearing on bank-notes as well as in fine art. A discovery like penicillin falls into a different category. It has certainly become a medical technology (for drugs and chemicals are just as much a part of technology as are machines); clearly, too, it is a benefit to humanity. But how do we visualize it, or describe it in non-scientific terms? We can only think of its packaging or of a vague mould in a laboratory; penicillin itself has little symbolic appeal. Conversely, the Apollo moon-walks had great symbolic appeal, fact and fiction blending together in the mythology of space travel; but it would be hard to justify them on directly utilitarian grounds. They are products of mass entertainment and power politics.

The human imagination works in symbols. Therefore when men look for poetic and artistic means of articulating faith in the future of man as 'product of his product', they do not feel obliged to present closely argued cases about the social benefits of a specific technology. Virtually any one of a wide range of technical innovations can stand symbolically for the whole of technology: tractors, power-stations, space walking, and many other symbols too. The symbolic field of technologies is interconnected. Yet this interconnectedness can work both ways, and it seems to be a rule that the Romance of Technology invariably goes sour. Tractors become symbols of noise or the violation of mother earth; power-stations, of industrial pollution. The space-walks in their turn come to represent US imperialism. The 'image' of penicillin is fairly untarnished, despite the dangers of over-prescribing by doctors, but DDT, the scourge of malaria and typhus, is now thought of in the richer countries more as a pollutant than as a blessing. Much of the quarrel over the Anglo-French Concorde project is due to its double-edged potency as a symbol – of progress or folly, depending on how you look at it – and all these connotations are now frozen in the aeroplane itself. The optimistic view of the Concorde will pick out its stylish sculptural form and graceful flight. The pessimistic view will dwell on the brutality with which it violates the human scale and natural equilibria. Similarly, though Brooklyn Bridge was seen as a positive symbol of the future for late nineteenth-century New York, the symbolism was asking to be turned on its head; hence Henry James elaborated on it as a mechanical monster in *The American Scene*.[1]

Some who work in scientific or technological fields may protest that they are soberly motivated by 'reason' and not by romantic or aesthetic urges. I shall not take the liberty of plunging into the depths of their psyches to expose a romantic idealism which they may have stifled. There is ample evidence to support my case in the mass media and popular art-forms, as well as in the 'high culture' of the past which has contributed to forming the dominant assumptions of our society today. I shall consider several examples from these fields in this chapter.

We could begin with some outrageous examples of technocratic romanticism run wild, such as Ian Fleming's much imitated series of James Bond thrillers, or E. E. 'Doc' Smith's cosmic epic, the 'Lensman' series. These are certainly worth looking at as examples of a genre of imaginative fiction which offers an extreme elation – an almost 'spiritual' liberation from the messy experience of everyday living – in exchange for a drastic flattening-out of human sensibility and tenderness into a corrupt one-dimensional world where ultimately men become machines programmed by obsessions. Here are two numbing extracts from E. E. Smith's *Galactic Patrol* (1937), which tells how a pack of interstellar pirates, master-minded by a super-scientist, is finally destroyed by an ace policeman, or Lensman: [2]

The helmet flew apart like an eggshell, blood and brains gushed out in nauseous blobs: but the delta-ray projector was so jammed that it would not soon again become a threat.

Surrender had not been thought of. Quarter or clemency had not been asked or offered. Victory of itself was not enough. This was, and of stern necessity had to be, a war of utter, complete and merciless extinction.

We shall consider the theme of space war briefly later in this chapter, for there is no doubt that this type of fiction is much in demand, in book, film and television form. If we go back in history to the eighteenth and nineteenth centuries, however, we can find more subtle embodiments of the Romance of Technology, in which critical reservation about the dangers of technology are sometimes incorporated. We can also trace a more primitive attitude where no incompatibility between technology and the natural order was yet perceived.

There are a number of preliminary observations which should be made. The humanist criticisms of technocracy articulated in Dan Dare only carried force because the *Eagle* was able to whip up such enthusiasm for technology in its innocent readers. Imagine our shock as children, after the first few issues had introduced us to the utopia of a technocratic world state in the 1990s, to find the whole Romance of Technology turned on its head when we got to Mekonta! It is a common pattern to find a critique of technocracy embedded in a glorification of the potential of technology, so that the discourse carries a double message.

Nevertheless, our analysis would be incomplete if we ignored the straightforward, uncritical Romance of Technology – or 'technological sublime', as it has been called.[3] This can be brutal (as in the glorification of war); it can also be innocent. Or rather, an innocent response to the drama of industrialization has been possible in the past. It was usually only a partial response, but when it was naive and uncalculated it sometimes approached the freshness of experience which, I have argued above, is more commonly our resource *against* the technological world-view. Such naivety in embracing technology is hardly ever found today – except in economically undeveloped countries that have not yet seen much of advanced technology, or among children and adolescents. We can find much of this innocence if we go back to the eighteenth and nineteenth centuries.

An important discrimination must be established here when we speak of a 'fresh' or 'innocent' way of embracing technology. I argue throughout this book that the technological world-view tends to reduce everything to objects, especially to instruments or obstacles, but our bodies persistently refused to be so reduced; and they offer an alternative mode of experience which is more honest and in a sense more concrete or 'real'. There is thus a fundamental contradiction between technology and the body, in the sense in which I am using the latter term (which, as the reader will see, owes a lot to the writings of D. H. Lawrence, Merleau-Ponty and Adrian Stokes). This fundamental contradiction is, however, complicated in two ways. First, the body *can* be 'technologized' – reduced to an objective or instrumental state: as an object of hate, of violence, of obsessive lust, of scientific analysis, of economic exploitation, or of psychological repression. Moreover, our pre-reflexive experience of technological manifestations – our 'gut-reaction' to them – is not always negative. Such manifestations can provoke wonder or aesthetic pleasure in a direct and uncalculated way, when spontaneous, visceral feeling short-circuits our rational arguments. For instance, we may condemn gambling as a sign of weakness of character and a social evil, but still be romantically stirred by the lights of Las Vegas and by the statistics of its electricity consumption. We may be vigorous opponents of the motor-car and advocates of the public bicycle, and yet feel a thrill of exhilaration when we are taken for a spin in a friend's Porsche. There would probably be no Romance of Technology at all without this kind of unguarded bodily acceptance to spark it off.

I remember how I loved the 'feel' of computers when I first started programming them: those flashing lamps, spinning discs, whirring printers, esoteric sesames in the air-conditioned temple of the computer-room at ICI's plant in a Garden City near London. And yet this euphoria is the most fragile of moods, since if we pursue it we find that we have been seduced by an obsessive taskmaster. If we succumb to this very special kind of gut-reaction, we are like the office secretary who is thrilled by the dynamism of her new 'whizz-kid' boss, but shortly finds that he wants her to work like a slave for him and listen to his troubles after office-hours. Late at night, when the devoted computer programmer hopes that his programme is going to work at last, the computer decides to give a 'core dump', spewing out yards of hexadecimal digits – everything that has happened to it, we might say, since it was last psychoanalysed; the programmer is kept up till dawn trying to find a 'fix' that will restore its mental health. In many large computer installations a few unfortunates have become anchorites, living only for the computer – occasionally to the extent of adding camp-beds to the operating-room equipment.

Most of us learn to be wary of the glamour of technology for fear of being trapped by it. The computers that I worked with soon lost their appeal, and became maddeningly temperamental, exacting and boring clients. Such disillusion is a feature of the sophisticated society that we have developed. In earlier times of modern industry it was not yet the rule.

The Romance of Technology in the eighteenth century has been admirably documented in Francis D. Klingender's *Art and the Industrial Revolution*, especially as regards visual iconography. He is particularly good on the response of poets and artists to Coal-brookdale, a place of great scenic attraction in Shropshire which became an important industrial centre because it possessed coal, limestone and a navigable river. This and similar sites were depicted by many late eighteenth- and early nineteenth-century artists. Klingender's book, published after the last war, brought to light a hidden face of English cultural history which had been ignored except by some specialists. Klingender was a Marxist and it is a Marxian tenet that bourgeois culture and 'high art' tend to repress or censor out their determining agent – the 'social mode of production'. Thus the capitalist version of English social history is dominated by the tradition of country houses, cathedral closes, market towns, second-hand bookshops and picturesque villages. As Klingender indicates, the Romance of Technology exerted a strong counter-force against this bourgeois urge to purify culture and art from the stain of industrial production – even in the media of expression such as painting and poetry that catered to bourgeois demand. Popular art has had no such inhibitions against including the material realities of production in its range of subject-matter (one thinks, for instance, of the tradition of industrial ballads that was especially strong in coalmining and on the railways).[4]

The paintings of Joseph Wright of Derby (1734–97) illustrate the freshness and innocence with which it was then possible to perceive technology. Wright was certainly not an inhabitant of Flatland; there is nothing in the least one-dimensional about him. He is now rightly recognized as a great English painter, if an uneven one – great both on technical grounds, as an explorer of the problems of depicting light-effects in oil-paint, and on account of his range of subject-matter, for he was a prolific artist who painted portraits and landscapes as well as spectacular firework scenes and volcanic eruptions. Erasmus Darwin, an important contemporary of Wright's whose work will be discussed later in the chapter, wrote of him:

> So WRIGHT's bold pencil from Vesuvio's hight
> Hurls his red lavas to the troubled night.
> From Calpe starts the intolerable flash,
> Skies burst in flame, and blazing oceans dash; –
> Or birds in sweet repose his shades recede,
> Winds the still vale, and slopes the velvet mead;
> On the pale stream expiring Zephyrs sink,
> And Moonlight sleeps upon its hoary brink.

The paintings of scientific and industrial subjects which I shall consider here are only one aspect of his total work; and it is important to my argument that science and industry could be interpreted by Wright as part of a continuum – to which the rest of his perceived world also belonged, rather than was opposed. He was strongly influenced by the great seventeenth-century Dutch school of painting which had been remarkable for the comprehensiveness of its subject-matter, giving us a vivid picture of what it was like to be alive in the Netherlands at that time.

(Even scenes of coarse manual labour had been painted by the Ostade brothers, scenes such as the interiors of butchers' shops, though admittedly these are not very common.)

First let us compare two paintings, both done when Wright was about thirty, both concerned with the marvel of human achievement; and let us mark the smoothness of the transition from the archaic to the up-to-date. *Three Persons Viewing the Gladiator by Candlelight* (1764–65) depicts three men studying the Borghese statuette of a nude gladiator, now in the Louvre. Benedict Nicolson felicitously comments in his book on Wright:

The nobility of the antique statue fills their minds, and justifies their earnestness. Its grace has lifted them above pettifogging everyday life, and from its contours their own features have borrowed refinement.[5]

It appears that Wright was by temperament a workmanlike craftsman, not of an 'intellectual' or speculative cast of mind. It is doubtful whether what Richard Wollheim calls the *'bricoleur* problem'[6] ever presented itself to Wright's conscious mind: that is, the problem of how certain material stuffs or processes become accredited as the vehicles for art, and others do not. Wollheim borrows this notion from Lévi-Strauss's comparison of human culture to a *bricoleur* or handyman who improvises only partly useful objects out of old junk. The problem is one that pre-occupies many modern artists, but Shakespeare posed it better than anyone when he wrote in *Much Ado About Nothing*, 'Is it not strange that sheepes' guts should hale soules out of mens bodies?'[7] The greatness of the *Gladiator* painting lies partly in its capture of this philosophical enigma at an intuitive level.

Centuries before Wright's act of painting, we can imagine a model posing for a sculptor. Here is what Adrian Stokes writes of the nude:

The human body thus conceived [as a whole] is a promise of sanity. Throughout history the totality of the nude may rarely have shone, yet the potential power will have made itself deeply felt. I propose that the respect thus founded for the general body is the seal upon our respect for other human beings as such (and even for consistently objective attitudes to things as such); an important factor, therefore, in regard not only to respect but to tolerance and benevolence. . . . The self-sufficiency where it is allowed to the nude, who may be the target of intense sexuality also as an independent object, accompanies our own integration or totality, our own integration of drives and character-traits. The respect for self-sufficient objects is the extension of self-respect.[8]

27

Wright's intense appreciation of the human body as subject-matter for painting is clear from the rest of his work. Here the living body of the gladiator, which is the work of God, and the mimetic skill of the sculptor, are equal grounds for the three men's awe. They gaze in awe at the presentment of the gladiator in the culturally hallowed medium of marble; and we in turn catch ourselves gazing at their presentment in the culturally hallowed medium of paint (or, more probably, in scaled-down reproductions of paint through engraving or photography). We have no sense of missing anything in the picture through ignorance of art-history; nor does Wright evoke any feeling of competition between the Ancients and the Moderns, though this was a favourite topic for discussion in his century. The whole experience of looking at the painting depends on a tissue of unexamined assumptions. We *know* that the gladiator who is depicted is not made of icing-sugar and about to be eaten by the men, and we *know* that the painting is not an advertisement for the men's tailoring of the day, though we cannot prove any of these assumptions. Everything about the picture seems fresh, unpremeditated and natural – whereas what is going on in it, in terms of cultural assumptions, is quite complicated.

I have risked labouring analysis of the *Gladiator* in order to show how Wright could move from a situation like this one, where he could count on his audience sharing his own assumptions – since antique sculpture was, and still is, so well known as an object of admiration – to situations where he dealt with new and unfamiliar marvels. In *A Philosopher giving a lecture on the Orrery* (1764–66), perhaps one of the greatest of all English paintings, he depicts a comparable indoor scene. There is more variety among the spectators: the scientist is speaking, one man is following him, another takes notes, another studies the orrery, two children barely restrain themselves from fiddling with it; on the left a woman broods (her eyes do not seem focused on the orrery), and just right of centre is a figure in silhouette facing away from us. An orrery is a clockwork device representing the motion of the planets round the sun in the Newtonian system, named after Charles Boyle, Earl of Orrery. It must have been more familiar to Wright's contemporaries than it is to us, but it is appropriately the subject of a lecture rather than of mere contemplation like the gladiator. We can obtain an idea of how an orrery worked from the second canto of Erasmus Darwin's poem *The Botanic Garden* (1789–91):

So, mark'd on orreries in lucid signs
Starr'd with bright points the mimic zodiac shines;
Borne on fine wires amid the pictured skies
With ivory orbs the planets set and rise;
Round the dwarf earth the pearly moon is roll'd,
And the sun twinkling whirls his rays of gold.

As with the *Gladiator*, the object of attention in this scene inspires awe on two levels: the marvel of God's creation, and the marvel of man's representation of it. But whereas the statuette of the gladiator evoked in cold stone the actual surface 'feel' or skin of the warm, living man, the orrery represents the *structural* relations of the universe and does not claim to represent its *visual appearance*. We are thrust into the realm of analytical, objective, schematic discourse, and are no longer in that of naive, subjective experience. We can imagine one of the men in the first picture thinking about the statuette: 'How did he [the sculptor] carve that bit there?' or, 'What is he [the gladiator] doing as he moves in that way?' or, 'Was it posed by a model?' We can even imagine him desiring momentarily to join in a tussle with the gladiator. These are kinaesthetic experiences – the feeling of muscular effort in one's own body – and nobody will deny that they are a vital resource for much art. The party looking at the orrery, however, with the possible exception of the children, is thinking about various structural relations and properties, abstracted from matter. The system before them – a clockwork simulation of the cosmos – was a central symbol for their age, and had to do with their notions of politics and society as well as science. This relationship between cosmology and social theory in the classical age has been well argued by the philosophical writer George Boas:

The myth of the [Hobbesian] social compact sought to explain psychologically the harmony of paths in civilized society, but the resultant picture of the absolute monarch controlling paths of his subject is duplicated later in Newton in the picture of the solar system, in which the orbits of the planets are compounded of their being pulled towards the sun and pursuing their own straight paths.[9]

It is possible to go further with the analysis of this painting. We may admire Wright's masterly stroke in hiding the spirit- or oil-lamp, which represented the sun in the orrery, behind the arm of one of the onlookers, though it is reflected from the dark-green base of the device. It is the only lighting on the scene, and the trick is rather like that of a photograph where the photographer has hidden the sun behind a tree to avoid glare. Is it over-fanciful to point out that the lecturer, shedding 'enlightenment' on his listeners, is surrounded by an audience of seven – the number of planets known at the time if the moon is included (before the discovery of Neptune, Uranus and Pluto)? I would not press the possibility and in any case it is most doubtful that Wright would have planned any such symmetry consciously. The rationalization is nevertheless a way for us to appreciate the peculiar felicity of the composition.

My main point is a simple one. Though both the *Gladiator* and the *Orrery* paintings are concerned with the awe that cultural objects can stimulate, they are concerned with two distinct kinds of awe. Yet Wright manages the transition smoothly, with no sense of opposition between one and the other. A briefer look at some of his other paintings confirms this reading of him.

6   *The Blacksmith's Shop* (1771) represents a simple enough technical process, the forging of an iron bar, but iron technology was booming at that time and must have had a symbolic value. Much of Wright's interest seems engaged by the painterly challenges of dealing with the diffusion of the white-hot light and evoking the muscular movement of the hammer-blows. Let us draw attention here to just one minor detail: the dimly lit sculpture of an angel sprawled over the arch. Francis Klingender suggests that this painting is an echo both of the forges of Vulcan painted by Jan Brueghel, Velasquez and other artists, and of Nativity or Adoration themes. Benedict Nicolson argues that it is probably a naturalistic depiction of an actual disused and patched-up chapel. Even if this is so, the resonances that Klingender draws attention to still seem to be there. What is interesting about the angel is its discreetness and marginality. If the painting were by, say, a Victorian Pre-Raphaelite like Millais, the angel would be highlighted so as to insist on a symbolic contrast. Wright is certainly not setting up a symbolic opposition between archaic and modern, the spiritual and the material.

The same can be said of *An Iron Forge, viewed from without* (1773) – which was bought directly from the artist's studio by Catherine the Great, and is now in the Hermitage at Leningrad. Here Benedict Nicolson claims that Wright has cut away the wall according to standard graphic convention to show the interior from without; Klingender says it is a ruin and he has some evidence on his side since much of the roof is missing too. My point here is again the continuum between the industrial scene and the rural surroundings. The setting is theatrically lit, but there is no feeling that the countryside has been violated; the iron-forging seems an extension of agriculture, as indeed 'cottage industry' was in a sense, until factories took over.

Wright's 'innocent' perception of technology enabled him to combine an optimistic zest for scientific and industrial progress with a tender appreciation of human beings, especially young people and children. Such an unforced, natural sense of continuum in experience between the analytic and the sensual, between the modern and the archaic, between science and art, became more difficult (though, as we shall see, not impossible) for people of imagination to sustain after the beginning of the nineteenth century: after Blake's 'dark Satanic mills', Chartism and other radical movements, Malthus's pessimistic theory of over-population, machine-wrecking, and Dickens's descriptions of the Black Country – a transition well documented in Klingender's book as far as the visual arts are concerned.

Wright, like any good artist, was a unique mixture of ingredients. He could not have worked as he did if he had lived outside the culture of the eighteenth century in general and English provincial culture in particular. Rather than set him up as representing his age, I would suggest that he is a key figure whom we must appreciate in order to understand what was happening in his lifetime and how our own history follows. His work is a kind of classical moment of equilibrium between the old order and the new. We value Wright especially for the sobriety of his imagination, and for his provincial integrity which can stand aside from the hectic sophistication of the metropolis.

In architecture, Ledoux's salt-works at Arc-et-Senans seem a comparable 'classical moment'. In poetry, no such calm equilibrium seems to have been found in the eighteenth century. John Dyer's long, blank-verse poem *The Fleece* (1757), about the cotton industry, is an interesting document, including a glowing tribute to the work-houses where paupers were sent; but it does not stir the imagination. A more significant example is Erasmus Darwin's *The Botanic Garden*, a poem embracing not only botany but also the whole field of pure and applied science.

Erasmus Darwin (1731–1802), grandfather of Charles Darwin, has been compared with Goethe as an eighteenth-century 'comprehensivist'. He was the leading spirit of the Lunar Society, whose meetings were attended by James Watt, Joseph Priestley and Josiah Wedgwood. He was a great biologist, and a doctor and inventor. His poetry was widely admired during his lifetime, but after some parodies it grew to be ridiculed, and it has been treated shabbily or patronizingly by literary historians, who are mostly, one must remember, men of humane culture with no special interest in science. It has been taken more seriously by Klingender and by Elizabeth Sewell.

Certainly Darwin is a minor poet compared to Pope. Darwin could never have conceived anything like the amazingly organized penultimate couplet of Pope's *Dunciad*:

> Lo! thy dread empire, Chaos! is restored;
> Light dies before thy uncreating word.

The literary merit here depends on scientific insight; it is a vision of what we now call entropy – the measure of a system's disorganization, or increasing statistical probability, in both thermodynamics and information theory – expressed in a theological metaphor from *Genesis*, unravelling our universe before our eyes and then knitting it together by Pope's own articulation of the poetic 'word'. However, we must remember that Darwin's project – his path of cumulative activity – was different from Pope's; he was not a dedicated poet or man of letters, but someone who turned his hand to poetry as part of a broader programme of interest. His literary production must be read as the hobby of an heroic all-rounder with an insatiable curiosity.

The Botanic Garden is a whimsical poem; 'camp' is what we might call it today. It is as if Darwin was precariously holding together in his own person the unity of a culture that was already in process of fragmentation and specialization. One cannot but admire, for instance, his famous set-piece on the steam-engine:

> Soon shall thy arm, UNCONQUER'D STEAM! afar
> Drag the slow barge, or drive the rapid car;
> Or on wide-waving wings expanded bear
> The flying-chariot through the fields of air.
> – Fair crews triumphant, leaning from above,
> Shall wave their fluttering kerchiefs as they move;
> Or warrior-bands alarm the gaping crowd,
> And armies shrink beneath the shadowy cloud.

But it would be a mistake to give the impression that the sense of continuity which we find in Wright and Darwin was universal in the eighteenth century. After all, the great landowners spent fortunes, often made from the new extractive and industrial pro-

cesses, in moving villages and people from the landscape to con-
form to received ideas of 'unspoilt' natural beauty. They artfully
hid roads and approaches, turned laundries into green houses,
brew-houses into pineries, so as to banish all reminders of economic
realities.[10] And in such a poem as Anna Seward's on Coalbrook-
dale (*c.* 1785)[11] we find an acute sense of violation of nature, as
well as exhilaration at the vastness and power of the new industry.

One famous painting by Turner, *Rain, Steam and Speed*, executed   7
in his seventieth year (1844), deserves comment by way of both
comparison and contrast with Wright's work.[12] Turner depicts a
steam-train, preceded by a small running hare, speeding over a
bridge across a river. Waving figures on the river bank cheer the
train on. This certainly represents an 'innocent' response to
technology, since clearly nothing was further from Turner's mind
than the dangers of pollution, mechanization or desecration of the
past which the railway had already at that date come to symbolize
for some others. The range of Turner's subjects for painting is
very wide – it included many kinds of natural and atmospheric
spectacle, monuments, naval pageantry, conflagrations of human
artefacts – and his sensibility is marked by a smooth continuity of
receptiveness, as Wright's is. Figures or human artefacts occur in
most of his paintings, for Turner's great theme is the confrontation
between man and nature. But here any similarity with Wright
ends. Most of what there is to be said about *Rain, Steam and Speed*
relates to the 'internal' history of painting between Constable and
Monet. The continuity or coherence of his work is sustained by
the painter's single-minded romantic belief in his own art, so that
he becomes a kind of entrepreneur or risk-taker.[13] We get very
little sense of the communal in Turner's work. It is not irrelevant
that he was usually careless in painting the human figure, though
not through any lack of technical ability. Contemporary critics
complained that he distorted human features for the sake of
colour, and that he was more interested in visual 'effect' than he
was in 'truth', i.e. representational accuracy.[14] If Turner's later
work represents, among other things, an astonishing anticipation
of 'abstraction' in painting – Jack Burnham calls this a case of
'historical transgression' of the myth that art progresses from one
stage to the next through time – it also anticipates the estrangement of art from everyday living and social involvement.

The physical impact of Turner's paintings is very fresh and
strong. Yet something has been forfeited, in exchange for this
sensual and psychic energy, since Wright: the feeling, which we

33

get from all the four Wright paintings considered here, of a human fellowship to which the subjects of the paintings belong, and from which neither the artist nor the spectator is excluded. Great though Turner's art is, it is also the victim of *hubris*, or staring into the sun as mortals are not supposed to do.

8   Faith in technology is still preserved in 1855 in a picture called *The Lackawanna Valley* by George Inness; but this is an American painting, and the United States became industrialized considerably later than England. As Leo Marx points out in his book on technology and the pastoral ideal in America, the whole composition expresses unity rather than disharmony. The industrial artefacts are enveloped by trees and hills; steam-puffs rise from the engine and the round-house but also from behind the church; grazing animals are not disturbed by the little train; a shepherd relaxes in the foreground; and the railway line moulds the composition of the painting into sinuous, complementary ovals. As we shall see later, the negative aspects of technology were admitted slowly and unwillingly by nineteenth-century America.

The Lackawanna Valley is like an industrial painting by Wright: both express continuity between nature and technology. But there is an important difference. The harmonies of *The Lackawanna Valley* are surely *willed*. The painter seems to be making a literary point by his juxtaposition of images and his pictorial composition. Wright was not motivated to *emphasize* harmony, since he took it for granted: the possibility of disharmony between the work of God and the work of man did not exist for him. Nor

9   does it exist even today for many agricultural communities that are just tasting the labour-saving benefits of simple mechanization.

Only in one painting of Wright's, the Tate Gallery's *An experiment on a bird in the air pump* (1767–68), do we get a hint of the negative aspects of science. Certainly Wright's intention must have been to glorify science and its popularization. None the less, the modern spectator is likely to feel sympathy with the two children who are frightened and cannot believe that the dying bird will be revived when the demonstrator reintroduces air through his gadget. Indeed we may sympathize with the tortured bird itself. This element of pathos contributes to the richness of a great painting, into which we can read perhaps some unconscious disquiet about the scientific domination of nature. Yet if there is disquiet, it is marginal. It is not the disquiet of Fellini's film *8½*, which opens with the hero trying to get out of his car in a traffic-

34

block as it fills with exhaust fumes. But then, almost two hundred years separate these two works of art.

It is sometimes said of the nineteenth century that its dominant ideology was one of progress. And yet so much nineteenth-century culture seems to yearn for a lost golden age or the presumed innocence of childhood, while the greatest artists and writers to whom we look back – Turner was only one of them – are so complex and individual as to make generalizations of this kind seem irrelevant. If most of the dilemmas of our own scientific and industrialized society can be traced back to the eighteenth century, it is in the nineteenth century that they begin to become richly tangled; and as it was a period that encouraged individualism to the point of eccentricity, there are dangers in attempting to impose any schematic historical theory on its culture.

In the course of the nineteenth century, intense anxiety was experienced about the various effects of industrialization. Klingender calls the early part of the century the 'Age of Despair'. Nevertheless these hundred years were also the age of electricity and other key scientific discoveries, of the railways, the postal service, the 1851 Great Exhibition in the Crystal Palace in London, the spectacular feats of the Brunels, the Stephensons and other civil engineers. These men were glorified by Samuel Smiles in his biographies of industrial leaders and other self-made men, the 'stars' of an industrial revolution in which engineering was the product of bold pioneers working in the full glare of publicity and criticism. Nor must we forget public health reforms and discoveries in medicine and anaesthesia.

Among the many enduring monuments to the nineteenth century's Romance of Technology is Decimus Burton's lucid glass 10 Palm House at Kew Gardens (1844–48), which seems to have blissfully eluded all Victorian pomposity. More typical, perhaps, of the dominant spirit of Victorianism is the palatial Abbey Mills Pumping Station at West Ham, part of the sewage system installed in London, after some revelations about cholera, by Sir Joseph Bazalgette in the 1860s. It was designed with lavish ornament rather in the style of a large Greek Orthodox church; the plan is cruciform and each arm of the cross originally housed two beam-engines. Floral and heraldic ornamentation abounds. An obituary of Bazalgette in 1894 noted that, defending himself against the charge of extravagant ornamentation, the engineer had pleaded that,

> as the public saw nothing of the great underground works continually in operation for the safety of their health, not to say the convenience of their entire existence in London . . . a little extra and apparently unnecessary ornamentation might safely be permitted in a building which would stand above ground.[15]

This was a characteristically Victorian way of translating technological pride into hallowed cultural forms, exaggerated in this case by the embarrassing character of the industrial process in question. The 'truth to materials' of the Burton glass-house was exceptional. Here the Romance of Technology is put *into* the technology, rather than sublimated into a dream of the past. The result is that this building, delightful to enter with its steamy atmosphere and lush vegetation, is also totally modern and 'futuristic' to look at from a distance today. Somewhere between the two extremes of the Palm House and Abbey Mills Pumping Station is John Roebling's Brooklyn Bridge in New York (opened in 1883), which combines a highly functionalist structure with twin Gothic arches in each of the towers.

Samuel Smiles was single-mindedly committed to the Romance of Technology and believed that engineers such as George Stephenson and Thomas Telford had embodied the qualities of 'self-help' which he extolled in his book of that name (1859). Here is a characteristic passage from Smiles's *Industrial Biography* (1863), a paean to steam, though less elegant than that of Erasmus Darwin:

> Yoked to machinery of almost infinite variety, the results of vast ingenuity and labour, the Steam-engine pumps water, drives spindles, thrashes corn, prints books, hammers iron, ploughs land, saws timber, drives piles, impels ships, works railways, excavates docks; and, in a word, asserts an almost unbounded supremacy over the materials which enter into the daily use of mankind, for clothing, for labour, for defence, for household purposes, for locomotion, for food, or for instruction.[16]

Smiles's biographies celebrate the entrepreneurial energy of Britain at that time, without much thought for the political incompatibility between his ideology of 'self-help' in the competitive jungle and the new ideology of workers' solidarity that was gathering force. For the modern reader Smiles's unremitting insistence on the Victorian virtues of work, duty, frugality, study, self-discipline and perseverance may be salutary; but it does not make for very lively reading. And the engineers and industrialists themselves are presented as perfect steam-engines of morality, rather than as fallible, embodied human beings. Smiles was one of the supreme Flatlanders.

In the 'serious' literature of the nineteenth century in England we do not find much to represent the Romance of Technology. The novel is an art-form that can accommodate most aspects of cultural life, and one thinks of some sympathetic – if sometimes also ironic and critical – portraits of scientists and industrialists in nineteenth-century fiction: of Daniel Doyle, a somewhat colourless inventor in Dickens's *Little Dorrit*; or of the ironmaster Rouncewell in Dickens's *Bleak House*. But these are marginal figures. The Romance of Technology did not captivate the greater nineteenth-century English novelists. George Eliot's *Middlemarch* is an exceptional case; for not only is one of its chief characters, Tertius Lydgate, an ambitious and progressive medical scientist, but the whole narrative is held together by its author's interest in scientific analysis and structural relations. Joseph Conrad, at the turn of our own century, was fascinated by the romance of the sea and man's mastery of it, but we find in some of his fiction – *Nostromo, Heart of Darkness, An Outpost of Progress* – that the railways, mining and colonial industries become symbols of a deep moral corruption that he saw afflicting civilization. And when we think of Dickens's treatment of industrialism we think first of his scathing denunciation of everything connected with it, in *Hard Times*, rather than of the more positive treatment of the railway in *Dombey and Son* as a romantic symbol of progress.[17]

A late sonnet of Wordsworth's, *Steamboats, Viaducts, and Railways* (1833), illustrates how perplexed literary Victorians were on the subject of their burgeoning industry:

> Motions and Means, on land and sea at war
> With old poetic feeling, not for this,
> Shall ye, by Poets even, be judged amiss!
> Nor shall your presence, howsoe'er it mar
> The loveliness of Nature, prove a bar
> To the Mind's gaining that prophetic sense
> Of future change, that point of vision whence
> May be discovered what in soul ye are.
> In spite of all that beauty may disown
> In your harsh features, Nature doth embrace
> Her lawful offspring in Man's art; and Time,
> Pleased with your triumphs o'er his brother Space,
> Accepts from your bold hands the proffered crown
> Of hope, and smiles on you with cheer sublime.

This is a lame sonnet, but one can see how hard Wordsworth is trying to be fair and open-minded. We may ridicule the generalized title, and the quaint convention whereby the poet speaks to a set of miscellaneous engineering products, as woefully lacking in poetic concreteness; and how are we to visualize, for example, the 'bold hands' of the steamboats offering a crown to Old Father Time? Yet Wordsworth was wise enough to see that what matters most in technology is not the visible monument – the actual specific locomotive or bridge that he might have described – but the new dynamic processes and technical facilities ('motions and means') that are liberated, and the new human potentialities that ensue. He does not commit himself to saying what these new forces symbolize, except that they are pregnant with change. He deliberately abstains from premature interpretation. The new 'motions and means' *are* at war with poetic feeling, as the crippled gait of the sonnet ruefully testifies. We may recognize here the honesty of a great poet in decline. (Eleven years later, in 1844, Wordsworth's open-mindedness shifted to opposition when he saw the Lake District threatened by a railway, and he wrote two sonnets and two letters in the *Morning Post* attacking the railway project.)

By contrast, Tennyson's *Ode, Sung at the Opening of the International Exhibition* (1862) manages the job of mourning the Prince Consort, and celebrating the Crystal Palace and free trade, with apparently total confidence. There is not a spark of originality, but it is a clear enough illustration in verse form of the official version of the nineteenth century's Romance of Technology.[18]

Clearly 'old poetic feeling' was fatally at war with the industrial revolution. This is one reason why Jules Verne (1828–1905), a popular commercial writer without artistic pretensions, is perhaps the most illuminating spokesman for the nineteenth century's Romance of Technology; his imagination was uniquely wide-ranging within the limits of his craft, and it was untrammelled by the need to strike a note of high seriousness.

Jules Verne started his career as a stockbroker and property dealer, but in 1862 he met the publisher Hetzel and signed a contract to produce books for him. He eventually wrote some sixty-four books in the series *Voyages Extraordinaires*. They are remarkable first of all for sheer sweep of subject-matter, though only a handful of them, such as *20,000 Leagues Under the Sea* (1870)[19] and *Around the World in Eighty Days* (1873), have become lasting international classics. Every continent of the world, and a wide range of topical events, were drawn on to provide background for his novels: from the Irish nationalist movement (*P'tit Bonhomme* or *Foundling Mick*, 1893) to the Indian Mutiny (*The Steam House*, 1880) and the anti-slavery movement (*Un Capitaine de Quinze Ans* or *The Boy Captain*, 1878). It is hard to think of any major nineteenth-century technology which Verne did not 'use'. His novels themselves exhibit an inventiveness in finding new combinations of elements which enacts the whole spirit of a pioneering industrial culture, as much as do their regularity of manufacture and their close eye for the market. The title-pages of some of the early French editions are marked: 'This work is honoured with subscriptions from the French Ministry of Public Instruction, adopted for school and public libraries, and chosen by the Town of Paris for distribution as prizes.' Moreover, he was translated into twenty languages and his novels bear signs of being devised for an international readership; for instance, the characters in a typical Verne novel belong to a range of different nationalities. Certainly Verne's work proves irresistible to modern French textual critics. One of the best studies of him is Jean Chesneaux's lively and useful *The Political and Social Ideas of Jules Verne*, which explores the paradox that Verne appears to have been fascinated by the romantic resonances of radical politics, behind the façade of a pillar of the patriotic bourgeoisie of Amiens.[20]

If there is one influence on Verne's work which needs emphasizing here, and which goes a long way towards clarifying his otherwise strange perspective on the world, it is that of the Comte de Saint-Simon (1760–1825). Saint-Simon is remembered today as the teacher of Auguste Comte (1798–1857), whose scientistic humanism or 'positivism' was influential in the nineteenth century, and also in his own right as one of the early 'utopian socialists'. Saint-Simon is now being seriously studied as a social theorist whose reputation does not rest only on his anticipation of modern socialism and communism. In the history of the Romance of Technology, Saint-Simon is especially important, for he was one of the first to make the new class of technical specialists aware of its power to sustain, destroy or change the institutions of Western civilization. He created a scandal during his lifetime by arguing that France would sink in the scale of civilization and prosperity, and become inferior to her equals among the nations, if she were to lose suddenly such people as her scientists, artists, architects, engineers, doctors, bankers, merchants, ironmasters, industrialists, masons, carpenters and craftsmen; whereas she could easily survive the loss of the whole royal family, her ministers and state counsellors, her prefects, judges, bishops and the ten thousand wealthiest landed proprietors living solely on rents.

This emphasis on the economic and (potentially) political power of technical specialists was to be eliminated from the mainstream of nineteenth-century socialism and communism. Theoretical Marxism, while perceiving the importance of science and relying on new technology to stimulate revolutionary conditions and free man from toil, has never encouraged political ambition in the class of scientists, technicians and managers. Indeed, it now has great difficulty in fitting the 'aristocracy of labour' and the 'bearers of science' into the capitalist/proletariat dichotomy. In practice, most communist countries are as technocratic as the rest of the industrialized world.

When Verne began his literary career only 'practical Saint-Simonism' – that is, minus the socialism – had survived, embodied notably in captains of industry like Ferdinand de Lesseps, railway promoters, and great financiers like the brothers Emile and Isaac Pereire, who named one of the first ships of the CGT (Compagnie Générale Transatlantique) the *Saint-Simon*. We can find the tradition of 'practical Saint-Simonism' carried on directly today in the American ideology of the 'managerial' society. This was promoted by Edward Bellamy (author of *Looking Backward: 2000–1887*, published in 1888); later by Thorstein Veblen, and Technocracy Inc., the engineers' movement of the 1930s; and finally by James Burnham in *The Managerial Revolution* (1941). Daniel Bell argues neatly that Frederick W. Taylor, the American founder of 'scientific management', should be seen to stand in the same relationship to Saint-Simon as Lenin stands to Marx. This is an intellectually inferior tradition compared to the great and inspiring socialist tradition; but since 'practical Saint-Simonism' is gradually extinguishing the socialist ideal, and is becoming for better or worse the dominant ideology in the world we know, there is some sense in getting to know its theoretical antecedents. [21] It is not surprising to find America as one of Jules Verne's favourite backgrounds for his novels, for it seemed to offer a model for a new society based on industry and free from the encumbrances of the European past.

Many readers – including Raymond Roussel and the Surrealists – have admired Verne's richly poetic descriptions, with their incantatory use of scientific terms. Here is one typical example plucked at random from Chapter 24 of *20,000 Leagues Under the Sea* and translated into English:

Finally, after two hours of walking, we had reached a depth of about 300 metres, that is to say the extreme limit where coral begins to be formed. But there, it was no more in single bushes, nor in modest copses of low woodland; it was an immense forest, great mineral vegetations, huge petrified trees, united by garlands of elegant plumarias, those lianas [tropical twining plants] of the sea, all of them adorned with tints and reflections. We were passing freely under their high branches lost in the shade of the waves, while at our feet tubipores, meandrines, *astrées, fongies, cariophylles*, formed a carpet of flowers sown with dazzling gems.

Such heady lexical connoisseurship reminds us that there is a Romance of the Encyclopaedia not unrelated to the Romance of Technology. It is not Verne's literary qualities, however, that concern us here. Nor shall I consider those of his novels which are concerned more with political themes (especially nationalist movements) than with aspects of science and technology – though science is an important factor in *all* of the novels, not just in the twenty out of sixty-four that deal with scientific forecasts.

Apart from the interest of Verne's more spectacular flights of technical imagination, we can see the pattern of his imagination at work on a small scale, and thereby gain an understanding of how technology can acquire glamour and symbolic appeal in the hands of a brilliant popularizer. Having made it once come alive for his public, he was able to build a strongly critical element into his treatment of technology. Nevertheless, the residue that remains for posterity, the quintessential Jules Verne, is his apprehension of the Romance of Technology.

Tribulations of a Chinaman (1879) is one of Verne's lesser-known novels. Kin-Fo, a rich young Chinese gentleman, is escaping from some enemies on a ship in company with his sea-sick servant, Soon, and two American bodyguards, Craig and Fry, employees of a Chicago life insurance company, the Centenarian. They escape through a port-hole in 'four sets of the swimming apparatus just invented by Captain Boyton'; this is a gutta-percha suit consisting of leggings, tunic and cap; it is waterproof and has an air-space between the inner and outer layer providing both buoyancy and insulation from cold; and it is complete with a waterproof bag, a light paddle, and a small sail with a mast attachable to the foot. After some adventures, Fry boils fresh 11 water on a small stove (powered by phosphuretted calcium which burns spontaneously on contact with water) and makes tea in a pot. 'The whole party then partook of the decoction, and even Kin-Fo and Soon, although it was not brewed in the Chinese fashion, had no fault to find with it.'

Captain Boyton's apparatus points historically towards several modern tendencies: the development of life-support systems for use in the sea and also in other environments inimical to man; consumer merchandizing, which has persuaded people to buy equipment for activities just as gimmicky as drinking tea in the sea; and the growth of new specialized sports. Thus though the tea-making feat, as Verne describes it, might seem to represent a purely technical possibility and nothing more, it sticks in the mind as representing an expansion in the permutability of resources. If man can engage in such a hospitable activity as sharing tea in such an inhospitable place as the sea, there is no limit in principle to the combinations of activity open to him. Many of the limitations of nature turn out to be cultural conventions in disguise.

This is a pattern we find repeated many times in Verne's work: either imagining some combination of elements which had never yet been realized, then thinking of objections against its realization and overcoming these objections; or alternatively starting with some existing invention and conceiving a bizarre use for it. Obviously the new transport and communications technologies were of particular appeal to him. We can easily share his enthusiasm: each age responds strongly to the symbolic appeal of its new means of transport and communication. We can also see the same pattern of imagination at work in a novel like *Les Indes noires* or *Black Diamonds* (1877), which looks frankly to the future, but with a convincing show of verisimilitude. This is about a utopian mining town built in a huge underground cave with a lake under the soil of Scotland, and lit by two powerful electromagnetic lamps. Verne's novel includes some didactic material about the history of coal and coal-mining, and he is at pains to point out that an actual underground cavern on the scale described exists in Kentucky: the 20-mile-long Mammouth (*sic*) grottoes containing '226 avenues, 11 lakes, 7 rivers, 8 cataracts, 32 unfathomable wells and 57 domes'. Hence Verne grounds his fiction squarely in the factual and credible. It should be added that though most of us would look upon the notion of living in an underground city with horror, it is possible that such a city may be built one day as land for building gets progressively scarcer; and several avant-garde architects have sketched out schemes for

14

such cities. The idea of an underground city in the moon has even been seriously proposed.

My second illustration of the pattern of Verne's imagination is concerned with prosthetics. *From the Earth to the Moon* (1864) was devised in an opposite fashion from *Black Diamonds*. Here he had a definite, though difficult, technological goal which had to be reached in the novel – flight to the moon – and he had to devise ways and means of getting there. The novel is set in America just after the Civil War. The plan of sending a projectile to the moon in a vast cannon has the function of peacefully channelling the enthusiasm for ballistics built up during the American Civil War, when (Verne imagines) the Gun Club was formed. Its members are all inventors of cannons or other guns. They are unoccupied and restive at the end of the war; but the president, Impey Barbicane, announces that he has conceived a 'great experiment worthy of the nineteenth century', which will be to send a projectile to the moon. The subsequent narrative – where eventually a party of men rather than just a projectile is sent – need not concern us. The membership of the Gun Club is, however, of particular interest, and their bellicosity is described in the following terms:

No-one will challenge the following calculation, obtained by the statistician Pitcairn; dividing the number of victims fallen under their aim by the number of members of the Gun Club, he found that each of the latter had killed an 'average' of 2,365 men and a fraction.

Considering such a figure, it is clear that the only preoccupation of the learned society was the destruction of humanity with a philanthropic aim, and the perfecting of weapons of war, considered as instruments of civilization.

It was a meeting of Exterminating Angels, though they were the best fellows in the world.

We must add that these Yankees, good for any test, were not satisfied with theory only, but paid with their own persons. Among them were officers of every rank, lieutenants or generals, soldiers of all ranks, those who were beginning a career under arms and those who were growing old on their gun-carriages. Many stayed on the battlefield, their names appearing in the Book of Honour of the Gun Club; of those who returned, the majority bore marks of their indisputable intrepidity. Crutches, wooden legs, articulated arms, hooks, rubber jaws, silver skulls, platinum noses, nothing was missing in the collection, and the above-mentioned Pitcairn also calculated that in the Gun Club there was only one arm for every four people, and two legs for every six.

Much later in the narrative, the Perpetual Secretary of the Gun Club, J.-T. Maston, who has a gutta-percha skull which he scratches with an iron hook, tries to persuade Barbicane to let him join the trip to the moon:

When the Secretary of the Gun Club heard Barbicane and Nicholl accept the proposal of Michel Ardan [a heroic Frenchman who has joined the team], he made up his mind to join them and make a 'four'. One day he asked to be part of the team. Barbicane, miserable at having to refuse him, told him that the projectile could not carry such a large number of passengers. J.-T. Maston went in despair to find Michel Ardan, who advised him to resign himself and emphasized some *ad hominem* arguments.

'Look here, old man,' he told Maston; 'you must not take my words amiss; but really, between you and me, you are too incomplete to present yourself on the moon.'

'Incomplete!' cried the valiant invalid.

'Yes! my good friend! Suppose we were to meet inhabitants up there. Would you want to give them such a sad idea of what happens down here, to teach them what war is, to show them that we spend the best part of our time devouring each other, eating each other and breaking arms and legs, on a globe that could feed hundreds of billions of people, and where there are hardly twelve thousand million? Come, my worthy friend, you would have us put out of the door!'

When Kingsley Amis tells us in *New Maps of Hell* that Verne's work is of 'poor' literary quality, I wonder if he has taken into account images like this one. At a literal level, Verne is indulging in a whimsical exaggeration of familiar contemporary prosthetics, so as to make the reader think hard about the nature of the human body and the extent to which defective parts of it can be replaced – very provocatively, since now science can replace some internal organs as well as limbs and bones, and can control artificial limbs with electrical impulses from the nervous system. But Verne's image goes further this time: it tells us how a technology perverted for destructive ends can boomerang back on the inventor. D. H. Lawrence is using a similar image in *Lady Chatterley's Lover* (1928), when he makes Sir Clifford Chatterley crippled by a war injury to drive home the point that he is morally crippled. In the context of Lawrence's naturalistic novel, this stroke appears to show the author unfairly and maliciously stacking the cards against Sir Clifford. Verne's context of fantastic exaggeration allows the image to come home with a poetic force.

The various substitutes for parts of their bodies that the Gun Club members have lost would now be called 'technological fixes', applications of technology to try and rectify the ill effects of technology. We now have considerable evidence that there is

44

an aggressive, disquieting element in the whole technological enterprise – not just in military technology – in so far as it involves treating people systematically as instruments. It is not only on the battlefield that we devour (or 'consume') each other.

From the Earth to the Moon is one of Verne's earliest novels. His later work indicates a growing disquiet and disillusion about progress, large-scale industry, the power of money, and the American dream. The scientists and engineers in his novels are no longer heroes but figures of fun, misanthropes, even madmen. A turning-point is his remarkable book *The Begum's Fortune* (1879). Here two scientists, a Frenchman Dr Sarrasin and a German Professor Schultze, share a vast inheritance from India. Each builds a utopian city in America. The French city, Franceville, has an enlightened, paternalistic regime. The German city, Stahlstadt, is a huge gun factory, directed by Professor Schultze as a military hierarchy, secretive and totally centralized. Schultze sets out to launch an attack on Franceville but fails. Not surprisingly, *The Begum's Fortune* was on a list of banned books during the Nazi occupation of France in 1940.

Verne's disillusion is also a keynote of his other later novels. In *L'Ile à Hélice* or *Propeller Island* (1895), he describes a luxurious floating city, inhabited by American millionaires, where everything can be bought; two rival groups of millionaires start to quarrel and the city is finally destroyed by a meteorite. In *The Astonishing Adventures of the Barsac Mission* (published posthumously in 1920)[22] Verne conceives of Blackland, a city in Africa based on political terrorism, ruled over by a despot, Harry Killer, surrounded by nine counsellors, a black guard of 50 men, and a caste of 566 Merry Fellows, who are white criminals recruited in Europe. They rule over thousands of black slaves, and there is an intermediate caste, the 'free workers', who work under contract for good wages; when their contractual period of work ends, they think they will be free to leave, but they are actually killed in the desert and their savings are returned to the dictator's treasury. The rulers of Blackland use automatically piloted electric gliders, monitoring radar screens and electric torture. The city plan is dominated by two towers, that of the Palace (representing political power) and that of the Factory (representing economic power). The Factory is run by Harry Killer's assistant, Marcel Camaret, who is an engineer. Camaret is described as a 'pure abstraction', a 'thinking-machine, prodigious, inoffensive – and terrible'. 'His body was scarcely developed and resembled that

13

of an adolescent.' The two towers both fall in the end, crushing Killer and Camaret.

It will be clear from the last few pages that Verne was no simple-minded romanticizer of technology; a critical element is built into some of his earliest work, while novels like *The Begum's Fortune* face the threat of the total perversion of science. None the less, this critical note gathers its resonance within the context of an enthusiasm for science and technology which Verne whipped up for his readers and on which his fame rests. His preoccupation with technology is surely of a piece with the limitations of his literary talent. Most of Verne's characterizations are sadly one-dimensional and the female figures tend to be completely de-materialized; priggishness and sentimentality abound. The reader seldom gets that feeling of freshness, of the unpremedi-tated, of a sudden matching of the text with his own experience, which is associated with great fiction – the feeling which makes a book itself suddenly go limp in one's hands. True, the popular novel is a literary genre which derives from epic; and we look in work done within this genre not for subtle characterization but for the exploits of gods and heroes. Michel Serres's book on Verne treats the novels as forms of myth or dream. The fact remains that there is little genuine vitality in the interplay of characters, and the narrative is sustained by various ponderous devices – suspense, topographic description, pedagogic asides, 'running gags' – and by stylistic tricks such as enumeration and 'blinding with science'.

In spite of the anti-technological undercurrents, a technological imperative is central to Verne's work in another way: in his need, stimulated by the exigencies and opportunities of the publishing trade, to ring every possible change on his basic formula. This procedure is sometimes very plain – for instance, in *The Steam House* (1880) he conceives of an exotic Indian house drawn on wheels by an elephant which is driven by a concealed loco-motive. It is as if, having established the Verne brand-image, he produced a new line for the market every six to twelve months. Verne is the multi-national conglomerate of literature. Where an artist's production becomes as industrialized as this, it is inevitable that there will be a loss of spontaneity and emotional warmth; Verne's genius was to compensate in other directions.

The other great progenitor, with Verne, of science fiction[23] was H. G. Wells (1866–1946). Wells wrote many novels unconnected

46

with science, and in his later years a number of didactic and historical books too; his eight 'Scientific Romances' ought, therefore, to be seen in the context of his total output.

Though Wells insisted that he was a journalist rather than an artist, he was also accustomed to being taken very seriously as a popular sage. When, near the end of his life, he began to go out of fashion, he was not easily able to come to terms with his new position. While Verne had no literary or pontifical pretensions, and it is therefore a pure bonus when we find things to admire in his work, Wells was consciously tackling the big problems of the day head-on, having identified them more lucidly than most. By the high standards which such a project demands, his solutions were surely inadequate. His prescriptions for a future world state at the end of *An Outline of History* (first published in 1920), now seem incredibly naive. It is easy to sympathize with F. R. Leavis for having expressed surprise in 1932 – while recognizing that Wells was disinterested and had good intentions – that he still commanded attention as a sage.

And yet the distance that now separates us from Wells allows us to be attentive once again to his genuine originality and imagination, and his contribution to the development of socialist thought. Raymond Williams,[24] for instance, suggests that in his novel *Tono-Bungay* (1909), Wells saw more clearly than anyone before him the connection between the ruling power of the industrial city and the ruling power of the country-houses, with their dangerous illusion of an idyllic rural order. We must also acknowledge that Wells was one of the first people to start thinking seriously about the development of alternative modes of science and technology, adapted to a new socialistic and ecological order, and respecting the animal world. Moreover, if we read the Scientific Romances as popular fiction – rather than setting up a competition between them and the great English novels of their time – they are as impressive as Verne's.

No one could accuse Wells of blind submission to the Romance of Technology. We have only to think of *The Island of Dr. Moreau* (1896), where a crazed doctor fabricates 'beast folk' in his laboratory, or of *The Invisible Man* (1897), where the albino Griffin robs his father to finance his experiment in achieving invisibility. Griffin later announces a 'reign of terror' – 'An invisible man is a man of power. . . . I am Invisible Man the First' – and the outcome of his researches is pain, violence, ruthlessness. In one still earlier tale, 'The Lord of the Dynamos' (1894), a superficially civilized negroid savage is employed by a brutal engineer in the deafening railway dynamo-shed at Camberwell in South London. Maddened by his working conditions, the savage comes to worship the dynamo, and finally sacrifices the engineer and himself to it by electrocution. 'So ended prematurely the worship of the Dynamo Deity, perhaps the most short-lived of all religions. Yet withal it could at least boast a Martyrdom and a Human Sacrifice.'[25]

The First Men in the Moon (1901), is a more ambiguous case. The Selenites who live on the moon are partly a 'burlesque' of the effects of specialization (as Wells says in his preface to the collected Scientific Romances in 1933); they are physically differentiated according to task like ants, though a much wider range of different demands are made on them. They are ruled by an aristocracy of 'big heads' and ultimately by the Grand Lunar – an ancestor of the Mekon – whose brain-case is many yards in diameter and has to be sprayed with cooling liquid by attendants. Their regime is a kind of technocratic police-state. But the Selenites also offer Wells a vantage-point for making an ethical criticism of man's technological presumption and lust for dominance. The Selenites are appalled by what they hear, from the visiting scientist from Earth, Mr Cavor, about mankind's love of war. They finally censor his radio communications with the Earth to forestall another visit by Earthmen.

Certainly Wells was capable on occasion of sharp satire, as in the following passage from Cavor's message to Earth in *The First Men in the Moon*, which carries with it something of the sting of both Swift and Marx:

The making of these various sorts of operative must be a very curious and interesting process. I am still much in the dark about it, but quite recently I came upon a number of young Selenites, confined in jars from which only the fore limbs protruded, who were being compressed to become machine-minders of a special sort. The extended 'hand' in this highly developed system of technical education is stimulated by irritants and nourished by injection while the rest of the body is starved. Phi-oo, unless I misunderstood him, explained that in the earlier stages these queer little creatures are apt to display signs of suffering in their various cramped situations, but they easily become indurated to their lot; and he took me on to where a number of flexible-limbed messengers were being drawn out and broken in. It is quite unreasonable, I know, but these glimpses of the educational methods of these beings have affected me disagreeably. I hope, however, that may pass off and I may be able to see more of this aspect of this wonderful social order. That wretched-looking hand sticking out of its jar seemed to appeal for lost possibilities; it haunts me still, although, of course, it is really in the end a far more humane proceeding than our earthly method of leaving children to grow into human beings, and then making machines of them.

Yet the mainspring of Wells's Scientific Romances – as of Dan Dare and Verne's *Voyages extraordinaires* – is always the positive energy and positive glamour of science and technology. This is what keeps the interest alive even when wicked characters get hold of the power.

Wells is much less interested than Verne in technical detail – as Verne himself pointed out when he read *The First Men in the Moon* ('I make use of physics. He fabricates'). Wells's power of characterization is on the whole superior to Verne's, and yet it is still undistinguished – at least in the novels classed as Scientific Romances; in particular his handling of love and sexuality is usually marred by a mawkish vulgarity. It is the effect of scientific precision, induced by a kind of conjurer's 'patter', that lends such excitement to his narratives.

In *The War of the Worlds* (1898), Wells is really in his element as a story-teller, though the total effect of the book is as equivocal as *The First Men in the Moon*. Martians with heat-rays land in the Home Counties of England. Their bodies are atrophied, lacking entrails and reproducing asexually, but instead they have built themselves elaborate machinery for transport and fighting. Their apparent intention is to breed Earthmen as food, but they are eventually thwarted by their inability to resist bacterial infection (a fine touch by Wells). *The War of the Worlds* represents a simpler and in a sense purer form of science fiction than *The First Men in the Moon*. There is no communication with the alien beings, and so no eliciting of the reader's sympathy with a new species, a new class of embodied consciousness. Space war is a logical culmination of the march of technology. Since this march has to use or displace anything that blocks its path, the inference follows that alien beings will be similarly motivated and will wish to use or displace Earthmen. I have urged that the Romance of Technology position can have a strong humanistic motivation, since it asserts man's ability to build his own future. This motivation, however, can all too easily be forgotten: we are left with the removal of obstacles as an end in itself rather than as a means to an end.

The War of the Worlds was no doubt partly intended as a satire against Western cerebrality, as the following passage suggests: 'Without the body the brain would of course become a mere selfish intelligence, without any of the emotional substratum of the human being.'[26] As a scientific statement this would be meaningless, since the literal concept of a brain without a body is impossible; even the Martians have mouths and whip-like tentacles which (an Earthly anatomist suggests) may have evolved from the hands. Yet Wells's meaning is quite clear. One could criticize the term 'substratum', with its implication that human emotions are simply a foundation, unchanged during the evolution of man, for the gradual superimposition of his reasoning powers, for it is surely more useful to think of human evolution as having been a dialectical process between mind and physiology, reason and emotion. This does not detract from Wells's main point here: the importance of the human sympathies.

If the underlying purpose of *The War of the Worlds* was humanistic and satirical, the resulting book, seen as a whole, seems to depart from satire and to be carried away by its own narrative energies. What, therefore, should be our reaction to the colour movie made of *The War of the Worlds* by Paramount (produced by George Pal), which is well known for its cinematic 'special effects' but commands no respect whatever as narrative? Here the setting has been updated and transposed to America, and the moral speculation of Wells is replaced by a nauseous religious-revivalist interest. A travesty of Wells, yes. But there are elements in the original novel which were asking for such debasement. Take the following passage, where the narrator is passing on to the reader his brother's report of the panic exodus from London:

After a fruitless struggle to get aboard a North-Western train at Chalk Farm – the engines of the trains that had loaded in the goods yard there *ploughed* through shrieking people, and a dozen stalwart men fought to keep the crowd from crushing the driver against his furnace – my brother emerged from the Chalk Farm road, dodged across through a hurrying swarm of vehicles, and had the luck to be foremost in the sack of a cycle shop.[27]

Am I wrong in detecting a kind of cruelty coming out in Wells's italicized 'ploughed'? It is not clear whether the shrieking people are killed, injured or merely divide like the Red Sea; they do not even get a complete sentence with a full stop to themselves as a memorial, but are stuffed into a parenthesis. You may say in Wells's defence that such scenes of violence are universal in situations of crowd panic – as indeed in military battles – and the author is merely describing a plausible incident. But it should be noted that the narrator is adopting the standpoint of the riot policeman or the stationmaster when he writes of the engines 'ploughing' through the crowd as if it was a field of earth. This is not the viewpoint of the people themselves. You may say that Wells is ironically articulating either the personality of the narrator through which the story is refracted, or else the brutalization of human sympathy under stress. I don't think so; when Wells is using irony he usually lays it on so thick that we cannot miss it. Another writer – Wells himself, perhaps, on another occasion – might take such a scene of panic and turn it into art through the seriousness or compassion of his prose. Here he seems to strike a false note. (Wells appears to have had some sardonic misgivings himself since he wrote jocularly in a letter to Elizabeth Healey: 'I'm doing the dearest little serial for Pearson's new magazine, in which I completely wreck and destroy Woking – killing my neighbours in painful and eccentric ways – then proceed via Kingston and Richmond to London, which I sack, selecting South Kensington for feats of peculiar atrocity.')

Wells's image of the engines 'ploughing' through the crowd offends because it reduces the human body to an object. You may say that I am making too much of this image and that Wells simply wished to generate a momentary *frisson* in the reader with the word 'ploughed', which is why he italicized it. But there is evidence elsewhere in *The War of the Worlds* that, despite his recognition of the body as representing man's emotional 'substratum' (in the passage I have quoted above), he also favours another model of the brain/body relationship. The narrator, speculating earlier in the book on the nature of the Martian machines, writes:

[These mechanical colossi] seemed amazingly busy. I began to ask myself what they could be. Were they intelligent mechanisms? Such a thing I felt was impossible. Or did a Martian sit within each, ruling, directing, using, much as a man's brain sits and rules in his body?[28]

This model of the brain 'driving' the body as a soldier drives an armoured car – or, we would now say, as a computer programme 'drives' factory machinery – seems to me characteristic of the technocratic cast of mind. It is a model that Wells could use unironically in his writings even though (as we have seen) he was also capable of appreciating some of the positive aspects of the body's emotions.

Wells writes in similar terms later in the same novel when he is describing the Martian physiology and culture:

We men, with our bicycles and road-skates, our Lilienthal[29] soaring-machines, our guns and sticks and so forth, are just in the beginning of the evolution that the Martians have worked out. They have become practically mere brains, wearing different bodies according to their needs just as men wear suits of clothes and take a bicycle in a hurry or an umbrella in the wet.[30]

This passage is based on an important truth of everyday experience – that when we use tools and machines of a human scale, these can seem virtually part of our bodies – but also on current ideas of late nineteenth-century intellectuals. Samuel Butler had articulated the theme satirically before Wells in his *Erewhon* (1872); this incorporates a sophisticated text, 'The book of the machines',[31] that imaginatively exploded the whole contemporary debate about analogies between organisms and machines, into a witty fantasy of a civilization which destroys all its machines in order to avoid being enslaved by a new evolving race. In George Bernard Shaw, we find the dream of evolving out of the prison of the human body. (At the end of Shaw's *Back to Methuselah* (1921), a character called the She-Ancient says, 'Yes: this body is the last doll to be discarded'.) The dream, which seems to have been shared to some extent by Wells, had its origins in the superimposition of evolutionary theory on a long tradition of Western teaching that reason must rule over the flesh. It has not been very successful, for our civilization has contained powerful counter-currents against the total reduction of the body to an instrument or encumbrance.

It is not surprising that both Wells and (still more so) Shaw are implausible when they try to dramatize the more tender human emotions. Essentially these depend on a recognition that the 'body' has a certain independence or plenitude vis-à-vis the rational faculties that we call the 'brain', is more than a substratum, has indeed 'its own reasons that reason does not know'. (Pascal wrote, 'The heart has its reasons that reason does not know'; but the word 'heart' often seems to be used as a substitute for the whole body of which it is a part, opposed to the 'head' which stands for reason. This substitution of part for whole – or *synecdoche*, to use the technical term of rhetoric – is aided in the original French by the assonance between *cœur* and *corps*. I have seen a sex-film, *Le Corps a ses Raisons*, advertised in a cinema off the Place Pigalle, whose title proves the point.)

There is a strange scene at the end of *In the Days of the Comet*, one of the latest of Wells's Scientific Romances (1906), the first part of which is distinguished by some vivid and caustic descriptions of economic life in the English industrial Midlands. Halfway through the novel, a comet passes by the Earth and gasses everybody, thereby effecting the 'Change', a moral awakening of mankind at both an individual and a communal level which results in a benevolent world government and a sudden transcendence of competition, aggression, jealousy and alienation. A chapter called 'Love after the Change' is Wells's opportunity to voice his progressive views on sex. His attack on the proprietary character of conventional bourgeois love and marriage recalls Shelley, in *Epipsychidion*:

> I never was attached to that great sect
> Whose doctrine is, that each one should select
> Out of the crowd a mistress or a friend,
> And all the rest, though fair and wise, commend
> To cold oblivion.

But it is clear that the body is an encumbrance in Wells's theoretical scheme. One of the characters – the narrator, Willie Leadford – speaks as follows:

You see, Nettie, these bodies of ours are not the bodies of angels. They are the same bodies – I have read somewhere that in our bodies you can find evidence of the lowliest ancestry; that about our inward ears – I think it is – and about our teeth, there remains still something of the fish, that there are bones that recall little – what is it? – marsupial forebears – and a hundred traces of the ape. Even your beautiful body, Nettie, carries this taint. No! hear me out . . . Our emotions, our passions, our desires, the substance of them, like the substance of our bodies, is an animal, a competing thing, as well as a desiring thing. You speak to us now a mind to minds – one can do that when one has had exercise and when one has eaten, when one is not doing anything – but when one turns to live, one turns again to matter.

The novel ends with the narrator, two women and Verrall, his former rival in love, forming a close group of 'friends, helpers, personal lovers in a world of lovers'. One longs to know in detail how this actually works out, but Wells will not tell us; the novel concludes by dissolving into a 'dreamland city . . . its galleries and open spaces, its trees of golden fruit and crystal waters, its music and rejoicing, love and beauty without ceasing flowing through its varied and intricate streets'.

We may compare this with a passage in the final chapter of Wells's *An Outline of History* (1925, revised edition): 'Hitherto a man has been living in a slum, amidst quarrels, revenges, vanities, shames and taints, hot desires and urgent appetites. He has scarcely tasted sweet air yet, and the great freedoms of the world that science has enlarged for him.' But it is not at all clear how we could give up our pig-sty of 'hot desires and urgent appetites' even if we wanted to. And what kind of socialism stands any chance of becoming a reality if it remains an effusion of the mind, refusing to be grounded in the concrete bodily experience of individuals? It is hardly surprising that the progressive rationalism which Wells stands for has excited strong counter-reactions, one of which is to try and abandon the scientific enterprise altogether. Anti-scientism, however, is itself an irresponsible and inadequate response to the dilemmas that face the world.

If we take a sidestep in time from H. G. Wells we find the roughly contemporary movement of Italian Futurism. Italian Futurism has been the most emphatic and least critical manifestation of the Romance of Technology in our century; and, as we shall see, it was very influential in spite of being almost provincial in its intellectual origins.

Industrialization came late and rapidly to the Italians. For this reason, F. T. Marinetti, the poet and cultural entrepreneur of Futurism, was able (with his friends) to respond to it with a brash, almost hysterical enthusiasm that was no longer possible in England, which had already experienced the thrills and dis-illusion of a Steam Age. The Futurists read Verne and Wells; also Walt Whitman, and some of the French symbolist poets and 'decadent' writers who used industrial imagery. Antecedents can probably be found in the nineteenth century for most if not all of the Futurists' explicit ideas and imagery. Their own original achievements were nevertheless many: to accept the challenge of mixing art with political agitation; to offer and provoke alternatives to the dead clichés of academic and museum art; and to exploit the publicity media. All these innovations were widely influential. Above all, it was their fascination with machinery, speed and the city that made them most seductive and notorious.

They ignored or rejected the eloquent critique of mechanization that had been a major debate of the nineteenth century in both England and America. Marinetti, for instance, gave a lecture at the Lyceum Club in London in 1912 attacking Ruskin for 'infantilism'. The positive worth of their version of the Romance of Technology makes us prepared to swallow a little rhetorical overexcitement, such as this famous passage in Marinetti's first manifesto, published in 1901 in the Paris *Figaro*:

We shall sing of great crowds excited by work, by pleasure, and by riot; we shall sing of the multicoloured, polyphonic tides of revolution in the modern capitals; we will sing of the vibrant nightly fervour of arsenals and shipyards blazing with violent electric moons; greedy railway stations that devour smoke-plumed serpents; factories hung on clouds by the crooked lines of their smoke; bridges that stride the rivers like giant gymnasts, flashing in the sun with a glitter of knives; adventurous steamers that sniff the horizon; deep-chested locomotives whose wheels paw the tracks like the hooves of enormous steel horses bridled by tubing; and the sleek flight of planes whose propellers chatter in the wind like banners and seem to cheer like an enthusiastic crowd.

In human terms, however, the Futurists' work was one-dimensional, in the sense in which I have used this term before. Thumbing through the illustrations in any book on Futurism,[32] one notes great technical inventiveness, energy, variety, and the most dashing visual originality. As Andrew Higgens points out in an illuminating essay[33] on this period, a parallel was seen between the artist's new freedom from the process of imitating the real world, and man's remaking of his environment through technology. But when we look at Futurist representations or evocations of the human body, we find that it has been treated exactly as a machine. Footballers, boxers, riders and dancers are given no privileged status over trains, trams, motor-cars, propellers and cannons. There are some exceptions: Boccioni's painting of people who have seen friends off at a railway station, *Those Who Stay Behind* (1911); or Anton Bragaglia's time-lapse photograph *Young Man Rocking* (1911), where one catches that tenderness which the human body can inspire – as it conspicuously did in Rodin and in the late nineteenth-century Italian sculptor Medardo Rosso, as well as in countless earlier artists. The Futurists despised the nude as a subject for art, as well as any sentimentalization of human relations. Their rejection of the debased sentiment of much nineteenth-century salon art is understandable, but they paid a penalty in blocking off an artistic resource – what Rousseau called *amour de soi* or *pitié*, sympathetic love of the human species – which until the twentieth century would have been thought indispensable for the practice of art in any accepted aesthetic theory. The Futurist version of the Romance of Technology readily embraced enthusiastic militarism, which is a special form of the refusal to distinguish people from

15

machines or obstacles. The first manifesto by Marinetti spoke of war as 'the world's only hygiene'.

In the 1910 'Technical Manifesto' – signed by Boccioni, Carra, Russolo, Balla and Severini – we read:

Our renovated consciousness does not permit us to look upon man as the centre of universal life. The suffering of a man is of the same interest to us as the suffering of an electric lamp, which, with spasmodic starts, shrieks out the most heartrending expressions of colour.

Andrew Higgens comments perceptively that the Futurists used the new reality 'to create a kind of programmatic romanticism, fully in the nineteenth-century tradition, confusing organic and inorganic in an arbitrary way in order to preserve some kind of exterior equivalent for strong feeling by transferring it to a new range of objects'. The masses are brought in simply to generate feelings of power and excitement.

This callous aestheticism – a dominant element in Futurism – contrasts with a sometimes attractive spontaneity and trust in impulse. One of the strangest of the Italian Futurist manifestoes is the 'Manifesto of Lust', which at one point seems to advocate a healthy sexual liberation:

Christian morality alone, following on from pagan morality, was fatally drawn to consider lust as a weakness. Out of the healthy joy which is the flowering of the flesh in all its power it has made something shameful and to be hidden, a vice to be denied. It has covered it with hypocrisy, and this has made a sin of it.

We must stop despising Desire, this attraction at once delicate and brutal between two bodies, of whatever sex, two bodies that want each other, striving for unity. We must stop despising Desire, disguising it in the pitiful clothes of old and sterile sentimentality.

Earlier the same text glorifies both rape after battle and the hard-driving energy of bankers and international traders. It is all the more difficult to 'place' this text because it is the work of a woman, Valentine de Saint-Point.

There are enough contradictions in Italian Futurism, and enough different colourful individuals involved, to make one hesitant in generalizing about it.[34] Perhaps D. H. Lawrence's summary, in a letter[35] written in 1914, is fair:

They want to deny every scrap of tradition and experience, which is silly. They are very young, college-student and medical-student at his most blatant. But I like them. Only I don't believe in them. I agree with them about the weary sickness of pedantry and tradition and inertness, but I don't agree with them as to the cure and the escape. They will progress down the purely male or intellectual or scientific line.

The Italian Futurists were followed by a comparable movement in Russia, in which a wing of the avant-garde – particularly Malevich, Lissitsky and Gabo – attempted to fuse enthusiasm for technology and the city with communism. Though the movement is of great importance in the history of modern art, it was doomed not merely by the growing repressiveness of Soviet cultural politics after four initial years of patronage of the avant-garde after the Revolution, but also by the incompatibility of Futurist rhetoric and Marxian political theory. Such artists were quite unable to develop a political ideology. There was a cult of Americanism among Russian intellectuals in the 1920s: an admiration for the mass-production of Ford cars, for skyscrapers, and for Taylorism (the scientific study of work habits with a view to greater efficiency). As Peter Wollen[36] observes, the artistic results – such as Tatlin's air-bicycle for the masses – are both grotesque and sublime, expressing 'the quest for the marvellous and the Utopian in contradiction with the exigencies of the practical and the utilitarian'.

After the First World War, the Italian Futurists' cult of the machine became more temperate. A more sober enthusiasm altogether was expressed by the Dutch group De Stijl, founded in 1917. This group admired the machine for its beauty, not as a cult object, and its members had a strong architectural orientation. Mondrian's paintings and Rietveld's furniture, which resulted from its activities, are certainly beautiful, in a different way from the products of Italian Futurism. Everything is so neat and tidy; there is none of the spontaneity and brashness of Futurism. De Stijl theory stated that the only satisfactory way of genuinely representing emotion in art was to drain away subjective and arbitrary details, organizing them intellectually into a pure, harmonious, geometric order.[37] The machine, with its programmability and accuracy, stood for the transcendence of nature. Some critics have commented that this view reflects the artificial and geometric character of the Dutch landscape.

As a theory, De Stijl served its purpose as a peg on which a number of talented individuals could hang their art. To the modern reader, it sounds too like an excuse for censoring out the difficult. And in practice, the dangers of the 'machine aesthetic' (a phrase coined by De Stijl's guiding spirit, van Doesburg) were enormous. Reyner Banham[38] has shown how it influenced the whole international movement in architecture.[39] When we look back now at the mainstream of modern architecture, it seems to have been very successful in building monuments to its own technology in the form of bridges and skyscrapers, that is, sculpture on a grand scale. It has made an appalling job of accommodating the human body, except for the bodies of a small number of privileged private clients who have had luxury houses made: no wonder that we are now witnessing a reaction against the whole enterprise of modern architecture and city planning, which is increasingly condemned as a noxious fusion of 'technological rationality' with a romantic faith in artistic genius; or that there is a new respect for the mock-Tudor semi-detached, and for folk architecture of various kinds.[40]

Architects run a special risk to their reputations because human beings have to live in their buildings; painters are less exposed. One painter, Fernand Léger (1881–1955), seems to have come out of the ideological ferment of the Futurist period with his innocence intact: by 'innocence' I mean the same kind of classical sense of continuum that characterized the painting of Wright in the eighteenth century. Léger achieved no personal 'breakthrough' in art to match the technical innovation of Picasso and Braque's analytical cubism; but if we value highly the qualities of sanity and comprehensiveness, then his work until the mid-1920s ranks high in the history of modern painting. Like Wright, he integrated within his art the conflicting forces that were working on it. Léger absorbed the Romance of Technology of the Italian Futurists, De Stijl and the French Purists (Ozenfant and Le Corbusier),[41] but without losing a classical painter's respect for the human figure. Thus we find many evocations in his paintings of machinery and the hectic pace of the city, but he was just as happy to focus a painting round two men and a cow, as in his *Paysages Animés* (1921). Douglas Cooper has aptly commented: 'Léger is the only contemporary painter who feels himself capable of confronting, without compromise, at once the rugosity of trees and the elaborate architecture of precision-built machines.'[42] If there is one painting of Léger's which sums up both his art and its relationship to the period, it is *The Mechanic* (1920), which illustrates the Purist doctrine that man is the most precise and perfect of natural machines, but which does not forfeit the mechanic's dignity and reality as a human being.

It is only when we compare Léger's paintings, inspired to a great extent by the city of Paris (at least as far as subject-matter is concerned), with Eugène Atget's photographs of Paris, taken at roughly the same time (between 1898 and 1914), that Léger's limitations as an artist become apparent. This was partly a matter of professional choice; by Léger's time the art of painting was beginning to specialize in perceptual exhilaration by means of the painted surface, leaving the tasks of documentary realism and sympathetic portraiture to photographers. None the less, Atget with his detailed and cumulative vision of what we would now call the ecology of the city – its trades, transactions, commodities and energies, the material interchanges between human bodies and the earth – seems to me a pictorial artist of more intelligent sympathy than Léger. Which leads one to suspect that the integrity and innocence of Léger's work may have been actually protected by a certain honest obtuseness on his part. As Ozenfant once remarked, 'Léger knows how to make a good Léger from everything.'

In the following text, published in 1924, Léger describes a visit to the academic *Salon d'automne* when an exhibition called the *Salon d'aviation* was being prepared next door:

The mechanics had seen me go by, they knew they had artists for neighbours, and in their turn they asked me for permission to go and have a look at the other side. They were good lads who had never seen an art exhibition in their life. They had clearly been brought up in the pure and fine tradition of raw materials, and they went into ecstasies over works which I will not concern you with.

I shall always be able to picture a sixteen-year-old boy with flaming red hair, standing in a new jacket with a blue criss-cross pattern, orange trousers, and one of his hands stained with Prussian-blue paint, blissfully gaping at nudes in gilt frames. There he was, without the slightest suspicion that his working clothes bursting with colour killed the whole show. There was nothing on the walls but hazy shadows in old frames: the dazzling boy seemed to be the child of some agricultural machine – he was the symbol of the exhibition next door, the symbol of the future when Prejudice will be destroyed.[43]

The cult of the engineer as a kind of Noble Savage was a feature of the period. Léger's text is an interesting one because the body is aligned *with* technology *against* art – a local inversion of the normal opposition in which the body is set against technology. For Léger, it is the salon art that is stereotyped, machines and the body that brim with life and colour. Nevertheless, it is clear that he is much more interested in appreciating the splash of colour that the young mechanic makes on his imaginary canvas than in understanding the boy's particular consciousness. We are a long way from the tradition of painting as a psychological and physiognomic exercise.

The classical moment achieved by Léger during his great period was short-lived, idiosyncratic, and – I would guess – unlikely to be retrieved again within Western industrialized culture.

Every generation seems to rediscover the Romance of Technology as if it were something new (only to clutch in due course at revolt against technology). At times a special gathering of forces – economic and cultural – results in a concentrated enthusiasm for technology during a limited period. I can only make guesses as to why these periods occur when they do; but they are certainly *concentrations* of a tendency which is visible in other periods as well. The first quarter of the twentieth century was clearly one time when the Romance of Technology was especially dominant. The 1960s was probably another, and at the end of the 1960s there occurred a break which enables us to look back on that decade with some detachment. Not everyone gave in to a frenzied enthusiasm for technology, nor has this suddenly given way to a rampant primitivism. Serious thought is to some extent independent of the swings of intellectual fashion. But the late 1950s and early to mid-1960s were a period of considerable hope in technology.

The economic background encouraged the attitude. The industrial recovery of both Japan and West Germany from defeat in the Second World War was a challenge. Fuel was cheap. The science-based industries such as plastics, electronics and computers were booming, especially in the USA. In the universities, a succession of ambitious new projects like automatic language translation and teaching-machines (or 'programmed learning') attracted research funds (the assumptions on which they were based now seem very crude and they surely found popularity only because of an uncritical deference towards science). The behavioural sciences and quantitative sociology – technicist approaches to human beings – were widely influential; and huge claims were made in various quarters for the importance of systems theory and cybernetics, information theory, and artificial intelligence.

60

The two groups of people who reflect fashion most accurately (apart from professional publicists) are politicians – because their job is to voice public opinion – and the young – because they are most vulnerable to the seduction of apparent novelty. Politicians everywhere made speeches during this period about the importance of technological progress; I remember in 1963 or '64 being surprised to see even Sir Alec Douglas-Home, a politician more associated in the public mind with grouse-moors and sofa diplomacy, pleading on television for the 'modernization of Britain', and this became the watchword of the British Labour Government in the 1960s. The latter even gave a new government department the Orwellian name of MinTech. As for the young, even some who had been imbued with the critique of scientism and industrialism put forward by men like D. H. Lawrence, Eliot and Leavis began to wonder if these formidable minds were not mistaken. Was there not another cultural tradition, the scientific culture described by C. P. Snow, which was a cumulative, collective search for a consensus of agreement about reality, rather than a series of solo performances? Should we not show more respect for the technical perfectionism and impersonal dedication of design engineers and computer programmers? Should not science replace the humanities as a common core for educational curricula?

During this period the Romance of Technology was expressed less strongly in literature – where it had too many entrenched positions to fight against – than in architecture, the visual arts and the 'media' (especially television and advertising). In architecture, Buckminster Fuller's stirring call for a new generation of 'comprehensive designers', and his attack on specialization, was a source of great inspiration, notwithstanding some flaws in his reasoning.[44] Many otherwise dissimilar projects in experimental or utopian architecture of the 1960s reveal a fascination with the *aura* of technology, its sheer glamour. Nicolas Schöffer proposed in 1969 a cybernetic city equipped with a sumptuous 'centre of sexual leisures' in the shape of a swollen breast. Reyner Banham proposed in 1965 an Environment-Bubble, pushing to an extreme the notion of the disposability of consumer goods, so that all human requirements come through electronic media incorporated under an inflatable dome, and all products are dispensed with, including clothes. The Archigram group, led by Peter Cook, executed a number of studio projects, attractively drawn and influential within the architectural world, such as the Plug-In

City (1964) – a basic extensible structure serviced by railways, helicopters and hovercraft – and Instant City (1969) – a travelling circus that could bring a wide range of metropolitan attractions to the provinces overnight. A proposal by Vjenceslas Richter,[45] called Heliopolis, includes a peripheral urban membrane that would rotate slowly around a central, static core. Farooq Hussain, another architect, envisages in his book *Living Underwater* (1970) that men will one day not only live in underwater cities but also submit to irreversible surgical operations to make their lungs function as gills.

Clearly this list of projects – selected from the output of avantgarde architectural studios of the 1960s – bears the specific aura of mid-twentieth-century technology. No longer do we find obsession with speed and force, but with 'spin-off' from cybernetics, and from the life-support systems developed for space and underwater exploration. We also find the influence of Buckminster Fuller's structural engineering and of Marshall McLuhan's theories about media. McLuhan's influence was strongest in the worlds of television and advertising. Arts graduates working for high salaries in making television commercials rejoiced to hear from McLuhan that 'the medium is the message'; in their state of professional guilt they were able to convince themselves that manipulation of other people's minds was somehow justified by its technological progressiveness.

Visual artists in the 1960s were also interested in exploring technology. One way of doing this was to use technological subject-matter for painting. Other artists actually tried to use new technologies in their work and a whole new branch of the arts called 'Technological Art' sprang up in the late 1960s. The culmination of the movement was the founding in New York of 'Experiments in Art and Technology' (EAT) by Billy Klüver, a laser physicist, and Robert Rauschenberg the artist, after an experiment in October 1966 called 'Nine Evenings: Theatre and Engineering'. EAT claimed a membership of 3000 artists and engineers by 1968, and its *magnum opus* was an ambitious pavilion at the World Fair in Osaka in 1970. Technological Art was in part a continuation of the 'machine aesthetic' and of the cult of the engineer which had characterized the 1920s. But, as one would expect, the new technologies and scientific disciplines began to influence art production; and artists began to use computers, lasers or fibre optics in their work, or to build ambitious theories based on cybernetics or information theory or behavioural psychology. Most of this work was ephemeral, and artists who dabbled in technology ran the risk of becoming monkeys driven by their barrel-organs rather than taking the initiative themselves.[46] At least some of this work, however, and some of the architectural projects I have outlined, show how technology can be reclaimed for creative purposes which it was not designed for, thus enabling us to elude technological determinism. I shall explore the implications of this in my concluding chapter.

The student movements in America and France, the publication of popular books like Roszak's *The Making of a Counter Culture*, the influence of men like Marcuse and Chomsky and Paul Goodman in attacking American technocracy, and the growing politicization of young scientists – all these were signs that, at the end of the 1960s, the Romance of Technology went sour for many people. One awaits with interest the next swing back. No doubt it will have features different from those of any previous period. Perhaps a refined form of systems theory or cybernetics will again fascinate people (as I admit they once fascinated me for use as a possible interdisciplinary language); or some new technology such as laser holography – that striking visual proof of post-Einsteinian physics – may become the symbol of a new age. But we may also predict that any future Romance of Technology will have important similarities with past enthusiasms, since man's situation is not fundamentally changed from that stage in history when he first began to become conscious of his 'open future'.

It may be contended that the Romance of Technology will not recur in future generations. The theory of 'post-industrial society'[47] is either over-stated (for the economic shift from manufacturing to services, and the expansion of professional and technical social occupations, hardly amount to a superseding of industrialism) or else false (for the evidence that culture is developing autonomously from economics, as Daniel Bell claims, is very weak). If, on the other hand, it is forecast that man will never again make the mistake of believing in industrial progress, but will try to achieve some sort of harmonious balance with nature, then I can only guess that the orphans of mid-twentieth-century technocracy will eventually find life intolerable without indulging again in romantic hope. If, again, it is forecast that industrialization of the world will be so complete and all-pervading that no such hope is necessary or appropriate, then surely men will rebel against it – and the dialectic of technophobia and technophilia will begin again.

Since the essence of the Romance of Technology is to feel liberated from the past, can we expect future generations to admit that in their own euphoria they are following a well-trodden historical path? Probably not – nor should we try to damp down their ardour. For without the Romance of Technology life in the future would be at best like that of a small, sleepy and superstitious provincial town. What is important is that due weight should be given to other human resources as well.

One important feature of our civilization needs consideration on its own: the city. A great deal of very diverse theoretical effort has been expended on the 'urban phenomenon', from the viewpoint of architecture, history, economics, sociology, political theory and most recently the study of signs (semiology). Some of this theorizing is very stimulating, but I propose here to consider cities from a strictly defined point of view, in relation to technology.

The city is in a sense co-extensive with technology, an aggregation of technical resources. Jane Jacobs[48] has argued against the traditional historical view that cities emerged gradually out of rural societies; in her view, the city was primary, the focus of trade and intercourse, and what we perceive as the countryside is really a set of land-allotments for servicing the city. We need not accept the whole of her historical argument (which is controversial) to see the point of inverting the usual image of the countryside as natural order and the city as an unnatural tumour.

The Romance of Technology is nearly always associated with an enthusiasm for cities, classically in Italian Futurism. Rejection of technology is nearly always associated with rejection of city life. Yet we cannot build an understanding of technology on a theory of cities. Too many competing theories of cities already exist; and more fundamentally, the city is a complex phenomenon which cannot be conveniently analysed into relationships with the human body. Admittedly we do not yet have a complete theory satisfactorily explaining the social implications of all technology. But there do exist some very powerful approaches to such a theory (these I shall discuss in Chapter 4), and above all we can in principle analyse down *all* technology into precise material relationships with the human body. Thus, for instance, a machine represents the solidified labour of a set of individual people; it is operated and maintained physically by a second set of people in order to produce output to be physically consumed by a third set.

Technology could be said to precede the city, rather than *vice versa*, in the sense that we must aim to build a greater understanding of cities on a greater understanding of technology, rather than the reverse. This point is made strikingly by Marx in the course of the passage in his *Grundrisse* on classical and Asiatic history – a sentence which goes some way to explain why he did not give his attention to formulating a systematic theory of the 'urban phenomenon', though his whole work is pervaded by a sense of the city as the milieu that would generate a new proletarian consciousness and solidarity:

The really large cities must be regarded . . . merely as royal camps, as works of Superfetation erected over the economic construction proper.[49]

'Superfetation' is a physiological term meaning 'a second conception occurring after a prior one and before the delivery; the formation of a second foetus in a uterus already pregnant . . .' (Shorter OED).

At an abstract level, technology and the 'urban phenomenon' have one key factor in common. Each is essentially an increase in the permutability of resources. With his technology man learns increasingly to put together resources that were never joined before – for even in chemical synergy, or in the splitting of the atom, the required elements or particles for these dramatic transformations were always there in nature. The city is essentially an increase in options and in interrelationships between man and man. Though this has a negative side – the city as a 'lonely crowd' of people joined by superficial instrumental ties rather than by the close bonds that unite a small community – it also has a positive aspect, and it is this which generates the Romance of the City. Clearly, the city gives even its poorer inhabitants a wider choice of work, entertainment and social opportunities than does a small community (except under very repressive regimes), while the affluent citizen of a great metropolis need not stir from the city's perimeter to be a citizen of the world,

One sign of real urban decay is when this range of options starts to be reduced. Thus the visitor to New York City is appalled to find parts of the marvellously landscaped Central Park deserted on weekdays, even when the sun is shining, for fear of mugging, and to be told that he cannot visit large sections of the city safely. It is not the Blacks in Harlem who are in a ghetto, as they can stroll freely in all parts of New York. The real ghetto is the respectable White area of Manhattan whose inhabitants do not dare to leave it. In some other American cities, such as Greater Boston, public transport does not even reach certain poor areas, and taxi-drivers refuse to go there.

These are extreme symptoms of gross urban decay, but the Romance of the City, like the Romance of Technology, invariably goes sour, even amidst affluence and freedom of movement.

There is a link, then, between the combinatory opportunities offered by the city and those offered by technology. It is my case that these opportunities deserve to be responded to as sympathetically as possible, rather than brushed aside. The next chapter is concerned with people who *have* brushed them aside: we shall see that their case for doing so is strong, and it must be responded to with equal sympathy before any attempt is made – as we shall attempt in the final chapter – to reconcile the contradiction thus exposed. In the final chapter I shall also return to the theme of the city, in its positive and negative aspects.

Chapter Three

The Recoil to the Body

The Recoil to the Body in Literature

The most imaginative early voices to be raised against the prospect of modern industrialization were those of Rousseau in Switzerland (who will be discussed in Chapter 4), and of Blake and Wordsworth in England.

Everyone knows Blake's lines:

> And was Jerusalem builded here
> Among these dark Satanic Mills?

where, as John Broadbent[1] has pointed out, the mills are not only industrial buildings but also 'anti-sex machines'. Everyone knows   16 the poems where Blake deplores the employment of children as chimney-sweeps, or the blackening of Wren's churches in London through consumption of domestic coal. But some of his most direct and striking attacks on industrialism are to be found embedded among the obscurities of the *Prophetic Books*. On the slave trade:[2]

> First Trades & Commerce, ships & armed vessels he
>   [Urizen] builded laborious
> To swim the deep; & on the land, children are sold
>   to trades
> Of dire necessity, still laboring day & night till all
> Their life extinct they took the sceptre form in
>   dark despair;
> And slaves in myriads, in ship loads, burden the
>   hoarse sounding deep,
> Rattling with clanking chains; the Universal Empire
>   groans.

On the alienating effects of mechanizing and fragmenting the labour process:[3]

67

Then left the sons of Urizen the plow & harrow, the loom,
The hammer & the chisel & the rule & compasses.
They forg'd the sword, the chariot of war, the battle ax,
The trumpet fitted to the battle & the flute of summer,
And all the arts of life they chang'd into the arts of death.
The hour glass contemn'd because of its simple
  workmanship
Was as the workmanship of the plowman, & the water
  wheel
That raises water into Cisterns, broken and burn'd in
  fire
Because its workmanship was like the workmanship of
  the shepherd,
And in their stead intricate wheels invented, Wheel
  without wheel,
To perplex youth in their outgoings & to bind to labours
Of day & night the myriads of Eternity, that they might
  file
And polish brass & iron hour after hour, laborious
  workmanship,
Kept ignorant of the use that they might spend the days
  of wisdom
In sorrowful drudgery to obtain a scanty pittance of
  bread,
In ignorance to view a small portion & think that All,
And call it demonstration, blind to all the simple rules
  of life.

For Wordsworth in similar vein, we may turn either to his great poem about depopulation of mountain lands, *Michael*, or to some scathing remarks on urban culture in his Preface to the *Lyrical Ballads* (1800):

A multitude of causes, unknown to former times, are now acting with a combined force to blunt the discriminating powers of the mind, and unfitting it for all voluntary exertion, to reduce it to a state of almost savage torpor. The most effective of these causes are the great national events which are daily taking place, and the increasing accumulation of men in cities, where the uniformity of their occupation produces a craving for extraordinary incident, which the rapid communication of intelligence hourly gratifies. To this tendency of life and manners the literature and theatrical exhibitions of the country have conformed themselves.

Early in the nineteenth century, the critique of industrialism became common, but it took a variety of different forms. Moreover, although affirmation of the human body is the most powerful defence we have against industrialism and technocracy, it was far from a universal reaction in the nineteenth century. The kind of affirmation I have in mind seems to have been made in the nineteenth century only by a few exceptionally clairvoyant individuals, such as Rimbaud and Walt Whitman and Nietzsche. (William Morris, Thomas Hardy and Havelock Ellis are three other names that might be added to the list, and it could be useful to go back earlier and consider the poetry of Burns and of Byron.) In the twentieth century it becomes a commonplace thanks to the influence of some key figures such as D. H. Lawrence and Freud; the latter summarized his point of view pithily in *The Ego and the Id*: 'The Ego is first and foremost a bodily Ego.'[4] At least, this was the pattern for literature and discursive thought. The role of the body has a somewhat different history in the visual arts, where there had been a long tradition in which painters and sculptors depicted nude models.

One caution remains: we should ask whether it is right to give so much attention to literature and the arts. Do the œuvres of a few individuals of outstanding talent give a complete and fair impression of changes in the social lives of ordinary people? Of course not. A complete study of the awakening of the body in the nineteenth century would have to cover a wide range of sub-cultures and experimental communities of which some records survive. That would be an essay in historical sociology. There are obvious conveniences in studying the work of exceptionally perceptive and original individuals. In doing so, we must remember both that they *are* exceptional, and that none the less there probably lived numerous 'mute, inglorious' Blakes and Rimbauds whose revolts against societal repressions do not live for posterity.

It is important to remember, in considering the apparent rarity of affirmation of the body in the nineteenth century, that in Western history the body has been – to speak very generally – a repressed element. The theological and philosophical tradition of the West has devalued it. Platonic philosophy and Christianity raised the soul above the body, and gave out that the body was to be transcended or even (in St Paul) 'mortified'. Ignatius Loyola taught his Jesuits to accept the maxim *Perinde ac cadaver* ('henceforth as a corpse') on entering the Jesuit Order, so passive did he expect them to be, and so indifferent to any care except the glory and praise of God and the salvation of their souls. This characteristic of Christianity should not be exaggerated, for it was sometimes balanced by a paradoxical glorification of the body – implicit in the fundamental doctrine of the Incarnation – which is one of the chief secrets of its greatness as a religion. Norman Brown has provocatively written

Christian asceticism can carry punishment of the human body to heights inconceivable to Plato; but Christian hope is for the redemption of that fallen body. Hence the affirmation of Tertullian . . .: The body will rise again, all of the body, the identical body, the entire body. The medieval Catholic synthesis between Christianity and Greek philosophy, with its notion of an immortal soul, compromised and confused the issue; only Protestantism carries the full burden of the peculiar Christian faith.[5]

Yet the matter is more complicated still; for at the heart of *Catholic* ritual is the symbolism and actual transubstantiation of the Host, where (in the words of the Catholic anthropologist Mary Douglas):

The white circle of bread encompasses symbolically the cosmos, the whole history of the Church and more, since it goes from the bread offering of Melchisedech, to Calvary and the Mass. It unites the body of each worshipper to the body of the faithful.[6]

Again, Christianity often showed great flexibility in absorbing pagan festivities; we can see this both in the sculptures of 'green men' in some English churches and in the Christian theatre of the Middle Ages in England and France. And the history of Christianity is punctuated by the emergence of various antinomian cults that have celebrated the body energetically.

Nevertheless, there will surely be no argument that the *dominant* ethos of Christianity has been one of repression of the body. This becomes particularly clear if we make a broad cross-cultural contrast with, say, Tantric Buddhism or the culture of the Balinese or the Mehinacu Indians or the Ancient Etruscans. Blake put the matter very well in his poem *The Garden of Love* (1794):

> I went to the Garden of Love,
> And saw what I never had seen:
> A Chapel was built in the midst,
> Where I used to play on the green.

> And the gates of this Chapel were shut,
> And 'Thou shalt not' writ over the door;
> So I turn'd to the Garden of Love
> That so many sweet flowers bore;

> And I saw it was filled with graves,
> And tomb-stones where flowers should be;
> And Priests in black gowns were walking their rounds,
> And binding with briars my joys and desires.

One of the most vivid recognitions I know of the effect of this Christian tradition in conditioning the young is the magical flashback scene in Fellini's film *8½*, where the protagonist, Guido, recalls his boyhood encounter as a pupil in a Catholic school, with Seraghina, a huge prostitute. He and some town-boys pay Seraghina to dance for them on the beach; afterwards, Guido is vindictively punished by the Fathers.[7] Here the point is that prohibition on natural bodily desires leads the adult either to unhealthy prurience and 'sensuality' or else to an equally unhealthy preoccupation with sex as a threat (such as is typically found today in women's vigilante associations set up to scrutinize television programmes).

If the tradition of mortifying the flesh runs right through Christianity, some commentators influenced by Marx have also offered a political explanation for the repression of the body. Sartre writes of the body as the 'presence within the oppressor of the oppressed in person',[8] so that the typical bourgeois attitude to the body is one of tight corseting. Horkheimer and Adorno have written stimulatingly (though not all this passage is very lucid):

The relationship with the human body is maimed from the outset. The division of labour which made a distinction between utilization on the one hand and work on the other, outlawed crude force. The more dependent the ruling classes become on the work of others the more they despise that work. A stigma attaches to work as it does to slavery. Christianity extolled the virtues of work but declared the flesh to be the root of all evil. . . .

The exploited body was defined as 'evil', and the spiritual occupations in which the higher people were free to indulge were asserted to be the greatest good. This process made possible the supreme cultural achievements of Europe, but the suspicion of the trickery which was apparent from the outset heightened the love-hate relationship with the body which permeated the thinking of the masses over the centuries, and found its authentic expression in the language of Luther. . . .

The love-hate relationship with the body colors all more recent culture. The body is scorned and rejected as something inferior, and at the same time desired as something forbidden, objectified, and alienated. Culture defines the body as a thing which can be possessed; in culture a distinction is made between the body and the spirit, the concept of power and command, as the object, the dead thing, the '*corpus*'. In man's denigration of his own body, nature takes its revenge for the fact that man has reduced nature to an object for domination, a raw material. The compulsive urge to cruelty and destruction springs from the organic displacement of the relationship between mind and body; Freud expressed the facts of the matter with genius when he said that loathing first arose when men began to walk upright and were at a distance from the ground, so that the sense of smell which drew the male animal to the female in heat was relegated to a secondary position among the senses. In Western civilization, and probably in all other forms of civilization, the physical aspect of existence is taboo – an object of attraction and repulsion.[9]

Horkheimer and Adorno, writing in America as refugees during the Second World War, went on to condemn the 'romantic attempts to bring about a renaissance of the body in the nineteenth and twentieth centuries', attempts which simply 'idealize a dead and maimed condition'. They cite as examples of this tendency Nietzsche, Stefan George the poet, and Gauguin the painter. One sympathizes with Horkheimer and Adorno's uncompromising conclusion:

The idolizing of the vital phenomena from the 'blond beast' to the South Sea islanders inevitably leads to the 'sarong film' and the advertising posters for vitamin pills and skin creams which simply stand for the immanent aim of publicity: the new, great, beautiful and noble type of man – the Führer and his storm troopers.[10]

But the tradition that I want to trace is a rather different one and its main literary representatives are Blake, Rimbaud and D. H. Lawrence. Blake and Rimbaud were antinomian, anti-authoritarian radicals. Between Lawrence and fascism there was a little more affinity; but there was antinomianism in Lawrence too. I think it can be shown that the affirmation of the body which writers of this quality practised in their work is relatively invulnerable to the crude exploitation that so offends Horkheimer and Adorno. It is quite true that the imagery of the body has been co-opted by advertising and the film industry for purposes of manipulation or titillation rather than of liberation; it is also true that the Nazis ruthlessly co-opted ideas which they could use for their purposes, and that the ideology of Nazism owes much to German Romanticism. I think it is over-fatalistic of Horkheimer and Adorno, however, to claim that the body of Western man is for ever 'maimed', since society is constantly being regenerated by new births and the process of renewal is surely our one inalienable resource against all kinds of societal malaise.

Whatever the historical explanation, it is the case that the recoil against technology since the eighteenth century has been in general deflected away from the body towards other positives. It is as if some kind of psychic censorship mechanism, such as operates (according to Freud) in dreams, but here acting on a whole civilization, displaced attention from the body to other, more easily accepted, positives.[11] Instead of a direct turning towards the body, there was an acceptance of some variant of the old theological doctrine of the Fall – the belief in a lapse from some earlier state of beatitude to a present state of corruption. The earlier state could be located in childhood (as in Wordsworth, to some extent in Blake, and in a great deal of sentimental Victorian literature); or in a state of nature (as in the myth of the Noble Savage popular in the eighteenth century and later); or in some imaginary golden age symbolized by the myth of the countryside, the peasantry, the 'land', or the Middle Ages. Raymond Williams[12] has shown that in English cultural history we can trace back almost indefinitely (certainly as far back as the Middle Ages) a nostalgia for the past; a defensive response to social change, though very common at the beginning of the nineteenth century, was by no means new. Nor has it ceased to be favoured today; for in the mid-twentieth century the American South was idealized as a nostalgic symbol of a lost civilization by the Fugitive Agrarians, the American literary movement of the 1930s led by John Crowe Ransom, just as the 'organic society' of a vanishing rural England was idealized by Leavis and the *Scrutiny* critics. Even the theory of 'alienation' as developed by the young Marx seems to be based ultimately on a version of the myth of the Fall of Man, though attempts have been made to argue that the state of disalienation, or non-alienation, was not intended by Marx to represent a historical fact, but is merely a theoretical construct that we are invited to hold before us as an encouragement to destroy capitalism. Yet another surrogate for the body that we must note was the characteristically Romantic notion of the 'organic' as opposed to the mechanical, a multivalent metaphor for the mind, society and the cosmos which runs right through the intellectual life of the nineteenth century.[13]

My case is that the most radical challenge possible to industrialization and the technocratic ethos has been, and still is, the direct affirmation of the body through a transgression of Western taboos. Some careful discriminations have to be made here. I do not mean transgression of these taboos through 'eroticism' in the sense of mechanical, genital sexuality. Such a version of eroticism is in fact no transgression at all, since there have always been accepted conventions of 'eroticism' in Western society, which offer an easy way – like the related conventions of bawdry – of evading the challenge and difficulty of confronting another human being in a relation of embodied love.

73

One of Herbert Marcuse's most persuasive theories is his reinterpretation of the Freudian notion of genital sexuality.[14] According to Marcuse, sexuality in the child involves the whole body. But our society insists that the body becomes desexualized for use as an instrument of labour – except for one zone of the body, the genital zone, which becomes the specialized instrument of pleasure. Genital eroticism must always have, because of the very architecture of the human body, a partly mechanical or instrumental function; when this is allowed to dominate, it induces degradation of the sexual partner and the more subtle degradation of one's own self-respect. As the narrator in V. S. Naipaul's novel *The Mimic Men* puts it: 'We violate no body so much as our own; towards it we display the perversity of the cat that constantly rips its wounds open.' In so far as Christian-humanist timidity and *pudeur* about the body are protections against this kind of degradation, they are not to be lightly repudiated. Embarrassment about sex is a response to its very real dangers. And it seems that as society becomes more extensively industrialized, genital eroticism tends to become more fully mechanized – more a matter of manipulative titillation, or again of repetitive routine, or virtuoso 'technique'. Certainly there is a commercial market for information about sexual mechanics and for appliances such as vibrators.

The newest mode of packaged mechanical eroticism has abandoned the assumption of genital supremacy. Primers on sexual technique show how all the commutative resources of two, or more, bodies, as well as various unguents, lubricants, boosters and prosthetics, can be simultaneously exploited to heighten pleasure. This is surely a symptom of the further technicizing of sexuality. We find an interesting anticipation of it by the Marquis de Sade at the end of the eighteenth century. Roland Barthes[15] writes as follows on Sade's 'erotic grammar' of bodily 'postures', 'operations', 'figures' and 'episodes': 'in every subject, all the zones of the body must be erotically saturated; the group is a sort of chemical nucleus none of whose "valencies" must stay free.' And Barthes quotes an amusing sentence from one of Sade's narratives: 'To unite incest, adultery, sodomy and sacrilege, he buggers his married daughter with a Host (*hostie*).'

Though Sade has been highly praised as a serious subverter of hypocritical bourgeois morality, it seems to me that his systematic fantasies are much more a symptom of the technological ethos than a recoil against it. Not only did he conceive of elaborate automatic *godemiché* machines for self-pleasuring; but also, as

Barthes points out, 'the whole living group is conceived and constructed like a machine'. Sade's sexual permutations have no more in common with the Recoil to the Body than has the technical perfectionism of Casanova.

Despite the rareness of direct affirmation of the body between the late eighteenth century and the early twentieth, some of the great poetry of the Romantic period carries a particularly strong libidinal charge. One thinks of Coleridge's *Kubla Khan* (1797):

> And from this chasm, with ceaseless turmoil seething,
> As if this earth in fast thick pants were breathing,
> A mighty fountain momently was forced:
> Amid whose swift half-intermitted burst
> Huge fragments vaulted like rebounding hail. . . .

or Keats's *Ode to Autumn* (1820):

> Season of mists and mellow fruitfulness,
>   Close bosom-friend of the maturing sun;
> Conspiring with him how to load and bless
>   With fruit the vines that round the thatch-eaves run;
> To bend with apples the moss'd cottage-trees,
>   And fill all fruit with ripeness to the core;
>   To swell the gourd, and plump the hazel shells
> With a sweet kernel . . .

This linguistic sappiness is not peculiar to the period: it is, on the contrary, a resource always available to poets, the proof that black marks on the page can be arranged to evoke concrete experience which thrills right through the nervous system.

Wordsworth's lyrics often seem to approach a more specific acceptance of the body on the part of this poet, who of all poets is perhaps (at his best) the subtlest in his unobtrusive questioning of received ideas (the flatness of the metre often leading us to expect cliché and get the reverse of cliché). For instance, his charming parable of *The Oak and the Broom* defends the values of flamboyance and light-heartedness against conscious social responsibility. In some other poems from Wordsworth's earlier period, 'idleness', 'wise passiveness' and 'spontaneous wisdom' are commended (*To my Sister, Expostulation and Reply, The Tables Turned*), which is getting near the kind of quiet trust in bodily plenitude that we shall find is one of D. H. Lawrence's most impressive positives. Wordsworth's articulation of nature and humanity makes him one of the greatest of poets. Yet the body is, as it were, elided in this articulation. A real passionate embodiedness is there behind the words – for instance in the Lucy and Matthew groups of lyrics – but it is not spelt out, and therefore amounts to no strong positive. The explicit positives to which Wordsworth habitually does have recourse are the innocence of childhood and the language of 'low and rustic life'. Both of these – though his arguments for using 'low and rustic' diction are no doubt justified by his poetic practice – remain locked into the myth that man underwent a Second Fall into a state of moral and cultural corruption.

Blake also makes free use of the myth of a Second Fall, but his affirmation of the body points to an ever-present resource for opposing the 'arts of death', rather than leaving us with a sense of destitution. Blake – that astonishing, idiosyncratic visionary and artist – must clearly be our starting-point because his affirmation of the body is explicit and transgressive, charged with erotic desire and yet clear of both prurience and sadism, founded on recognition of the body's intuitive life in general rather than of sexuality in the narrow sense. His candid acceptance of, and delight in, the embodied state speaks with singular directness to our own century: and it is this part of his work that we shall examine.

There is one eighteenth-century precursor of Blake's morality of instinctual release, the crazed poet Christopher Smart.[16] His glorification of the bodily vitality of animals, especially his cat Jeoffry, in the rhapsodic poem *Jubilate Agno* (1756–63), is especially impressive, anticipating the poetry of Walt Whitman. In *A Song to David* (1763) Smart runs right against the long-sought-after calm and temperance of the Augustans:

> Use all thy passions: love is thine,
> And joy, and jealousy divine,
>   Thine hope's eternal fort;
> And care thy leisure to disturb,
> With fear concupiscence to curb,
>   And rapture to transport.

As John Broadbent[17] comments, 'The Augustans were anthropocentric but they did not look on each other as bodies in case they fell into distemper.'

Blake's psychological radicalism was very uncompromising and it is not surprising that he was neglected till many decades after his death.

> Children of the future Age
> Reading this indignant page,
> Know that in a former time
> Love! sweet Love! was thought a crime.

(Songs of Experience, 1794)

Are not the joys of morning sweeter
Than the joys of night?
And are the vig'rous joys of youth
Ashamed of the light?

Let age and sickness silent rob
The vineyards in the night;
But those who burn with vig'rous youth
Pluck fruits before the light.

(Miscellaneous Poems and Fragments)

Abstinence sows sand all over
The ruddy limbs & flaming hair,
But Desire Gratified
Plants fruits of life & beauty there.

(Miscellaneous Poems and Fragments)

He who binds to himself a joy
Does the winged life destroy;
But he who kisses the joy as it flies
Lives in eternity's sun rise.

(Miscellaneous Poems and Fragments)

Those who restrain desire, do so because theirs
is too weak to be restrained; and the restrainer
or reason usurps its place & governs the unwilling.

(The Marriage of Heaven and Hell, 1793)

Damn braces. Bless relaxes.
Exuberance is beauty.
Sooner murder an infant in its cradle than nurse
    unacted desires.

(The Marriage of Heaven and Hell)

If Blake sometimes gets near to isolating genital sexuality, this is
completely balanced by his humour; one thinks of the angel in one
of his poems who

    wink'd at the thief
And smil'd at the dame,
And without one word spoke
Had a peach from the tree,
And 'twixt earnest & joke
Enjoy'd the Lady.

(Miscellaneous Poems and Fragments)

When Blake writes

    In a wife I would desire
What in whores is always found –
The lineaments of Gratified desire.

(Miscellaneous Poems and Fragments)

he is commending not the sexual exploitation of women, but the ability of some whores to wrest from their work a kind of bodily liberation denied to most housewives.

Among the many modern readings of Blake, one in particular is worth mentioning here because its author, Theodore Roszak, has written as eloquently as anyone in recent years against technocracy and urban industrialism. Roszak proposes a triad of heroes for our time – Blake, Wordsworth and Goethe – representing what he calls the 'Old Gnosis'. In his long commentary on Blake Roszak observes:

Blake foreshadows both Nietzsche and Freud: cool head outlaws hot blood; Urizen [the god of reason in Blake's mythology] drives the passions into dungeons of unreason. Science increases the pressure upon sensual joy: empiricism becomes *empiricide*, the murder of experience, Science *uses* the senses but does not *enjoy* them, finally buries them under theory, abstraction, mathematical generalization. At the foundations of Urizen's palace, Luvah-Orc lies writhing, burning for vengeance.

'Damn braces: Bless relaxes.' 'He who desires but acts not, breeds pestilence.' Blake saw: there is no cure for civilization's discontents by way of repression. So the image of Wild Orc enchained is Blake's symbol of war: 'Energy enslav'd'. The last resort of embattled vitality is blind, indiscriminate destruction.

Easy at this point to mistake Blake for Wilhelm Reich or D. H. Lawrence. But Energy, while 'from the body', participates in Eternity. With Blake, *everything* moves toward Eternity. . . . Blake could strike the Rabelaisian note; but only in passing. Sex belongs to the garments of the soul.[18]

Roszak is wrong, I believe, to reduce Lawrence's beliefs to mere sexual liberation. The sexual liberation advocated by Reich is another matter. Reich's preoccupation with the orgasm seems to me mechanistic[19] and much less morally impressive than Marcuse's belief in a diffused, polymorphous sexuality, or than Blake's equally diffused belief in 'exuberance'. Roszak's strategy is to 'spiritualize' Blake, implying that only those who have risen above the crude material level of existence are qualified to understand his poetry. This line of argument is fairly consistent and has distinguished antecedents; and many people no doubt prefer to pursue Blake in this fashion. I can only repeat that my present book is written within a general framework of historical materialism, at least to the extent of attempting to understand cultural phenomena first of all in terms of the material interchange between men and men, and men and nature. Sex and morality, in this view, are not levels of experience to be transcended; they pervade all experience. Nor does the discipline of a 'materialist' perspective prevent one from interpreting and appreciating poems written by such a man as Blake, who regularly had 'visionary' experiences; for what we are reading is a text, not the soul of William Blake. Blake's poems, like many other literary texts produced by men of genius at odds with the literary taste of their day, reveal an elaborate private mythology and a playful exuberance of language which can certainly be read without recourse to 'spiritual' categories. Of course, Roszak is perfectly entitled to retort that a 'materialist' approach to Blake is doomed to be inadequate, and that man's only hope of salvation is a mystical or religious revival. I have mentioned his interpretation of Blake here as a convenient way of clarifying a point at which my argument breaks away decisively from Roszak's; the reader can then decide which reading of Blake is correct.[20]

After Blake's death in 1827 there is a gap in literary history before another writer of comparable stature takes up the theme of liberating sexuality and affirming the body – and he is equally astonishing: the French boy-poet Arthur Rimbaud.

The tragic career of Rimbaud is well known: his production between the ages of sixteen and nineteen (1870–73) of some dazzlingly original verse and prose, his stormy love-affair with Verlaine, followed by a wretched life as works manager in Cyprus, and subsequently trader, explorer and gun-runner in the Middle East. During this latter period he refrained from any literary production, and recalled his poetry with distaste, while his letters show no special mastery over words. In 1891 he was stricken by a tumour in his right knee and returned to Marseilles, where the leg was amputated. After terrible suffering (described in a letter from his sister to his mother) he died in November of that year of generalized cancer, at the age of thirty-seven.

One would look in vain in Rimbaud's writings for any kind of reflective critique of society such as Blake and Wordsworth expressed. Rimbaud reacted to the changing circumstances of his life with the emotional spontaneity of a child in the language of a man; he never, in the conventional sense, 'grew up', and no doubt this explains some of the misery of his later life. In his writings we find scattered references to the more Romantic aspects of the city, of factories and of scientific progress, which anticipate Italian Futurism; as he wrote at the end of his cryptic prose work *Une Saison en Enfer* (1873), 'Il faut être absolument moderne'. But this 'futuristic' imagery never dominates and seems to be introduced merely *en passant*.

Rimbaud's habit is to attack the immediate tangible *symptoms* of an unhealthy society, projecting into words his own psychological turmoil and anarchistic rebelliousness. In *A la musique* (1870) he writes bitterly of the promenade in the Place de la Gare in the provincial town of Charleville in northern France, where he was brought up:

> Sur la place taillée en mesquines pelouses,
> Square où tout est correct, les arbres et les fleurs,
> Tous les bourgeois poussifs qu'étranglent les chaleurs,
> Portent, les jeudis soirs, leurs bêtises jalouses.

Against the lushness of the body and green countryside, in which Rimbaud delighted (as we shall see in other poems), are opposed the shabby geometry of the municipal garden and the wheezing decrepitude of the town worthies. After further scene-setting, the poem concludes:

> – Moi, je suis, débraillé comme un étudiant,
> Sous les marroniers verts les alertes fillettes:
> Elles le savent bien; et tournent en riant,
> Vers moi, leurs yeux tout pleins de choses indiscrètes.
>
> Je ne dis pas un mot: je regarde toujours
> La chair de leurs cous blancs brodés de mèches folles:
> Je suis, sous le corsage et les frêles atours,
> Le dos divin après la courbe des épaules.
>
> J'ai bientôt déniché la bottine, le bas . . .
> – Je reconstruis les corps, brûlé de belles fièvres.
> Elles me trouvent drôle et se parlent tout bas . . .
> – Et mes désirs brutaux s'accrochent à leurs lèvres . . .

In another poem, *Les Assis* (1871), Rimbaud was apparently paying off a score against the local librarian who had refused to let him read some valuable books, and he delivers a bitterly savage attack on the dried-up, disfigured old men in the library, locked into their chairs. His poems contain an element of pure teenage rebellion – one reason for their perennial appeal to young readers. The more 'symbolist' and 'hermetic' texts – where the language seems to carry itself on through its own energies rather than through reference to a real world – are of great literary interest. How high one finally rates them depends on whether one insists (as Leavis insists) that great literature must be normative and sanative, or on the contrary (with some modern French Marxist critics like Julia Kristeva) that the most important poetry is that which subverts bourgeois norms of meaning, sanity and morality. But there can be little argument about those early poems of his which still affirm the vitality of the body, before the period in Paris when Rimbaud seems to have deliberately debauched his body in the cause of his art. The adolescent narcissism of the early poems, and their occasional misogyny and bitterness, are liberated by an extraordinary tenderness and freshness.

One of his earliest poems was *Soleil et Chair* (May 1870):

> Le Soleil, le foyer de tendresse et de vie,
> Verse l'amour brûlant à la terre ravie,
> Et, quand on est couché sur la vallée, on sent
> Que la terre est nubile et déborde de sang;
> Que son immense sein, soulevé par une âme,
> Est d'amour comme Dieu, de chair comme la femme,
> Et qu'il renferme, gros de sève et de rayons,
> Le grand fourmillement de tous les embryons!
>
> Et tout croît, et tout monte! . . .
>
> – Oui, l'Homme est triste et laid, triste sous le ciel vaste,
> Il a des vêtements, parce qu'il n'est plus chaste,
> Parce qu'il a sali son fier buste de dieu,
> Et qu'il a rabougri, comme une idole au feu,
> Son corps Olympien aux servitudes sales!
> Oui, même après la mort, dans les squelettes pâles
> Il veut vivre, insultant la première beauté! . . .
>
> C'est une bonne farce! et le monde ricane
> Au nom doux et sacré de la grande Vénus!

Sex and the body are hallowed for Rimbaud – this is the starting-point of his experiments in the 'disordering of all the senses'. Everywhere he sees them cheapened and violated, as in his moving poem *Le Cœur Volé* (1871), which – it has been guessed – may have been written after some unpleasant sexual experience in Paris:

> Mon triste cœur bave à la poupe,
> Mon cœur couvert de caporal:
> Ils y lancent des jets de soupe,
> Mon triste cœur bave à la poupe:
> Sous les quolibets de la troupe
> Qui pousse un rire general,
> Mon triste cœur bave à la poupe,
> Mon cœur couvert de caporal!
>
> Ithyphalliques et pioupiesques,
> Leurs quolibets l'ont dépravé:
> Au gouvernail on voit des fresques

Ithyphalliques et pioupiesques.
O flots abracadabrantesques,
Prenez mon cœur, qu'il soit lavé!
Ithyphalliques et pioupiesques,
Leurs quolibets l'ont dépravé!

Rimbaud's respect and love for the body are apparent even in those of his poems which are classed as erotica (*Stupra*, the date of which is uncertain). Among his lesser-known texts is an amusing anti-clerical narrative called *Un Cœur sous une soutane: Intimités d'un séminariste* (*c.* 1870). Here is the Father Superior interrogating the young novice:

'Young J. made a report to me in which he says that he notices you spreading your legs more and more flagrantly every day, during study. He claims he has seen you stretch right out under the table, like a young – like a great lout. These are facts which you can have no answer to. Come close to me, on your knees, right near me. I want to question you quietly. Answer me: do you spread your legs much when studying?'
  Then he put his hand on my shoulder, round the neck, and his eyes became bright, and he made me say things about this spreading of legs. Why, I prefer to tell you that it was disgusting, because I know what such scenes mean!

Perhaps his most haunting poems are those which, without becoming hermetic, explore the deepest questions of childhood and parenthood, adolescence and sexuality: poems such as *Les Chercheuses de poux* (1871), about a child whose hair is being searched for lice by two women; or *Les Sœurs de charité* (1871), with its splendid beginning:

Le jeune homme dont l'œil est brillant, la peau brune,
Le beau corps de vingt ans qui devrait aller nu,
Et qu'eût, le front cerclé de cuivre, sous la lune
Adoré, dans la Perse, un Génie inconnu,

Impétueux avec des douceurs virginales
Et noires, fier de ses premiers entêtements,
Pareil aux jeunes mers, pleurs de nuits estivales,
Qui se retournent sur des lits de diamants;

Le jeune homme, devant les laideurs de ce monde,
Tressaille dans son cœur largement irrité,
Et, plein de la blessure éternelle et profonde,
Se prend à desirer sa sœur de charité.

At one level this is an effusion of adolescent sexual fear – he goes on to describe 'Woman' as a 'heap of entrails'. But the tone is so astringent, so shifting, that the overall impression left is of a totally sincere puzzling-out of complexities.

There is something uniquely poignant about the transition from this romantic poetry of such precocious mastery to Rimbaud's second career in the Middle East when he was thrust into the rawest economic and political realities: supplying basic commodities such as skins and coffee for the European market, and witnessing the diplomatic machinations of the colonial powers. Perhaps the nearest to his later story in imaginative literature is some of Conrad's fiction: *An Outpost of Progress* (1898), *Heart of Darkness* (1902). When Rimbaud writes back home asking for books, they are not the works of the latest symbolist poets, but treatises on hydraulics, metallurgy, naval architecture and the like; he also asks for technical instruments for his explorations.

In a sense, every idealistic acidhead of our own day who decides, in his early twenties, to knuckle down and accept 'the system' is recapitulating, in a less extreme form, the career of Rimbaud. One starts to read the letters of Rimbaud from the Middle East back to his family with wry amusement.[21] Then the terrible climax begins to close in, and the story becomes tragic in the strictest sense of that word. In 1891, when he is in Harar, he goes on a wild ride on horseback to subdue a violent pain in the right knee; the excited horse bruises the bad knee against a tree. After the amputation of his leg in Marseilles, he is stricken with a huge cancer near the stump which makes his doctors (in his sister Isabelle's words) 'dumb and terrified'. His body begins gradually to die round him.

Sometimes he asks the doctors if they see the extraordinary things that he perceives and he speaks to them and tells them his impressions with gentleness, in terms that I could not reproduce. The doctors look into his eyes, those beautiful eyes which have never been so beautiful and so intelligent, and say to each other 'It is singular'. There is something in Arthur's case which they do not understand.

It would be impertinent to offer a total interpretation of Rimbaud's life on such scanty evidence as we have, though there have been interpretations galore. All one can say definitely is that the early Rimbaud pushed liberation – sexual, intellectual, artistic, even political – further than practically anyone else dared, and with a poetic skill which makes us aware (as with Blake) of how these various domains of experience hang together. Then, at an age when normal people are just groping towards maturity, he took refuge in a repression that was equally consistent and far-reaching: a repression of his passions, his mind, his genius, his political conscience. There is a grim irony in the final slow crucifixion of the body in which he had once rejoiced.

The French critic Etiemble has devoted four large volumes to demystifying the 'myth of Rimbaud'. While Etiemble is right to send us back from biographical gossip to the texts, this is surely the kind of myth that is useful. Rimbaud's second career seems like some ghastly travesty of an exotic tale by Jules Verne.

As we have seen, the nineteenth century had special difficulty in coming to terms with the problems of the body and sex, and the mainstream of art and literature took refuge in various modes of disembodied spirituality. A particular note of poignant yearning became common, the vague nostalgia for an irretrievable past located in childhood or in history: often indulged sentimentally but occasionally recognized for what it was, as in the delicate irony of Chekhov's play *The Cherry Orchard*. The gradual acceptance of the needs and rights of a body no longer anointed with spiritual grace is a great intellectual saga. A full account of it would have to deal with the influence of such people as Nietzsche,[22] Havelock Ellis and above all Freud, and then go on to trace how it toppled into the obsession with sexual mechanics that disfigures so much of present-day culture. Instead, I shall focus my concluding discussion of the Recoil to the Body in literature on the work of two great early twentieth-century writers, W. B. Yeats and D. H. Lawrence.

It is interesting that the four writers I have chosen as representing the affirmation of the body in modern literature – Blake, Rimbaud, Yeats and Lawrence – have all a second characteristic in common, that each was attracted, to different degrees, by mysticism, private mythologies and hermetic vocabulary. The same *dramatis personae* could no doubt be used to illustrate some plea for the subversion of modern technology by a synthesis of neo-platonism, alchemy, spiritualism and ancient Mexican rites. I would urge that, on the contrary, the human core of each of these writer's work lies in the area of intimate psychic, physical and social experience labelled here for the sake of brevity as 'the body'; and that their mystical and mythopoeic excursions are for the most part devices for maintaining a precarious sanity amid the disintegration of cultural certainties. Perhaps these writers each felt menaced by the growing authority of the scientific world-view, while unable to accept its assumptions and its very mode of gathering experience; as Blake put it, 'I must create a system, or be enslaved by another man's.'[23]

Certainly Yeats and Lawrence took the mystical aspect of their work only half seriously. Both are fundamentally writers who confront the specific experience of the twentieth century, including rapid industrialization and the dominance of the scientific world-view.

Of the two, Yeats offers the simpler formulations, inclining at his best to a majestic certitude and at his worst to crude posturing. (There is a tendency nowadays to praise Yeats on the grounds that his synthesizing spiritualism and exoticism anticipates some comparable confusions that are fashionable today, but this is to pay him a back-handed compliment.) The industrialized modern world is present in his poetry only by implication: first (in the early verse) in his urgent need to escape from it, later in his venture of building psychological or spiritual defences against its insidious embrace. Yeats was fond of contrasting the dashing spontaneity of artists against the servile calculation of the practical world. But he was well aware that what was at stake, in his antipathy to scientism and industrialization, was not a matter merely of life-styles but of opposed modes of experience acquired by learning. This is put lucidly in his short poem *The Dawn* (1919), where all of science is rejected in a grandiose gesture:

> I would be ignorant as the dawn
> That has looked down
> On that old queen measuring a town
> With the pin of a brooch,
> Or on the withered men that saw
> From their pedantic Babylon
> The careless planets in their courses,
> The stars fade out where the moon comes,
> And took their tablets and did sums;
> I would be ignorant as the dawn
> That merely stood, rocking the glittering coach
> Above the cloudy shoulders of the horses;
> I would be – for no knowledge is worth a straw –
> Ignorant and wanton as the dawn.

There is a clear contrast here between the scientist's imposition of an abstract, quantitative grid on the world, and the artist's naive, intuitive mode of experience. One source of this conviction of Yeats's is no doubt the ringing lament for chivalry, destroyed by 'sophisters, economists and calculators', that Edmund Burke was inspired to write by the humiliation of the Queen of France.[24]

Yeats's later poems are preoccupied with physical ageing, and the stance becomes more ironic. Sometimes a wry endorsement of the proverb 'Si jeunesse savait, si vieillesse pouvait':

> Bodily decrepitude is wisdom; young
> We loved each other and were ignorant.
>
> <div align="right">(<i>After Long Silence</i>, 1933)</div>

Sometimes a bitter defiance:

> You think it horrible that lust and rage
> Should dance attention upon my old age;
> They were not such a plague when I was young;
> What else have I to spur me into song?
>
> <div align="right">(<i>The Spur</i>, 1939)</div>

Sometimes a yearning for spiritual transcendence of the body, as in the famous *Sailing to Byzantium* (1928).

When one reflects on what is truly lasting and unique in Yeats, it is surely his extraordinarily fine evocations of the life of the body. This is the positive that runs right through his work, though it is often damped down by a proliferation of symbolism and allusion, rather than let rip as here:

> Minnaloushe creeps through the grass
>   Alone, important and wise,
> And lifts to the changing moon
>   His changing eyes.
>
> <div align="right">(<i>The Cat and the Moon</i>, 1919)</div>

> O body swayed to music, O brightening glance,
> How can we know the dancer from the dance?
>
> <div align="right">(<i>Among School Children</i>, 1928)</div>

One could hardly ask for a more sensitive registration or dramatization of the superimposed rhythms of lovers' bodies than the first eight lines of *Leda and the Swan* (1928):

> A sudden blow: the great wings beating still
> Above the staggering girl, her thighs caressed
> By the dark webs, her nape caught in his bill,
> He holds her helpless breast upon his breast.
>
> How can those terrified vague fingers push
> The feathered glory from her loosening thighs?
> And how can body, laid in that white rush,
> But feel the strange heart beating where it lies?

And in his consistent repudiation of the cerebral Yeats comes near to what is, I think, the central message of Lawrence:

> God guard me from those thoughts men think
> In the mind alone;
> He that sings a lasting song
> Thinks in a marrow-bone.

> (*A Prayer for Old Age*, 1935)

My treatment of Lawrence will concentrate on *Women in Love* (1921) and *St Mawr* (1925), and is indebted to F. R. Leavis's commentary on these works.[25] Though Lawrence's genius was a seriously flawed one, his great fiction stands as a model of sanity.

One point which Leavis does not make, and which Lawrence himself would no doubt have disavowed, is that *Women in Love* offers a strikingly Marxian or historical materialist analysis of contemporary alienation. In other words, the various psychological malaises suffered by most of his characters are not attributed merely to the decline of religious belief and to man's consequent exposure to existential realities. Lawrence makes a clear connection between these forms of psychic malaise and the socio-political contradictions inherent in a specific economic system, namely industrial capitalism, though he rejects any communist or socialist resolution of these contradictions. In fact, the fundamental crisis of England that he diagnosed in the 1920s has changed surprisingly little. The trend towards social justice has gathered speed, but Lawrence assumed this and did not regard it as a fundamental issue. *Women in Love* reads today with astonishing freshness and urgency, despite some obvious failings of restraint and balance which even Lawrence's warmest admirers admit.[26]

In particular, Lawrence makes a very convincing and resonant identification between machinery and psychological obsession, where a single mental function – of whatever kind, sex, the intellect, aestheticism, ambition, ideology – comes to dominate and restrict consciousness. One of the key themes in the book is the transition in the running of the Crich family coal business from the feudal, paternalistic direction of Thomas Crich to the new technocratic direction of his son Gerald:

Immediately he *saw* the firm, he realized what he could do. He had a fight to fight with Matter, with the earth and the coal it enclosed. This was the sole idea, to turn upon the inanimate matter of the underground, and reduce it to his will. And for this fight with matter, one must have perfect instruments in perfect organization, a mechanism so subtle and harmonious in its workings that it represents the single mind of man, and by its relentless repetition of given movement, will accomplish a purpose irresistibly, inhumanly. It was this inhuman principle in the mechanism he wanted to construct that inspired Gerald with an almost religious exaltation. He, the man, could interpose a perfect, changeless, godlike medium between himself and the Matter he had to subjugate. There were two opposites, his will and the resistant Matter of the earth. And between these he could establish the very expression of his will, the incarnation of his power, a great and perfect machine, a system, an activity of pure order, pure mechanical repetition *ad infinitum*, hence eternal and infinite.[27]

The imagery is derived historically from Carlyle and Friedrich Schiller, who wrote in 1795, in his *Letters upon the Aesthetical Education of Man*, of the 'monotonous sound of a perpetually revolving wheel' as figuring the 'degeneration' of Western culture; but Lawrence's use of the image is much more complex. His characterization is equally subtle: Gerald, one of the chief figures in the novel, is by no means portrayed as cruel or heartless. On one level he is the most amiable and sympathetic of men; his obsessiveness and destructiveness only appear at a deeper level, so that the reader's sympathies move for and against him – the total effect being most challenging, if occasionally rather obscure.

I will focus here on a justly praised scene in Chapter 9 of *Women in Love* where one of the key themes of the book is articulated symbolically. The Brangwen sisters, Ursula and Gudrun, are walking home from the school where they teach, across an industrial landscape of the English Midlands, when they come to a level crossing. The gate is shut as the colliery train is approaching. Gerald Crich (later to become Gudrun's lover) trots up on a red Arab mare, looking 'picturesque'. The locomotive gets closer and noisier; the mare winces away, but Gerald pulls her back. The locomotive begins to pass through the level crossing; the mare panics and rears but Gerald forces her back. Ursula protests: 'The fool! Why doesn't he ride away till it's gone by?'

But he leaned forward, his face shining with fixed amusement, and at last he brought her down, and was bearing her back to the mark.

The mare spins round and round on two legs, and Ursula shrieks at Gerald in protest.

A sharpened look came on Gerald's face. He bit himself down on the mare like a keen edge biting home, and *forced* her round. She roared as she breathed, her nostrils were two wide, hot holes, her mouth was apart, her eyes frenzied. It was a repulsive sight. But he held on her unrelaxed, with an almost mechanical relentlessness, keen as a sword

pressing into her. Both man and horse were sweating with violence. Yet he seemed calm as a ray of sunshine. . . .
Gudrun looked and saw the trickles of blood on the sides of the mare, and she turned white. And then on the very wound the bright spurs came down, pressing relentlessly.

There is a similar scene in *St Mawr* – a very compelling *nouvelle* of Lawrence's whose vitality and authenticity compensates for a bitterness that was eating into his later work. Here a stallion is the hero. St Mawr is a dangerous horse – when he is badly ridden. He has already killed two men in riding accidents before he is bought by Lou for her husband Rico, a fashionable artist. During a riding-party over the moors on the Welsh border of Shropshire, St Mawr rears and is pulled over by Rico. Rico is lamed and another young man is kicked and disfigured. The point is that (as Lou later discovers) St Mawr had understandably recoiled from the presence of an adder in his way; Rico refused to respond to the living intuition of St Mawr, and tried to force him down by sheer dominance of will. Rico is described as:

tall and handsome, and balanced on his hips . . . You could not imagine his face dirty, or scrubby, and unshaven or bearded, or even moustached. It was perfectly prepared for social purposes. If his head had been cut off, like John the Baptist's, it would have been a thing complete in itself, would not have missed the body in the least. The body was perfectly tailored. The head was one of the famous 'talking heads' of modern youth, with eyebrows a trifle Mephistophelian, large blue eyes a trifle bold, and curved mouth thrilling to death to kiss.

Taking the two horse-scenes together – from *Women in Love* and *St Mawr* – we are clearly very far from the obsession with sex that is still sometimes attributed to Lawrence through over-emphasis on his minor or unsuccessful works. Leavis, in his commentary on *St Mawr*, quotes aptly from an essay by Lawrence:

The body's life is the life of sensations and emotions. The body feels real hunger, real thirst, real joy in the sun or the snow, real pleasure in the smell of roses or the look of a lilac bush; real anger, real sorrow, real love, real tenderness, real warmth, real passion, real hate, real grief. All the emotions belong to the body, and are only recognized by the mind. We may hear the most sorrowful piece of news, and only feel a mental excitement. Then, hours after, perhaps in sleep, the awareness may reach the bodily centres, and true grief wrings the heart.

(*Apropos of Lady Chatterley's Lover*)

Leavis comments himself:

By 'body', then, Lawrence means all that deep spontaneous life which is not at the beck and call of the conscious and willing mind, and so in that sense cannot be controlled by it, though it can be thwarted and defeated. St Mawr, the stallion, *is* that life.[28]

The two horse-scenes beautifully subvert classical Platonic and Christian images of the body properly bridled and curbed by reason or the soul. (They also offer a justification for the much criticized English love of horses, which is in fact a national strength, celebrated most finely in the serene *Mares and Foals* series of paintings by Stubbs.) The body – the horse – does not stand simply for the emotions; it has, Lawrence urges, a kind of reliability or plenitude of its own. He makes the point in two of his letters:

We can go wrong in our minds. But what our blood feels and believes and says, is always true. The intellect is only a bit and a bridle. . . . I conceive a man's body as a kind of flame, like a candle flame, forever upright and yet flowing: and the intellect is just the light that is shed on to the things around.

(*Letters*, to Ernest Collings, 17 January 1913)

In modern symbolism, the Horse is supposed to stand for the passions. Passions be blowed. What does the Centaur stand for, Chiron or any other of that quondam four-footed gentry? Sense! Horse Sense! Sound, powerful, four-footed *sense*, that's what the Horse stands for. Horse-sense, I tell you. That's the Centaur. That's the blue Horse of the ancient Mediterranean, before the pale Galilean or the extra pale German or Nordic gentleman conquered. First of all, Sense. Good Sense, Sound Sense, Horse Sense. And then, a laugh, a loud, sensible Horse Laugh. After that, these same passions, glossy and dangerous in the flanks. And after these again, hoofs, irresistible, splintering hoofs, that can kick the walls of the world down.

(*Letters*, to Willard Johnson, 9 January 1924)

Lawrence was well aware of the dangers of animalism and primitivism as the mere safety-valves of a sophisticated society. Rupert Birkin in *Women in Love* says to Hermione Roddice (an intellectual hostess):

Even your animalism, you want it in your head. You don't want to *be* an animal, you want to observe your own animal functions, to get a mental thrill out of them. It is all purely secondary – and more decadent than the most hide-bound intellectualism.[29]

There are other passages in the same novel which cast a critical eye on primitivism, notably primitive art, though here I think (*pace* Leavis) that there is a loss of lucidity on the novelist's part, as there is in the Alpine finale when Gerald dies in the snow. Certainly Lawrence was very vulnerable himself to the primitivist temptation, and many of his novels end with flight from the unpalatable realities of industrialized society to a simpler way of life. There is certainly no serious attempt in his work to do justice to the positive aspects of industrialism.

It is often complained of both Yeats and Lawrence that they were not only illiberal and anti-socialist, but also that each flirted for a short time with fascist ideas. The charges are true enough on the level of behavioural fact, but many admirers of each writer feel able to take these idiosyncrasies in their stride, as conditions of eccentric greatness. The party-political milieu was not one that men of their temperament understood, and it often brought out the worst and silliest in them; their feeling for society functioned at a deeper level. The argument against them can be turned round. Nazism has cast such a shadow over our culture that we cannot do justice in our thought to the political positives that Yeats and Lawrence believed in, particularly charismatic leadership. Other, more liberal, figures of the same period who steered well clear of any fascistic temptations – men like Bertrand Russell, Wells and E. M. Forster – have earned our respect, but seem lacking in that profound, visceral feeling for the long-term crisis of the age that distinguishes Yeats and Lawrence on the one hand, and some committed Marxists on the other. No doubt there will sooner or later be a reaction in favour of the traditional concept of authority, as opposed to demagoguery, and we will remember that there can be good charisma, good leadership, good *esprit de corps*, as well as bad.

How should we react to aspects of Nazi propaganda and cultural life – Stefan George's erotic poetry, the German youth movement, the heroic recruiting posters for the SS, Leni Riefenstahl's films of the Berlin Olympics and the Nuremberg rallies, Richard Walter Darré's anti-urban 'blood and soil' movement – that seem to recall Yeats's and Lawrence's glorification of the body? And what of Drieu la Rochelle's remark: 'The deepest definition of Fascism is this: it is the political movement which leads most frankly, most radically towards the restoration of the body – health, dignity, fulness, heroism – towards the defence of man against the large town and the machine'? [30]

Similarly, Alfred Rosenberg, the Nazi propagandist, edited a magazine in 1929–30 which published a column called 'News from the Asphalt Deserts'. Yet we do not condemn all promoters of rural and pastoral myths as being latent Nazis, just because Rosenberg knew how to exploit anti-urbanism for propaganda purposes. If a human resource is really potent, it can be co-opted for manipulation or other infamous purposes, and even in some circumstances retain something of its original value. With a few exceptions, such as Riefenstahl's disturbingly powerful films, most Nazi exploitation of the power of the body was crude and *kitsch*, and was in any case eventually overshadowed by a massive technocratic state apparatus. It is true, however, that the exploitation of the body by Nazism remains something of an enigma – the perverse culmination of a whole tradition of German Romanticism. As Horkheimer and Adorno pointed out – in the passage quoted earlier in this chapter – there is a parallel between the Nazi use of the body and the use of the body in the advertising and film industries of our own society. Just as the boy depicted in an SS recruiting poster now seems tragic and confused rather than heroic or evil – a hastily conscripted peasant in uniform – so there is pathos today in the colour photographs of models who are induced to sell their physical beauty in a commercial appeal to the public's snobbery, greed or fear. If we do not always feel this pathos in the publicity of our own time (it is more striking in the publicity of the past) the reason is that we are so saturated with the tricks of consumer marketing and propaganda that we take abuse of the body for granted. Verbal language may deceive us less easily because it occupies a central place in our culture, and we all learn analytical techniques for distinguishing sincerity from insincerity in verbal discourse. The body as a whole is still a repressed element in our culture, and we tend to *believe* (or find it hard to disbelieve) the sincerity of the politician when he looks us straight in the eye over the TV screen, or that of the actress whose flashing teeth urge us to buy her brand of toothpaste. In both cases a verbal message is lent considerable persuasiveness by the controlled use of certain tricks of bodily deportment, which work largely at an unconscious rather than a conscious level. Until we become more aware of the body's power and resourcefulness, we will not feel a sufficiently educated outrage against its manipulation and exploitation. Rather than campaigns for literacy or numeracy, we may need a campaign for corporacy.

At this level of experience – deeper than that of party and nationalist politics – it is positive guidance that both Yeats and Lawrence offer. The heroine of *St Mawr*, Lou, dreams of a kind of intelligence 'burning like a flame fed straight from the source'. If we compare this to Yeats's

> He that sings a lasting song
> Thinks in a marrow-bone.

it is clear that neither Yeats nor Lawrence is making a crude opposition between Mind and Body, Reason and Emotion. (They may have done so occasionally, since both liked to strike postures, but I am concerned here with each artist's most mature and realized work – the appreciation of which always matters much more than the cutting of a 'representative' cross-section of an artist's output.) Reason is the faculty which gives man his responsibility, just as the rider is responsible for his horse and himself. But the mind must proceed through a keen sensitivity to the body's sure intuitions, and is indeed fed by the body, which has a sort of 'mind' of its own. The body is in no way there to be *used* by the mind.

I have found very useful Lawrence's image of true intelligence burning like a candle, while false intelligence burns like electric light, by means of the forcing of energies through devious 'mechanical' channels.[31] It seems to me a principle that has the widest moral and aesthetic validity. There is no question of reducing it either to an obsession with sex on the one hand, or to aesthetic Nazism on the other, though one must concede that if the body can be salutary it can also be satanic. (Only the very naive believe good and evil to be two spaces separated by an impermeable barrier.) If we accept that the body yields what I have called a 'plenitude' or 'reliability' when it is attended to with respect, then much of what passes for intelligence today seems a smart cerebral contrivance.

But *does* the body have this plenitude and reliability? What about the less appealing aspects of the 'visceral'? At least three of the Seven Deadly Sins – Envy, Ire and Lust – work visibly and palpably through the body; are we better off for them? It is true that the human body often seems to behave like a mechanical doll which is wound up, rolls its eyes, waves its arms, cackles with laughter, stamps its feet, jerks its sexual organs, and relapses to a state of rest. The moral or rational potentials of the body that I have tried to bring out in this book must be seen, by contrast, as essentially diffuse and slow-dissolving: they are, for example, unease that things are not as they should be, or a sudden surge of tenderness for a friend, or a mood of irritation inexplicably provoked over a friendly exchange of words. It is precisely when we feel anger towards a jay-walking pedestrian, lust towards a cinema poster, or jealousy at the success of an enemy, that our bodies swing into a kind of 'machine mode'. Sexual ejaculation is a form of reflex. Other human actions, such as losing one's temper or laughing hysterically, have much in common with what the student of animal behaviour calls 'fixed action patterns', sequences of acts which are brought into operation by an initial stimulus and can only be modified by the intervention of subsequent stimuli – and not terminated until the 'programme' has run its course. We are culturally conditioned to control these forms of behaviour in ourselves, and to be aware of the dangers of slipping into the early stages of 'programmes' which are capable of taking us over. If this were all there were to the way the body works, then the proper job of the human mind would clearly be to keep the body rigidly under control, to stop it 'going off' into rages, hysterias, orgasms and fits – the job that some philosophies and religions do in fact seem to assign to the mind. That such a model of the mind/body relationship is dangerously crude will surely be agreed by readers of Lawrence, and the need for a more subtle and flexible model is surely confirmed by ordinary daily experience too.

Many distinguished writers since Lawrence and Yeats have worked out individual variations of the Recoil to the Body. There is Henry Reed's poem *Naming of Parts* (1946), where the depersonalizing jargon of army training is contrasted with naive perception of the erotic rhythms of the natural world outside the parade-ground:

> We call this
> Easing the spring. And rapidly backwards and forwards
> The early bees are assaulting and fumbling the flowers:
> They call it easing the Spring.

And there is F. T. Prince's *Soldiers Bathing* (1954) about soldiers stripped to swim – a poem which argues that war crimes are caused by inability to accept the full implications of sexuality, but is best remembered for its pictorial immediacy:

> 'Poor bare forked animal',
> Conscious of his desires and needs and flesh that rise and
> fall,
> Stands in the soft air, tasting after toil
> The sweetness of his nakedness: letting the sea-waves coil
> Their frothy tongues about his feet, forgets

His hatred of the war, its terrible pressure that begets
A machinery of death and slavery,
Each being a slave and making slaves of others. . . .

Again, Octavio Paz the poet has written (1970):

The time of progress, technology and work, is the future; the time of
the body, the time of love and of poetry, is the present, not eternity.

Paz sees the 'embrace of bodies' and the 'poetic metaphor' as two
resources we have against technological vacuity:

In the first: union of sensation and image, the fragment apprehended
as cypher of the totality and totality parcelled into caresses that transform the bodies into a fountain of instantaneous correspondences. In
the second: fusion of sound and meaning, marriage of the intelligible
and the felt. The poetic metaphor and the erotic embrace are examples
of this moment of almost perfect coincidence between one symbol and
another that we call analogy and whose true name is happiness.

T. S. Eliot's *The Dry Salvages* of 1941 (though it is concerned with
much else too) begins with a powerful appreciation of the role of
the river in large cities as a reminder of primitive natural force
amid the questionable achievements of civilization; and it is of
the body too that Eliot writes implicitly:

> I think that the river
> Is a strong brown god – sullen, untamed and intractable . . .
>   the brown god is almost forgotten
> By the dwellers in cities – ever, however, implacable,
> Keeping his seasons and rages, destroyer, reminder
> Of what men choose to forget. Unhonoured, unpropitiated
> By worshippers of the machine, but waiting, watching and
>   waiting.

The Recoil to the Body can also be seen in twentieth-century
social fiction, in, for example, Evgeny Zamyatin's *We* (1920), the
better-known *Brave New World* by Aldous Huxley (1932) and
George Orwell's *Nineteen Eighty-four* (1949). All three satires are
nightmares of contemporary technocracy extrapolated towards the
future, and all three have some features in common, such as the
totalitarian deformation of language by the State. The differences
between the technocratic bogeys in each of the three are obvious
enough. Zamyatin is preoccupied by the threat of the subjection
of men to the dictates of mathematics, engineering and time-and-
motion study. Huxley concentrates on the threats of biological
engineering, drugs, Pavlovian conditioning, high-consumption
economics and what Marcuse was later to call 'repressive de-

sublimation' – the systematic pleasuring of the senses by exploitative institutions under the pretext of liberation of the body. Orwell's particular horror is the tyranny of a dehumanizing ideology. Airstrip One, or England in Orwell's 1984, contains sophisticated technologies, such as the two-way telescreen and the speak-write, which serve the interests of the regime; yet all except members of the Inner Party are kept in the economic deprivation of England in the 1940s.

Each author is grimly pessimistic about men's ability to resist determination by the technocratic state, and it is a telling criticism of this genre of nightmarish fiction that in general it underestimates the human ability to resist. Nevertheless, each author is virtually obliged, by the literary form he has chosen, to set up a polarity between his projected nightmare of technocratic hegemony and some opposite and potentially restorative values. In each case, these positive values focus on the subversive potential of the body, though in different ways.

In 'The One State' of Zamyatin's *We*, normal sexual relations between men and women are promiscuous, but they are confined to regular 'Sexual Days' when the 'Right of Blinds' is permitted (otherwise there is no privacy, for all walls in the State are of glass). Before intercourse, the stub of a small pink coupon from a book has to be torn off. The exact social organization of Zamyatin's dystopia is a little obscure: for instance, the principle 'Every number has the right of availability, as a sexual product, to any other number', is reminiscent of similar theories held by Sade, but its application would result in administrative headaches which Zamyatin does not discuss. It is certainly clear that the subversive aspects of sexuality have been systematically defused by the State. Huxley's *Brave New World* is much the same; but here the dissolution of the family has gone so far that childbirth is replaced by artificial insemination, and constancy in sexual relationships is generally deprecated. The population is subjected to compulsory VPS (Violent Passion Surrogate) treatments every month: as the Controller explains, 'We flood the whole system with adrenin. It's the complete physiological equivalent of fear and rage. All the tonic effects of murdering Desdemona and being murdered by Othello, without any of the inconveniences.'

Both Zamyatin and Huxley postulate in their anti-utopias that the civilized body has been conditioned into meek submission to 'happiness'; but set against the civilized majority, in both novels, are Reservations of savages. In Zamyatin:

Naked, they took to the forests. There they learned from the trees, beasts, birds, colours, sun. They became hirsute, but to make up for that they had preserved warm, red blood under their hirsuteness.[32]

Throughout the text of *We* runs the reverberation of a 'wild simian echo issuing from the shaggy depths', disturbing the crystalline purity of a totally logical State. The narrator, as he writes his diary, cannot avoid the sight of his own shaggy hands: 'I don't like to speak of them and I have no great love for them – they are the vestige of a savage epoch.'

This Darwinian theme in *We* is never adequately developed in the structure of the narrative, and the book as a whole is consequently rather a mess. Huxley develops the 'savage' theme more amply, and adopts a less naive tradition of primitivism; he had at least read Malinowski on the Trobriander and Margaret Mead on the Samoans, as well as Rousseau and D. H. Lawrence, even if he stirred them all up into a primitivist soup. The 'civilized' visitors to the New Mexican Reservation in *Brave New World* – accustomed as they are to 'feelies', scent organs and eau-de-cologne on tap – are disgusted by the body-odours of their Indian guide. The Indians, when they are not being intimidated by the gas-bombs of civilization, take part in ritual dances complete with snakes and flagellants.

There is a serious case for the view (if we may come back to reality for a moment) that it is the so-called primitive or tribal societies of the world, including European peasant societies, for whom we should reserve the word 'civilized'. Bodily intimacy between individuals in their everyday relations, including production and consumption, is a feature that nearly all these societies have in common, though the solutions they have developed to the problems of social and economic organization are extremely diverse; and it can be argued that these 'organic' relations are more important to men than any of the improvements brought by technology and the Western idea of progress. Robert Jaulin, the French anthropologist, writes[33] that the West and White society represent not Civilization, not even *a* civilization, but a 'movement of death' – ethnocide or Decivilization. And this threatened inversion of the deepest assumptions of our society about its superiority is latent in many texts since Rousseau dealing with 'primitive' cultures. It is not wholly reducible to the theological myth of the Fall of Man; or, to make the point another way, the theological myth may articulate a historical truth. Huxley failed to bring this point out clearly. At the end of *Brave*

New World a Savage who has been introduced to civilization becomes violently obsessed by hatred of sex and the flesh; and the finale is a mass orgy in which a huge crowd on the Surrey hills, incited by the media, joins in his 'whipping stunt'. This set-piece seems to me confused as well as lurid; but Huxley appears to be trying to show that the most primordial of man's instincts and habits are not immune to technocratic manipulation and exploitation.

The weakness of *Brave New World* (and of much of Huxley's other work) is that it is all 'in the head'. The message of the book, presented with much wit, is that everyone is liable to be totally reduced to a set of conditioned reflexes – everyone except the author, of course, and the reader, who is flattered into buying the book with the lure of sharing the author's Olympian omniscience and immunity to conditioning. The author's confidence trick would be exposed more obviously if there were a narrator, but Huxley gives us only slices of behaviour and mental processes, selected and recorded without explanation as if by some disembodied telescreen. If Huxley had introduced an 'I' into the story, the credibility of a totally conditioned society would have passed away. We cannot believe that an embodied consciousness who is addressing us is totally conditioned; the mere act of collaborative dialogue results in our imaginative substitution of ourselves for him (or her), and in order to understand what we are being told we have to make the assumption that he (or she) is free, and we are free. Huxley's mode of narration – the convention of omniscient objectivity combined with an assumption that the individuals in the story cannot elude their conditioning – is actually a symptom of the cerebrality, denial of the body and behaviourism which *Brave New World* purports to satirize.

This is why Orwell's *Nineteen Eighty-four* is a more sincere book, if less coruscating. For here is a narrator – or rather, an intermittent diarist – with whom we can empathize: Winston Smith. Winston serves three intertwined narrative functions. First, he is an objective 'native informant', a device for disclosing ethnographic details of life on Airstrip One to the reader. Second, he serves to illustrate in his own behaviour how individuals are determined by the technocracy's language and brainwashing. Third, he serves as a critic of the system – and one who is able to elude its conditioning temporarily. It is when he speaks to the reader with his own critical voice that Winston Smith becomes compelling; and the shock of later finding him write or act like any other indoctrinated Party Member is the more acute because we feel ourselves in his shoes.

The technocracy of 1984 is sexually repressive in a straight-forward way, compared to the subtler 'repressive desublimation' of *Brave New World*. If the mores of *Brave New World* are un-comfortably close to Japan in the 1970s, those of *Nineteen Eighty-four* are an accurate parody of Soviet Russia and some other communist countries. In Zamyatin and Huxley's anti-utopias, the body is technicized and its subversive potential paralysed, so that those two authors had to look elsewhere for positives – in the field of primitive anthropology. Orwell does not paralyse the body in this way, and one of the climaxes of the book is when Julia removes her Junior Anti-Sex League sash before making love with Winston in their country rendezvous. It is made explicit that Winston's transgressions of the sexual code are political acts directed at the Party. Unrepressed sexual desire and gratification survive in the proles as a kind of compensation for their brutalization by the regime; and Winston comments that 'out of those mighty loins a race of conscious beings must one day come'.

Orwell has been widely criticized (for instance, by Raymond Williams) for his condescending and romantic attitude to the proles in *Nineteen Eighty-four*, and for the one-dimensional poverty of the sexual relationship between Winston and Julia – an injustice to the *real* ability of human relationships to survive oppression. But if we think a little further abour Orwell's book, another perspective – more disquieting – suggests itself. Is not the effect of *Nineteen Eighty-four* to demonstrate that Orwell's narrative itself is conditioned by the pressures of *his own* society? If Winston Smith's marriage has been a failure, if his sexual tastes are prurient, if his affair with Julia is novelettish, if everyone in the book including the two lovers is eventually unfaithful – we must go a little further than objecting that there may be stronger guarantees against *Nineteen Eighty-four* happening than anything Orwell shows us.

Was not Orwell, when he wrote this book, in the same position as Winston Smith – sometimes able to speak to the reader as an inheritor of English literature at its greatest (Winston wakes from sleep one day with the name of Shakespeare on his lips), and yet reduced to a victim of alienation and repression? Great novels are not a feature of our time; the next best thing, perhaps, is a novel like this one whose one-dimensionality of execution *enacts* the one-dimensionality of its subject-matter, and so proves its case better than it would have if Winston and Julia had enjoyed a convincing relationship of profound and enduring love. The novel works artistically because the reader accepts the invitation to empathize with Winston Smith's predicament, and occasional images stand out as genuinely potent: for instance, Winston's insistence on writing his diary with ink, a dip-pen and rare cream-laid paper, rather than use the standard technology for writing laid down by the Party – a touch which convinces the reader that Winston is, after all, a free embodied being with a sense of history.

Most attempts to write fiction dealing with sexuality (*the* great theme of novels in general) have finished up with results that were far more one-dimensional than anything of Orwell's; such manuscripts are eventually consigned sheepishly to the dustbin. One reason why *Nineteen Eighty-four* is more than a mediocre piece of fiction is that it is, above all, about the processes of conditioning and impairment of the body's spontaneity. Orwell, unlike Huxley, does not remain above the fray.

The Recoil to the Body: Away from the Word

So far this chapter has drawn almost entirely on literary sources. Yet language is merely one – highly developed, specialized and efficient – resource of the body, and it is common for assertion of the body to take non-verbal – sometimes even defiantly anti-verbal – forms.

One of the chief traditional subjects for painting and sculpture has always been the human figure, and in particular the nude. It has been a principle of academic art that beauty and truth are vested in the nude human form, and that the nude remains perennially modern. The convention of depicting the nude remains – as Kenneth Clark points out in his instructive book *The Nude* – our chief link with the classical tradition, now that Greek mythology has been almost forgotten.

In my last chapter I had to anticipate the question of the human body as subject-matter for art, in dealing with Wright's *Gladiator* painting. But Adrian Stokes's words that I quoted there – that the nude is a 'promise of sanity' – seem to me to sum up the matter well (see p. 27). John Berger[34] has expressed a contrary and provocative point of view: that the depicting of the female nude often amounts to a degradation of womanhood, reflecting back to the male patron his fantastic, private supremacy.[35] 'To be nude', Berger writes, 'is to be seen as naked by others and yet not recognized for oneself.' Berger acknowledges that painters of nudes *can* transcend the conditions of their patronage, but considers this a relatively rare event. Perhaps Berger's criticism applies with greatest validity to French art of the eighteenth century, to paintings by Watteau and Boucher, and sculptures by Clodion. (It is significant that, as Clark points out, nudes of this period are often depicted from the back – a practice which is potentially a threat to the model's personal dignity, though it can also symbolize an exquisite trust.) What is very much to the point is that male nudes painted by women are very rare in art-history, perhaps because women artists had virtually no access to models or to training in anatomy; and supporters of Women's Lib would do better to encourage such painters as Sylvia Sleigh of New York, who are painting male nudes, than to denigrate the whole tradition of the nude as an art-form.

It is true that the relationship between artist and model has a kind of asymmetry which is sometimes disquieting; but this is irrespective of the gender of the model. John Addington Symonds wrote as follows of a sixteenth-century Florentine sculptor: 'Jacopo Sansovino made the statue of a youthful *Bacchus* in close imitation of a lad called Pippo Fabro. Posing for hours together naked in a cold studio, Pippo fell into ill health, and finally went mad. In his madness he frequently assumed the attitude of the *Bacchus* to which his life had been sacrificed, and which is now his portrait.'[36] Adrian Stokes was probably more representative of figurative artists when he wrote[37] that he was always solicitous for the comfort of his model. Similarly, an American photographer of the 1930s, William Mortensen, wrote in a manual on the problems of posing models:

I cannot pass over this subject without pausing to pay tribute to the late Arthur Kales for his remarkable skill in dealing with models. No one knew so truly as he how to obtain the finest response from a model, and no one ever treated his models with greater kindliness and tact. He worked with many models; but whether he was dealing with Ruth St. Denis, a bucolic beauty-contest winner, or the humblest Hollywood extra – all were treated with the identical fine consideration and impersonality. These relationships were marked with the same delicacy that characterised the unforgettable bromoil transfers of this great pictorialist.

The nineteenth-century attitude to the nude was rather para-doxical. Painters of the nude had always tended to dress their subjects in mythological guise to lend them respectability (and until the nineteenth century, nudes without a narrative pretext of some kind are rare); while a host of satyrs, fauns and centaurs had been conscripted to represent man's bodily drives, as were those angelic children who make love to animals in neo-classical friezes.[38] Nineteenth-century orthodoxy could allow Ingres to paint with impunity what Clark calls a 'whirlpool of carnality', 17 his circular painting of women in a Turkish bath, but only because Ingres's own views on paintings were orthodox and his scene was so clearly unreal. The employment of nude models in art schools was widely criticized as immoral, though the ritual of a young woman reclining on a velvet 'throne', warmed by a one-bar electric fire, while bearded artists twitch at their easels, survives to this day as a hallowed part of the tradition of painting. David Storey's recent play *Life Class*, set in a provincial English art-school, uses the degeneration of this tradition to symbolize a general loss of civilized values: a nude female model is subjected to cocky banter by a talentless class of art students and eventually appears to be violated sexually by one of the boys on her 'throne'.

18 Several painters of the nineteenth century – such as Courbet, Etty, Manet, Degas and Renoir – rebelled against, or ignored, the prudery of the day, and depicted realistic nudes with great artistic success. Delacroix painted a few nudes but preferred to paint horses and wild animals – a psychological substitute, perhaps, for the human form, just as the horse must have been for Stubbs. If the academic tradition of drawing, painting and sculpting 'from the life' had died before the mid-to-late nineteenth century – in other words, if Victorian prudery had gone one stage further than it actually did in its campaign against the life-class – one may surmise that the nude would have become a primary focus of attention as one of the most liberating art-forms. As it was, the salons were kept full of nude studies, whose style of execution was usually highly academic, that is to say rule-bound and (as it were) 'mechanical'. Nowadays some of this academic work has acquired a certain nostalgic charm. One is interested to learn, for instance, how marble was considered the right material for sculptures of the nude because of 'its fine grained purity and colour that complemented flesh'.[39] But to many of the progressive sculptors of the period, the nude was a dead art-form.

'Inveterate Salon visitors', writes Albert E. Elsen, 'could count upon an "eternal population of women", sleeping, waking, performing their toilette, bathing, reclining, being taken by surprise, experiencing their first romantic shiver, and grieving at the tomb, all in the service of the renewal of beauty and the sexual education of the young.' The very original sculptor Medardo Rosso was expelled from art-school in Milan for assaulting another student who petitioned for nude female models. It became a mark of modernity for late nineteenth-century sculptors to depict clothed rather than nude models, especially if the clothes signified labour and poverty. The nude convention had become fetishized and drained of all freshness; and it needed challenging. Brancusi, coming to his maturity as a sculptor some years before the First World War, felt that salon nudes were like 'toads'.

Rodin, however, had challenged the convention in a different way by radically revitalizing the nude, and the human figure in general, as a subject for sculpture. The main achievement of Rodin, according to the sculptor-critic William Tucker, is to have created 'a new and abstract language of sculpture, concerned with structure and material volume and space, but centred on a sense of the physical, of the character and performance of the human body'. It is widely agreed that much 'abstract' sculpture from Brancusi to Henry Moore and Anthony Caro is concerned with inventing forms analogous to, but not identical with, the human body. Or, as Adrian Stokes put it, in the rather cryptic style, with psychoanalytic allusions, characteristic of this writer: 'The idea of beauty . . . projects the integrated ego in the terms of a corporeal figure.'[40] Again:

There is a sense in which all art is of the body, particularly so in the eyes of those who accept that the painted surface and other media of art represent as a general form, which their employment particularizes, the actualities of the hidden psychic structure made up of evaluations and phantasies with corporeal content.[41]

Rodin provides a clear historical link with the later modernist movement in sculpture. None the less he also remains squarely within a tradition of figurative sculpture that was founded in Ancient Greece, just as Courbet, Renoir, Gauguin and Matisse remain within a tradition of figurative painting founded in the Renaissance (or before then in Ancient Rome). The human figure was laden with its glorious past, and it was available to be re-vitalized as a subject by all these artists; but it was never *inherently* a revolutionary subject, and was often a reactionary one. John Berger's scathing remarks about paintings of nudes apply perfectly well to much of the run-of-the-mill academic work that was done in the nineteenth century. Indeed, he is probably right, if the history of painting is to be considered in quantitative terms, to point out that the vast majority of all paintings of the nude ever

19

20

executed are bad art.[42] Yet it is an article of faith for most Western lovers of art that such an approach to the study of art is perverse and unrewarding. As I mentioned in Chapter 1 (see p. 17), the 'ethnographic' approach to art (here represented by Berger) cannot be reconciled with the 'critical' approach.

It would be a mistake to consider the body in painting and sculpture purely as subject-matter. What is equally important in modern art is the notion of the body of the artist in relation to his materials. Turner's famous 'Varnishing Days' at the Royal Academy in London are of great interest here. He used the Varnishing Days[43] not just to touch up his paintings, as was the usual practice, but to apply much of the colour; he would send in paintings merely 'laid in' with white and grey, to finish them off amid a group of spectators. As Jack Burnham has pointed out,[44] Turner anticipated the tendency of present-day painters to emphasize the *act* of painting. Turner seems to have wished to underline what we would call today 'art as process' or 'art as performance'. (He was described by a contemporary as a 'magician, performing his incantations in public'.) We can find this emphasis still earlier in the many Renaissance paintings where the artist at his easel is reflected in a mirror, or (turning to sculpture) in Michelangelo's four unfinished slaves in the Accademia, Florence, who wrestle with the stones out of which they are carved.

The implicit message in Turner's behaviour at the Royal Academy seems also to be conveyed in a piece made by Rodin in 1917 just before his death. He had a plaster cast made of his right hand (later cast into bronze) and put a small bronze female torso in it: art happens not by some magical transubstantiation of materials, but through the intelligent labour of the hand. As Hegel wrote of the hand, it is the 'animated artificer of man's fortune; we may say of the hand it is what a man does'.[45] The sculptor's hands turn metal into life; in this work of Rodin's, the process is varied and a living hand is transfixed for ever into cold metal. The bronze hand was generated from an actual fleshly hand and its surface bears a precise one-to-one correspondence to the surface of its model; whereas the bronze torso was presumably generated from a clay or plaster model and bears only a remote relationship to any individual woman. (The academic tradition of the broken torso, which Rodin revitalized, resulted from the historical accident that antique sculpture had often survived in a fragmentary state.) So this simple work by Rodin represents a kind of meditation on the physical facts and cultural conventions of sculpture. (In other pieces too Rodin drew attention to these facts and procedures: for instance, when he failed to disguise the marks on his pieces caused by moulds and damp cloths, or by his own 'editing'.)

In the early twentieth century Duchamp and other artists determined to challenge the importance hitherto attributed to manual fabrication in art. They drew attention to the importance of *selection* by the artist from a range of possibilities. This development was abetted by the spread of photography. Many present-day artists are persuaded that skill, especially manual skill, is quite irrelevant to art, and that the essence of art is mental decision-making, though a substantial body of painters and sculptors survives to defend the traditional media.

The strongest argument for the permanency of painting and sculpture as forms of art is surely the recognition of the importance of the body of the artist, and hence of the spectator's body too. The tools and techniques of painting and sculpture are so hallowed by cultural tradition that the artist is trained to regard them as the natural and inevitable means by which he works. Thus he feels that everything he produces is his. To put this in terms adapted from the early Marx (terms which will be discussed in some detail in the course of the next chapter), painting and sculpture are the opposite of such essentially 'alienating' activities as working on an assembly-line, auditing accounts, or appearing in *Oh Calcutta!* They are 'disalienating' or liberating work, in which technology has been pared down to a few very familiar and unquestioned facilities: brushes and paint and canvas, or chisel and stone.

To take sculpture first: the academic nineteenth-century view was that clay was essential for the making of rapid sketches. Sculpture issuing from the 'feverish thumb' in clay was then transferred not to stone, but to bronze. Certainly the practice of moulding clay is a technique which interposes minimum technical apparatus – not even a brush and palette – between the body and its art-work. Adrian Stokes, however, gives primacy to the act of carving. The carver relates to his stone (according to an elaborate set of analogies that Stokes developed, with less than perfect clarity) as the ploughman relates to the land, or as the dancer relates to the space which he assaults, or again as man relates sexually to woman. Modelling becomes for Stokes a female activity, more favoured by the twentieth century than carving.[46] But both carving and modelling are processes deeply rooted in bodily experience.

Various attempts have been made by painters to explain the peculiar psychic satisfaction they obtain. For instance, analogies have been made with the child's fondling its faeces, or with sexual ejaculation. It has been argued that the elimination of colour – or, rather, its austere reduction – in much modern art reflects sexual repression. Conversely, colour painting is in a subtle way one of the most erotic of art-forms. On a cruder and more biographical level, it is worth noting that many people outside the circles where modern art is revered must have found the paintings of Picasso very puzzling, but understood and appreciated his romantic reputation as a lover and sensualist.

In recent years, the assertion of the process of painting has become a fashionable doctrine, resulting in, for instance, deliberate clumsiness of fabrication – anything to avoid a machine-made or illusionistic look. (By contrast, the traditional ambition of the figurative painter had been that his art should resemble nature so closely as to be mistaken for nature. Thus the material reality of charging a surface with paint had been dematerialized.) Jasper Johns and Yves Klein both used actual human bodies as brush-substitutes to apply paint to a surface, but the greatest originator was Jackson Pollock, as the following description of Pollock's development by Charles Harrison suggests:

21

The adoption of the drip-and-spatter technique and of dried-out brushes, sticks and trowels as tools, can ... largely be accounted for in practical terms: Pollock was enabled by this means to maintain a relatively upright position, a distance away from the floor and the canvas. The painting-at-arms-length stance cannot be sustained for a painting on the floor as it can before an easel or a wall. The point of balance for Pollock became the hips, not, as before, the shoulder; the natural rhythm – and Pollock was a 'rhythmical' painter from the start – became inevitably more expansive, involved longer, more sweeping movements of the hand controlling the application of paint. He gained more sway over the canvas.[47]

The 'spirituality' of early twentieth-century European abstract artists (Malevich, Mondrian, Kandinsky) was no longer an acceptable option for the post-Second-World-War American abstract expressionist generation. According to Harrison:

The European abstract artists somehow managed to derive, from their inability to make sense of man's changed and fraught relationship to the material world, an optimistic belief in a future which would be characterized by the 'spirituality' of all relationships. The Abstract Expressionist, confronting a more developed condition of the same alienation of man from the world he had previously painted, saw nothing to which he felt a relationship he could embody, nothing he could affirm, with the confidence with which he could affirm his own existence and his own mortality.[48]

It may be objected that modern painters and sculptors often use quite advanced technology of various kinds. Does this result in their work becoming 'alienated'? No – or rather: not necessarily. When technology develops in direct answer to the requirements of artists, it may be called liberating as opposed to repressive. Acrylic paint is perhaps an example of this, in that painters have been able to use it to obtain desired results unattainable through earlier media. More important than the *level* of the technology (primitive or sophisticated) is the fact that painting and sculpture each inherit a ritualized cultural tradition for the bodily manipulation of materials.

This point will be clearer if we consider an analogy from the history of musical instruments: the piano. The modern piano is not the product of a very simple technology; on the contrary, it requires quite sophisticated engineering. Most pianists are totally ignorant of what goes on inside their instruments. Yet we do not normally think of the pianist as being 'alienated'. Indeed, his work seems as far removed as one can imagine from the work of, say, an assembly-line worker. (It is the pianola or player-piano, with its punched paper tape input, that reduces the operative to an alienated appendage.) The reason is that piano-playing is both a culturally hallowed tradition or ritual, and a skill requiring a more-than-mechanical co-ordination and sensitivity of mind and body. Generations of children have been brought up to accept the piano as a kind of 'natural' medium – even as *the* medium – of musical composition and performance (whereas a less familiar instrument like the sousaphone can often strike us as contingent or peculiar; we are provoked to wonder why it is so and not otherwise).

The bodily act of striking an instrument to produce sound is as primordial as that of charging a surface with a graphic mark. The pianoforte in music, and the paintbox and palette in painting, represent a graded systematization of artistic practice. Both, in a sense, may be regarded historically as 'liberating technologies' in that they have provided a technical base for traditions of artistic creativity. Today both are found alienating by *some* practitioners, those who desire to return to the immemorial founts of art, bypassing technological intervention and the repressive architecture of concrete concert-halls and museums of modern art. This means returning to the simplest physical processes, the simplest forms of interchange between the body and the material environment; perhaps making one's own instruments of expression, or getting friends to make them. [49]

Much of the figurative function of painting has been taken over by photography, as everyone knows. The photographic portrait is an important art-form. The convention of 'posing' is crucial to the integrity of photographic portraiture, being proof of an implied contract between photographer and subject. [50] The contract is sometimes broken when the photographer holds the subject up to ridicule through the context in which the photograph is made public, as in the exhibitions of photographs of 'freaks' by the late Diane Arbus. 'Candid' shots, or shots that seem to catch the subject in an instantaneous grimace, often seem an intrusion or violation, especially if the subject happens to be poor, old, deformed, mad or naked. The photographer becomes an exploiter of the body of another through his technological advantage; and at worst becomes a kind of chic vulture. The point is tellingly made by a moving sequence of three shots by William van der Weyde, a New York commercial photographer of the late 1890s, documenting the execution of a Negro, wearing the broad stripe, by electric chair. The first shot shows him being led into the room, accompanied by a clergymen, warders and sombre-faced officials. The second shot shows him being sat in the chair. The third shows him blindfolded, as the electric chair is switched on. The whole sequence is ethically and artistically justified by the second shot; for here the convict is looking straight at the cameraman. Had he wished, he could have deflected his gaze and so dissociated himself from the photographer. As it is, his face expresses dignity and responsibility, and it is not necessary to know whether his sentence is just or unjust; at that instant of frozen time he commands all our respect and sympathy. [51]

In painting and sculpture, music and photography, certain stuffs and processes – like paint, or breath driven through convoluted tubes – become accepted as the 'natural', 'right and proper' media of expression. In the performing arts – dance, acting, mime, recitation, singing – the body itself becomes the medium of expression. This fact could set us asking whether the body does not always remain the principal medium of expression even in painting – not simply in the 'action painting' of Pollock and others, but in easel painting too. And what about modelling and carving? playing the flute? playing the piano? Delicate theoretical points are raised by these questions, while it is an obvious yet also rather startling fact that the performing arts are able to dispense with all these adventitious aids. In our present culture they make use of ancillary technologies, such as lighting, make-up properties, scenery, amplification, and indeed the whole range of electronic apparatus which is used to record and disseminate performances. But the performing arts do not need these aids in principle. They do not even need clothing or shoes.

Dance, as a universal medium of expression, can be studied both historically and ethnographically across a wide range of cultures. (There are only a very few danceless peoples, Curt Sachs tells us in his *World History of the Dance*.[52]) We should not make the mistake of regarding all dance activities as psychologically therapeutic or expressive of bodily harmony, since some forms of trance dance and dancing mania have the effect of putting to sleep (literally) part of the dancer's brain and causing him to act in a non-responsible manner. Some of these dance-forms (not all) may fairly be called pathological. It would also be a mistake to regard all forms of dance as representing a reaction against rational and technological modes of experience. Alan Lomax, probably the world's leading anthropologist of dance, has offered the stimulating but controversial argument that certain kinds of dance – for instance those involving synchrony between hand and foot, three-dimensional movement, and varied movement – are characteristic of male-dominated, authoritarian cultures which are increasing man's manipulative control over the environment. The characteristic entertainments beloved of industrial-managerial societies like our own are symphony orchestras, brass bands, football and the ballet. Other kinds of dance – for instance, those involving high synchrony, sinuous curves of the trunk, and erotic, in-gathering movement – are characteristic of non-authoritarian cultures enjoying group solidarity and complementarity between males and females.

Frank Kermode has stated the position of dance well in his essay on Loïe Fuller, the celebrated music-hall dancer of the 1890s. In fact, Loïe Fuller's historical importance is more as a pioneer of spectacular lighting than of the more primitivist forms of twentieth-century dance (the line of her body became more and more concealed by drapes as her career developed, and Mallarmé wrote of her, 'Her performance, *sui generis*, is at once an artistic intoxication and an industrial achievement'). But Kermode also makes some comments on dance in general:

The peculiar prestige of dancing over the past seventy or eighty years has, I think, much to do with the notion that it somehow represents art in an undissociated and unspecialized form – a notion made explicit by Yeats and hinted at by Valéry. The notion is essentially primitivist; it depends upon the assumption that mind and body, form and matter, image and discourse have undergone a process of dissociation, which it is the business of art momentarily to mend. Consequently dancing is credited with a sacred priority over the other arts.[53]

The fundamental principle is that dance comes to be regarded as 'the most primitive, non-discursive art, offering a pre-scientific image of life, an intuitive truth'.[54] This new interest in dance as the most repristinating and 'disalienating' of art-forms was accompanied earlier in the present century by the study of the anthropology and folklore of dance ritual, including the Catholic liturgy, and by a new psycho-physiological approach to dance.

The new view of dance was also accompanied by a critical approach to classical ballet. As Alan Beattie – an English experimental theatre-artist – has argued, the underlying thrust of ballet technique is to protest against the law of gravity by rising in an upward direction. Ballet's social origins are in the European courts, and it is pervaded by ideals of purity, chastity, elegance and virtuosity. Thus it tends not to assert the body as such but to try and escape the encumbrance and corruption of the body through art. What Curt Sachs has written about the cross-cultural phenomenon of the 'expanded dance' and 'leaping dance' is especially true of ballet:

We are often reminded of that European school of architecture which more than any other grew out of the ecstatic soul – the Gothic. It too is a conquest and denial of the terrestrial burden, a defiant triumph of the vertical, a single, irresistible pushing aloft.[55]

Beattie makes a more questioning analogy between the pure verticality of ballet and that of glass skyscrapers, and quotes Reich on the 'uptightness' of 'tight-assed Western culture'. There is also constant danger of the body in ballet becoming a mere mechanical instrument. Only rarely in classical ballet does a genius like Nijinsky break through the limitations of the medium.

Nijinsky discarded the 'sauce' of the dance, according to the French critic Jacques Rivière in his review of *Le Sacre du Printemps*, and returned to the 'natural pace' of the body 'in order to listen to nothing but its most immediate, basic, etymological signs'.

25

Rivière defined two degrees of 'sauce'. First, more obviously, lighting, drapery and veils. But second:

What still envelops the dancer even when he has discarded his accessories? His very leap, his passage, his flight through time, the arabesque he describes by his movement.[56]

A ballet like *Le Spectre de la Rose* is visually delightful but artistically indistinct. ('In it the body of Nijinsky literally disappears into its own dance.') However, in *Le Sacre du Printemps*:

whenever the body offers tendencies and opportunities, the movement breaks off and begins afresh; each time the body feels possible starting points in itself, the dancer again springs into movement. He is constantly taking possession of himself again, like a bubbling spring whose every surge must be successively drained off; he goes back into himself, and the dance becomes the analysis, the enumeration, of all those urges to move that he discovers within himself. . . . The body is no longer a highway for the flight of the soul; it curbs its thrust, and by its very effort against the soul, it becomes completely permeated by it and exteriorizes it. . . . The dancer is no longer carried along by a light and emotionless inspiration. Instead of grazing things in his flight, he lands upon them with his whole weight, marks each one with his total, heavy fall.[57]

This acceptance of gravity – implying an acceptance, too, of man's 'terrestrial burden' rather than a single-minded desire to transcend it – was to be very characteristic of the Modern Dance movement, especially through the influence of Mary Wigman, the pioneer German expressionist dancer. She emphasized the need both to grapple with gravity and to yield to it, in a two-way pull – the upward surge and the downward ebb – expressive of man's struggle. Many practitioners of Modern Dance lay stress on the use of the ground. Other innovators, such as Isadora Duncan, put special emphasis on an 'organic' (i.e. non-mechanical) idea of 'fluidity' of bodily action, demanding, for example, a much more mobile spine and haunches than the classical tradition. Duncan also advocated a minimum of costume, but she invented no steps, whereas Martha Graham is thought by some experts to be the greatest single innovator in the whole history of the dance; and her conceptual framework – with its allusions to earth, nature and the flow of natural forces – is explicitly primitivist.

26

The international tradition of professional dance – including ballet and both the American and European schools of Modern Dance – represents a set of rich and sophisticated techniques.[58] One of the greatest difficulties for the non-dancer is that the dance world is both very inbred and genuinely non-verbal in its orientation. Many dancers and choreographers believe that their art is one which cannot be done justice to by any verbal analogue. There is not one even passably good book explaining the development of Modern Dance. This is one reason why Alan Beattie is right in his criticisms: 'In many respects modern dance could and should be a paradigm and model for the organization of bodily energies. But we have to acknowledge its failure: its fringe status in contemporary society, and its impotence, irrelevance and triviality in the face of our current cultural concerns.' Beattie sees dance as merely one of several dominant styles of 'body art' in our culture – others being sports, showbiz and beauty culture: 'All of these follow the same socio-economic pattern: wherein a select and remote corps of skilled, highly-paid and glamorous professionals perform to a passive and paying audience.' Beattie considers that we can learn from studying non-Western, pre-industrial dance forms, and that our own high-art dance forms must seek a rapprochement with social dance, and specifically with the Rock sub-culture. Another related school of thought is that of 'creative movement' specialists, influenced by the German dance theorist Rudolf von Laban. They believe that everyday movement is essential to the formulation of personality, and that knowledge of movement can be socially valuable in such contexts as psychotherapy, general education and vocational guidance.[59]

There is no doubt about the present popularity in our society of dance both as a pastime and as a spectacle. Various forms of social dance continue to enjoy a wide following, from the fairy-tale, courtly refinement of ballroom dancing to the blasting beat of rock. But it is especially significant that New York – where everyday experience of 'natural scenery' has become tragically impoverished – has become the world centre for the Modern Dance movement. It was an American dancer – Joseph Scoglio of the Ballet Rambert – who first made me realize, in a talk on choreography, how visual experience of the choreographed human body becomes a substitute for visual experience of the countryside when the latter is no longer available. That the landscape of nature and the landscape of the body are closely associated in our minds is shown by many poetic texts.[60] However, in this book I have taken the argument further back, urging that it is the body which is primary, and that the countryside, with its harmonious contours, textures, odours and protuberances, its springs and shelters and seasons, is (among other things) a kind of metaphor for the body.

Highlights from *Dan Dare* (1950–51)

1 Arrival at Mekonta.

2 Venus at War.

3 Sir Hubert assaults the Mekon.

4 Dare picks up the Mekon.

5 *Opposite above*, Joseph Wright, *A Philosopher giving a lecture on the Orrery*, 1764–66.

6 *Opposite below*, Joseph Wright, *The Blacksmith's Shop*, 1771.

7 *Below*, J. M. W. Turner, *Rain, Steam and Speed—Great Western Railroad*, 1844.

8 *Bottom*, George Inness, *The Lackawanna Valley*, 1855.

9 Prize Certificate for Farm Machinery, Hanover, 1852.

10 Decimus Burton, Palm House, Kew Gardens, near London, 1844–48.

11 *Left*,' "There's your stove", said Fry'; from Jules Verne's *Tribulations of a Chinaman*.

12 *Above*, The hearth of the Gun Club; from Jules Verne's *From the Earth to the Moon*.

13 *Below*, View of Stahlstadt; from Jules Verne's *The Begum's Fortune*.

14 The underground coal-mining city in Jules Verne's *Black Diamonds*.

15 *Left*, Giacomo Balla, *Gi running on a balcony*, 1912.

16 *Below*, William Blake, *Pity*, 1795.

17 *Above*, Jean Auguste Dominique Ingres, *Le Bain Turc*, 1862.

18 *Right*, Gustave Courbet, *La Source*, 1868.

19 *Left*, Auguste Rodin, *Study for Jean d'Aire*, bronze *c.* 1889.

20 *Below*, Constantin Brancusi, *The Kiss*, 1908.

21 *Opposite*, Jackson Pollock in his Hampton studio.

22–24 William van der Weyde: sequence of three photographs of an unidentified execution by electric chair, 1890s.

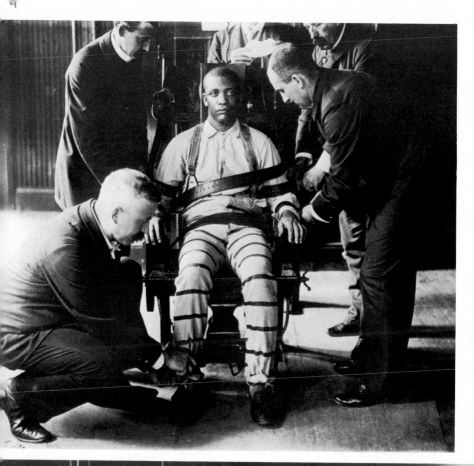
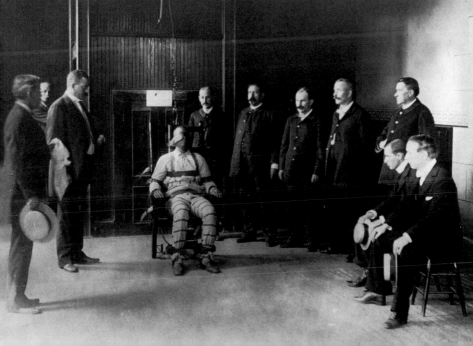

25 *Opposite*, Nijinsky as the Gold Slave in *Scheherazade*, 1911.

26 Martha Graham performs in *Errand Into the Maze*; the set was designed by the sculptor Isamu Noguchi.

27 The Living Theater in *Frankenstein* at the Round House, London, 1969.
Activities at various levels are going on inside the huge 'head' (shown in
lighted outline) of the Creature: dreams of sea, shipwreck, drowning.

Whether or not dance really has a 'sacred priority' over the other arts, there is something about it that is eminently hard to analyse and paraphrase, as if it played havoc with our unconscious. The fact that so much of both ballet and Modern Dance suffer from glaring defects – ranging from self-indulgence, narcissism, nostalgia and tweeness to formalism and avant-gardist pretentiousness – does not detract from their great power. In our predominantly verbal culture, an almost totally non-verbal art-form is widely practised and appreciated – though it exists alongside, rather than at the centre of, our cultural life.

Verbal language is widely and influentially regarded as *the* distinctively human capability, and has been extensively studied as such. In fact, the 'algebra' of verbal language is just one means whereby the body's physical organs and energies (of the mouth or the hand) are articulated to convey meaning. This is not to deny that it is a very concentrated and efficient means, which has been the vehicle for some of man's greatest cultural achievements.

Verbal language no doubt contributed substantially to the evolutionary success of early man, but may now be a part of the over-specialization of industrial man (even granting Octavio Paz all he says about the erotic fecundity of the poetic metaphor[61]); for science, technology, law, business and all the professions demand a specifically verbal articulateness. While it would be senseless and destructive to belittle verbal language, there is a great deal of sense in attempting to restore our awareness of other potentials of the body. One example is the 'language' of manual gesture which appears to be natural in young children, but is abandoned in the course of upbringing in favour of speech – by all except the deaf community, some of whom rely on it almost exclusively.

There is a complicated debate to be resolved here, calling for the interdisciplinary attention of sociologists and anthropologists, psychologists, linguists, ethologists and others – and it is outside the scope of this book. Nevertheless, the debate is a useful context for considering some recent important trends in the history of the theatre.

Theatre (or drama) has tended to be almost a department of literature in our culture. To follow Nelson Goodman,[62] theatre is a 'two-stage art', like music, rather than a 'one-stage art', like painting: that is to say, composition of a text (or a score, in the case of music) precedes, and is distinct from, performance. You can argue that looking at a picture is analogous to a stage-director interpreting a play, or to a pianist interpreting a sonata; but in that case painting becomes two-stage, and theatre and music three-stage (since we must take account of the audience's experience of the performance as the third stage). This distinction is neatly analysed by Goodman – whose book, *Languages of Art*, also includes a useful study of the problem of why notation systems are used in some art-forms but not others. It is a distinction which corresponds to 'theatre' as it is conceived by most people in our society, but would not be accepted by some theatre-artists today.

The theatrical innovator most influential in questioning the conventional literary view of the theatre was Antonin Artaud (1896–1948). Actually, many of Artaud's specific theatrical innovations can be traced back to earlier directors or artists (Appia, Gordon Craig, Reinhardt, Stanislavsky and the Dadaists). Nor would I argue that Artaud's conception of the body is one that harmonizes fully with my main argument. Artaud seems to have seen human existence as an incessant conflict and the human body as essentially bad – an opposite position to that of both the 'life-affirming' authors, like Blake, Rimbaud, Lawrence, Yeats and Whitman, and most of the innovators of twentieth-century dance. Artaud's life was one of intense physical and mental suffering and his importance is that of a ruthless, uncompromising self-questioner rather than that of a moral and imaginative exemplar. The current treatment of his work as holy writ by some French intellectuals seems to me exaggerated, though his influence in the 'uncrowning of the Word' in the theatre is indisputable:[63]

A theatre which submits *mise en scène* and stage-direction – that is, everything which there is specifically theatrical in it – to the text, is a theatre for idiots, madmen, inverts, grammarians, grocers, anti-poets and positivists, that is for Westerners.

('*Mise en scène* and metaphysics')

It is not a question of suppressing speech in the theatre but of changing its destination, and above all reducing its place, considering it as something other than a means of leading human characters to their external ends, since the theatre is always a matter of how sentiments and passions conflict with each other, and between one man and another, in life.

('Eastern theatre and Western theatre')

Language in the theatre was to become rather like the language in dreams as revealed by Freud (though Artaud was hostile to the theories of psychoanalysis).

In 1931, Artaud discovered the Balinese theatre at a colonial exhibition in France, and wrote admiringly of its synthesis of dance, song, mime and music; of its rejection of psychology; and of its subordination of words to gestures, cries and movements. The Balinese actor, he wrote, was a 'living, moving hieroglyph': 'and these three-dimensional hieroglyphs are in their turn embroidered with a certain number of gestures and mysterious signs corresponding to I know not what fabulous and obscure reality which we Westerners have irrevocably repressed' ('On the Balinese theatre'). Artaud showed no sensitivity to the political implications of witnessing a degenerate version of Balinese culture in the context of a colonial exhibition – whereas one cannot imagine, say, D. H. Lawrence, Aldous Huxley or Orwell missing this. Yet Artaud did not make the mistake of assuming that the Balinese theatre was more improvised, less governed by conventions, than Western theatre. On the contrary, he approved its coded stylization, a 'sort of spiritual architecture'. Artaud's general perception about the importance of the body to the Balinese has been borne out by the subsequent ethnographic researches of Bateson and Mead.

The movement in modern theatre represented by Artaud is far from being the only one (many continue to believe in the theatre as an arena for the clash of articulated ideas); and when we examine it in detail we find that it is not very coherent. It is true that certain theatrical methods fashionable in some circles today have a 'family resemblance' and are related to Artaud's teachings: the relegation of the text to a subordinate position; the priority given to the actors' bodies; emphasis on instinctual release rather than reason; the extension of the stage into the auditorium and out into the streets; provocation of the spectator. But when we examine the two most important companies that have practised such methods – Grotowski's Theatre Laboratory and the American Living Theater – we find fundamental divergences both from each other and from what Artaud believed in.

Jerzy Grotowski, the Polish director, is highly regarded by theatrical professionals for his insistence on rigour and on imaginative authenticity – the refusal to fake. His best-known principle is that of 'poor theatre', the result of his attempt to define the specific character of theatre as opposed to other types of performance and spectacle. 'We consider the personal and scenic technique of the actor as the core of technical art.' Grotowski's company gradually eliminated stage, make-up, costume, lighting and sound effects – criticized by him as the 'synthetic' or 'rich theatre'. (We may recall Jacques Rivière's tribute to Nijinsky for presenting the body of the dancer without 'sauce'.) The text becomes 'a spring-board and a challenge', resulting in a highly ritualized performance involving a 'direct, living, palpable commerce' between actor and spectator, in spaces specially designed for a restricted number of spectators. He emphasizes the importance of the actor's training, borrowing techniques from psychotherapy and yoga as well as from traditional theatrical sources (such as the exploration of the body's vocal 'resonators').

Grotowski is an important director, but it is not necessary to describe his work in detail here.[64] It is enough to say that he follows Artaud in an insistence on rigour and technique (belittling vulgar notions of 'inspiration') but departs from him ideologically: he relies on a personal synthesis of relatively traditional ideas, borrowed from Catholicism, Jungian psychoanalysis and Aristotle's theory of catharsis, as well as other sources.[65]

The practice of the Living Theater, founded in New York by Julian Beck and Judith Malina, also has a lot in common with Artaud's theories while diverging from them significantly – in some important details (such as the Living Theater's enthusiasm for narcotics) but more generally in its easy-going adolescent anarchism, which was so characteristic of American youth in the 1960s. The Living Theater was whole-heartedly in favour of liberation of the body, a recurrent theme in its practitioners' performance; they believed that a sexual revolution was necessary to exorcise violence and so bring about a peaceful revolution. For instance, in *Paradise Now* (1968) there was a scene in which the actors lay on the stage and caressed the bodies nearest to them. Spectators joined the scene; then couples detached themselves and sat upright in an Indian posture where each partner's arms and legs are curled round the other's trunk.

27 The Living Theater's performances were also full of attacks on the 'industrial-military complex'. In *Frankenstein* (1965) an actor, presented as a spokesman for international industry, enunciated through loudspeakers a series of slogans culled at random from such works as Sir Leon Bagrit's *The Age of Automation* and Bertrand Russell's *Power*. In so far as the Living Theater contributed to fuddling the brains of a generation of young people in the late 1960s, it can only be deplored; nevertheless, it illustrates the theme of my present chapter clearly, in its pronounced anarchism, sensuality and primitivism.

Artaud and Grotowski are less extreme cases. Each appears from his writings to hanker for a 'scientific' basis for his art, and each respects method and discipline. Method and discipline seem to be essential to art, and are rejected only in brief periods of effervescent utopianism such as characterized American youth in the 1960s. On the other hand, one is a little sceptical of the claims made by theatrical and dance innovators that their work has a 'scientific' basis; certainly the claim is made by many of them and appears to satisfy some psychological or didactic necessity, providing a weapon against popular notions of artistic inspiration, freedom and genius. Many conflicting tendencies now coexist in the theatre, and some of the most successful of today's directors are those who are able to integrate lessons learnt from the radicals I have mentioned, with a renewed emphasis on the text and a rigorous approach to costumes and settings.

The enterprise of abandoning the textual foundation of drama was almost certainly ephemeral, but the restoration of a fuller sense of the physical power of the actor/spectator relationship is probably more permanent. Advocates of the theatre claim that, whatever debasements it may have endured in modern times, it is in principle the greatest of all art-forms, since it allows the expressive power of the human body and that of language to be combined to maximum advantage. This is convincing as a theoretical statement. But as the period of 'retreat from the word' comes to an apparent end in the theatre – the phrase is George Steiner's,[66] though he is one who deeply deplores any such retreat – it is worth putting on record the work of one extreme group that has never become famous but which has probably pushed one line of theatrical development as far as it can be, or needs to be, pushed. The work of the RAT Theatre, which I have chosen to illustrate an extreme primitivist recoil against technocracy, must be related to certain developments that became popular outside the theatre at about the same time: Encounter Groups (which try to break down the psychological hang-ups of individuals through group sessions which are something between a children's party and watered-down Yoga), and some types of fringe psychotherapy that try to evoke early stages in human evolution through screaming, because traces of those early stages are held to survive in the civilized unconscious.

The RAT Theatre was founded by Peter Sykes and is based in Staffordshire; it also undertakes regular tours in Europe, where the 'theatre of physical expression' has been on the whole more appreciated than in Britain. The company believes in pushing both mind and body to the edge of endurance. One of its 'constructs', *Hunchback* (which I saw in 1972), works on the legend of the hunchback of Notre Dame. In the course of development, the theme took on a new significance for the group. *Hunchback* explores how a society deals with alien beings in its midst; how an alien sub-culture attempts to integrate itself into existing cultural patterns; and how the established society attempts to resolve the problem. The audience is alternately trapped into complicity with persecution, and appealed to directly and individually for sympathy. At the end of eighty minutes, the cast is physically exhausted; the actors have abused and pursued each other, crushed each other down on to the seating, fought each other ferociously. The work has little of subtlety or understatement, and is marred by a persistent note of hysterical self-pity, but its intensity is unforgettable. Words are used very sparingly and all the emphasis is on the actor's bodily presences.

One of the RAT Theatre's other constructs, *Blindfold*, explores a relationship between a drooling cripple and a group of blind dependents. A catastrophe has wiped out the whole of society except this one survivor, who survived because society had conditioned him to keep alive at the lowest possible level. He has rescued some unborn children from their dead mothers' wombs, but has blindfolded them from birth to ensure that they will always be totally dependent on him. The blind are totally unaware that their provider is a cripple, unaware that he possesses the faculty of sight; they only know the cripple as the source of all their needs, and as their antagonizer.

RAT Theatre seems at present rather too reliant on the magnetism and technical inventiveness of its young director and leading actor, Peter Sykes, but it has certainly carried its principles to a consistent, if lurid, outcome. The rawest physical relationships between actor and actor, and between actors and spectators, are the substance of the work, while verbal discourse is inherently suspect as a means by which the weak members of society are manipulated and the strong increase their strength.

'Body art' is a term which covers a number of very different manifestations in the visual arts, by artists whose background was usually in painting and sculpture, rather than in dance or theatre. One or two artists, such as Lygia Clark, a Brazilian working in Paris, illustrate the thesis of Recoil to the Body particularly clearly: in her 'living structures', a small group of participants is bound together by elastic bands or transparent plastic sheeting, so that each person's gestures affect the gestures of everyone else. This is an erotically charged, anti-intellectual exploration of the body, comparable to that developed by Encounter Groups.

Another trend has been called 'ritual art' and is well analysed by Jack Burnham,[67] who has argued, citing anthropological authorities, that ritual and art both seek equilibrium through 'control of analogies and oppositions'. It has long been known that dance and theatre originated in ritual and still carry with them much of the pregnancy of ritual; the practice of 'ritual art' by artists trained to make gallery exhibits merely suggests that the barriers between exhibition art and performance art are breaking down – as they have been breaking down since the days of Dadaism. Some 'ritual art' – particularly that practised in Austria by a movement called the Wiener Aktionismus – is appallingly lurid and dehumanized. In a typical performance in the late 1960s, a chicken's head was cut off and the still struggling body had its neck thrust into a woman's vagina. This kind of phenomenon appears to reflect deep disturbance in the minds of some of the generation who grew up under the Nazi regime, whereas the work of Darryl Sapien and Michael Hinton in the United States may at least approach the authentic feel of completeness that a true traditional ritual can give, persuading the spectator or participant that some satisfactory order has been imposed on the flux of experience. In Sapien and Hinton's *Untitled Ritual*, performed in 1971 at the San Francisco Art Institute, the two artists were nude, one painted orange and the other blue, and smeared with vaseline. Each was tied by a long rope to an opposite wall of the room. After some initial manoeuvres, they ended by wrestling to the limit of their strengths on a 10-foot-diameter circle of steer manure, till the colours on each became homogenized.

The artistic value of these recent examples is very variable. But what is unimpressive as an ordering of experience through art may still have sociological significance, if it is sufficiently representative. It remains to consider briefly the role of the body outside the arts, and here the sociological approach is most helpful.

John O'Neill has well described the phenomenon of 'body politics'.[68] According to O'Neill, America was taught in the 1960s by men as diverse as Norman Brown, Herbert Marcuse, Jerry Rubin, Cassius Clay, Eldridge Cleaver and Frantz Fanon to 'understand the deep political structures of sex, language and the body'. In the 1960s, demonstrations, street art, sit-ins and belly-laughs were used, literally and palpably, to *embody* arguments as a challenge to verbal mystification and lies. This kind of political dissidence carries a 'non-verbal rhetoric'. Its latest manifestation is the craze for 'streaking' (running in the nude through crowded parts of a city) that broke out in early 1974, though for centuries nakedness has been used as a token of subversion.

The control of most societies depends on the use of language for technical, manipulative and political purposes. Recruitment of the young into elite groups usually means – more than anything else – training them to develop specialized language skills. What is new in our own society is an extreme sophistication in the use of language, ranging from technical specifications of all kinds to the copy-writing of advertisements and propaganda. The sane and moderate way of resisting these forms of domination is to place a high value once more on plain face-to-face speech by individuals to each other. This may explain, perhaps, the swing away from rhetorical ability among very successful statesmen in industrialized democratic countries (though not in nations like France where literary elegance is still very widely esteemed): people of literary taste and education may deplore the verbal clumsiness of an Edward Heath or a Gerald Ford, but part of the recipe for their popular reputation for honesty seems to have been linguistic restraint.

During the political crisis of the United States that came to a head in the late 1960s, one of the claims of the dissident young was that verbal language was being used for euphemistic glossing of cruelties, for bullying and peddling and straight lying; and some of them began to despair of verbal rationality as a resource for political solutions. Of course, we may say, they were 'wrong' to do so, because language is as powerful in opposition and protest as in control and manipulation: Nixon was toppled through the efforts of journalists and lawyers, not those of the Yippies and the Weathermen. Nevertheless, that generation forces us to answer such questions as, 'Why do we always insist that protesters *give reasons* for their actions?'

In the 1972 programme at the London ICA called 'The Body as a Medium of Expression', we explored the speculation that 'repressed groups will tend to find their most effective and confident expression through the body's wider resources rather than within the enclosure of verbal language, in so far as they opt for self-assertion rather than for integrating with the norms of the majority'. The speculation was perhaps over-generalized (in the interests of provoking debate), but it seems to fit the classic case of the blacks well enough. White racial theory (succeeding to earlier doctrines that had placed the Negro lower than the White Man in the Great Chain of Being) attempted to define scientifically how the black body was set off from the white body; at the same time, in the economy many blacks were treated as tools under the slavery system. Blacks were stereotyped within the white unconscious as mindless brutes, or phallic symbols. Recently the black has asserted his body by claiming to be free from the puritanical hang-ups of white American culture; and, whatever other hang-ups he may suffer from, this is a great boost to his morale. Since the beginnings of jazz, and perhaps much earlier, young whites have sought psychological regeneration by imitating Afro-American culture and life-styles. At present the Black Power movement is entering a less romantic and more pragmatic phase in the USA, while little is left of the original idea of *négritude* in Africa. And neither in the USA nor in Africa are there any convincing signs that any viable black social alternative to Euro-American industrialization is being developed. None the less, there has been a marked strengthening in the image and self-image of blacks over the last ten years.

Paul Willis's study[69] of a motor-bike club in Birmingham, England, suggests that the working-class youths who were its members may fall into a similar pattern. These boys are regarded as barbarians by the dominant middle-class culture, while as workers they are called on to operate and service the machines and factories that help to sustain it. The codes central to the culture of the 'motor-bike boys' are concerned with clothes, speed, fighting, rock music and dancing, or (to put it more generally) with an enhanced sense of bodily attractiveness and the development of a collective mystique. Willis also argues interestingly that their taste in dance and music is intimately related to the experience of riding fast. These non-verbal modes of expression are 'protected', according to Willis, because they are ignored by the middle-class culture and are thus not vulnerable to manipulation; they can be used to express opposition to, or detachment from, middle-class culture. Equally important, the motor-bike boys described by Willis appear to have found a way of mastering the technology that they 'consume' – the motor-bike – rather than being mastered by it. We will come back to this question in the last chapter.

I shall pass by here the complex question of minorities and sub-cultures (though I have argued elsewhere[70] that such minorities as sexual deviants can and do assert themselves as sub-cultures in various ways through assertion of bodily resources which are ignored or repressed by the dominant majority). I hope to have said enough to convince the reader that the richness and diversity of the body is only now coming to be fully recognized, both in the arts and in everyday interaction between human beings. A wealth of academic research on the social aspects of the body is now generally accessible.[71] Taken all together, this amounts to a fairly substantial cultural phenomenon.

My case is that this interest in the body, while in many ways sanative, cannot be understood except as a reaction against the dominance in our culture of logic and analytical, quantitative, objective reason. (I do not mean that we are truly rational: it is a superstitious, and irrational, regard for a narrowly defined rationality which dominates us.) John Broadbent[72] has a somewhat different interpretation. He has argued that this interest in the body (an interest which he criticizes as sentimental, since it excludes the body's unattractive aspects) is due to the collapse of all coherent world-views in which people could make sense of the microcosm (man) and the macrocosm (the universe) in terms of each other – something that was possible until about the seventeenth century:

We know too much; so much that the truth has become unknowable in its quantity and complexity, and unrelatable to anything else. . . . The cosmos is expanding at the speed of light, and will collapse again. Civilization is growing exponentially, and will collapse again. The scale of quite familiar and diurnal things has suddenly enlarged – even in England, counties have supernova'd into regions; lorries and planes swell into juggernauts, jumbojets, super-tankers; and their noise drowns the church-bells which . . . used to be the loudest noise in England. Unable to register these expansions, we turn in to the one thing whose boundaries we can still define, the body.

The reader will recall Charles Harrison's remarks (see p. 106) on the American abstract expressionists.

Broadbent sees the Recoil to the Body as the result of too much undigested 'science' which we have not caught up with in quality of 'true' knowledge. I have interpreted the Recoil to the Body as primarily a reaction against technological endeavours to control the environment (and hence ultimately the universe). There is no incompatibility between the two interpretations. The growth of science and technology has given man immense hopes of imposing order on the chaos of his experience. Ironically, the result offers a model of the universe which is just as hard to believe in as any theological or occult dogma, while relating much less satisfyingly to one's actual experience of living. The Recoil to the Body has a salutary aspect which I have tried to bring out in this chapter; it can also be a pathological symptom of our perplexity, a mere refuge against what we cannot comprehend.

Where can we go to get out of the impasse? Nowhere, except by affirming man's unique opportunity and absolute responsibility to make his own future through his own product. Yet it was exactly by waxing enthusiastic about the potential of man's inventiveness and his control over the environment that our culture got into the state of confusion in which it dived 'into the body' to escape.

If it is true that a fundamental contradiction exists between the claims of technology and the claims of the body, then no way out of the impasse exists. Yet we shall see that it is something to have recognized the fundamental contradiction, to have seen it even as *the* contradiction. Only by seizing the contradiction between 'technology' and 'the body' will our culture avoid a perpetual recurrence of the Romance of Technology and the Recoil to the Body in repeated thesis and antithesis.

Chapter Four

Towards a Theory of Technology

In Chapter 5 we shall consider various ways of confronting the contradiction between the Romance of Technology and the Recoil to the Body. The present chapter is intended less to advance the argument in a linear fashion, than to reinforce it by drawing on a different corpus of material, the theory of technology. As we shall see, this field of study is fragmentary and inconclusive, but it provides useful corroborations and parallels for the propositions I have already developed.

The theoretical perspective is, after all, very important and intimately related to the practical aspects of technology. And the only way to approach the question of a general theory of technology is by a careful study and correlation of the most thoughtful texts yet contributed to this field, among which happen to be some writings by Marx and by Rousseau – though I must repeat, to avoid any misunderstandings, that the borrowing of Marxian concepts as analytical tools does not commit one to Marxist projections of the future.

In the course of the book, 'technology' and 'body' have gathered a whole complex of emotional connotations round them, since I have used each word as a shorthand term for rather complex clusters of meaning. In this chapter they should be read as neutrally and literally as possible: that is to say, 'technology' means here the sum of methods of material interchange between man and nature, and 'body' means the material human form.

The Evidence of Marx

I take Marx's writings as a starting-point not because of the authority with which they are credited by some, but because nobody has yet formulated a more adequate conceptual framework for considering what is one of the key issues of our time, perhaps *the* key issue: the social use of technology. In fact, Marx is ambiguous on some important points, and we have to ask about any interpretation of his texts not only 'Is this faithful to what Marx actually wrote?' but a separate question 'Is this theory correct?' It is essential to go back to his original writings, rather than depend on what his interpreters have written; though it can also be useful to contrast various divergent interpretations of him.

Marx applied his mind primarily, as a political economist, to the dominant technology of his society, industrial machinery. Any *general* theory of technology would have to be valid for different types of technology – such as the therapeutic technologies of surgery, medicine, drugs and so forth – which, even if we accept many criticisms of private medicine and the drug industry as well founded, have surely developed in a very different way from industrial machinery. The transport technologies, service industries and communication media have also become important in the twentieth century. We would clearly have to understand the specifics of each of these types of technology and their history before we could begin to formulate a convincing general theory of technology. The history of therapeutics simply does not seem susceptible to a Marxist analysis. According to Marxian theory, however, the dominant mode of production in a given society will determine – or strongly influence – the development of all its social institutions, including its other technologies. And certainly it is true that the administration of health services and the marketing of drugs have been strongly *affected* by the pressures and influences of managerial capitalism. It is worth going along with this approach to see where it takes us, since Marx was so clearly correct in emphasizing the all-pervading importance of capitalist manufacture and industry in the modern world. At the same time, we must bear in mind that his writings do not purport to offer a general theory of technology.

The principal text is Chapter 15 of *Capital*, 'Machinery and Modern Industry'. Marx begins this chapter with some historical distinctions, which I shall summarize here:

1 Between a tool, or instrument of handicraft, and a machine.

2 Between the co-operation of a number of machines of one kind, and a complex system of machinery.

3 Between a system where the workman has to participate with his labour in transforming the raw material, and an 'automatic' system, where the workman has only to attend the machinery.

Marx also distinguishes two main periods in the development of modern industry from handicraft:

1 *Manufacture*, the factory system, based on the division of labour which Marx analyses historically in the preceding chapter of *Capital*, Chapter 14. The period of manufacture thus defined lasts from about 1550 to the last third of the eighteenth century.

2 *Modern Industry*, associated with the construction of machines by machines, which was facilitated by the steam engine. The labourer becomes a 'mere appendage to an already existing material condition of production'.

In historical practice, machinery has (according to Marx) strengthened the capitalist's exploitation of the labourer, which had already been abetted by the growth of factories. We can pass over Marx's exposure of specific abuses by nineteenth-century industrialists, such as the employment of children in factories, and the prolongation of the working-day; the force of the main line of argument has survived all the industrial reforms enacted since he wrote. Marx's fundamental proposition is that:

Machinery is put to a wrong use, with the object of transforming the workman, from his very childhood, into a part of a detail-machine.

The 'intellectual desolation' imposed on the machine-minder must be distinguished from 'that natural ignorance which keeps the mind fallow without destroying its capacity for development'. The machine is 'dead labour' which 'pumps dry' living labour. These quotations are all from Chapter 15 of *Capital*. In Marx's early *1844 Manuscripts*, he had already described the machine as mortifying the worker's body and ruining his mind, till the worker becomes a mere fragment of his own body, a rump, an 'abstraction'.[1]

There are several points to emphasize straightaway. First, when Marx writes of *labour*, *exploitation* and so forth, he is not using abstract theoretical terms; we are constantly reminded of the sweating, suffering body of the labourer. Marx repudiated the philosophical concept of the 'disembodied mind' which has been so taken for granted in much Western thought, but which calls for historical analysis as part of an ideology associated with certain religious assumptions and certain social conditions. Marx stated his philosophical position in the *1844 Manuscripts*; and though in his later work he is more concerned with his critique of social institutions than with any philosophical study of man, there is no reason to think that he abandoned his basic view of man as an embodied consciousness:

The forming of the five senses is a labour of the entire history of the world down to the present.[2]

To say that man is a corporeal, living, real, sensuous, objective being full of natural vigour is to say that he has real, sensuous objects as the objects of his being or his life, or that he can only express his life in real, sensuous objects.[3]

Secondly, in analysing the functioning of any machine, we must think both of the mental and bodily labour that went into making it (and into making the tools or machines that were used to make it), and also of the mental and bodily labour required to operate it. Marx gives us, in Chapter 15 of *Capital*, a vivid image of the machine or capital as 'dead labour' (elsewhere 'congealed labour') that sucks living labour dry. The labourer is reduced under the capitalist system to a kind of industrial waste. The force of this analysis is not affected by modern efforts to 'humanize' the factory by means of good working conditions, short hours, well-designed equipment, 'job enrichment' and so forth. Marx's texts must be related to the tradition of nineteenth-century social criticism headed by Carlyle, Ruskin and Morris, which shows how the fact of mechanization comes to pervade *all* human experience: the human being is reduced to a repetitive, instrumental function, outside the factory as well as inside. In the last chapter, we saw how Lawrence gave the critique of mechanization a particularly powerful expression in *Women in Love*, while repudiating communist theories. If the industrial system were to be reformed, so that it consisted entirely of 'model factories', Marx's critique of mechanization would remain forceful; for mechanization spreads so far outside the factory walls as to eat into the soul of society. As Carlyle put it, 'Men are grown mechanical in head and in heart, as well as in hand.'

It is certain that Marx wished his critique of capitalist mechanization to be interpreted at a much deeper level than that of factory reform and economic justice. For instance, he writes in the *1844 Manuscripts*[4] of the alienated state of the capitalist or non-worker, who develops a 'theoretical attitude' to work through his lack of relationship to real production. This particular aspect of early Marxian theory has been imaginatively turned into art in our own day by the film director Antonioni, when, for example, the affluent and disturbed heroine of *The Red Desert* (Monica Vitti) prepares to open a shop with no stock in an empty backstreet.

Marx's critique of the malaise of capitalist society is usually called the theory of 'alienation' (it is, of course, equally applicable to state-communist societies nominally founded on Marxism-Leninism). The theory of alienation has encouraged some very imaginative multi-dimensional analyses of the relationship between psychic disturbance and social exploitation, especially in the work of Marcuse (which interestingly parallels Lawrence's fictional explorations). But it has also led to some rather arid controversy about the true interpretation of Marx (Althusser claims that bourgeois intellectuals have tried to emasculate or de-politicize Marxism by concentrating on the theory of alienation), and it is an extraordinarily difficult term to deploy precisely.[5] This debate need not affect our discussion of technology and the body.

The central ambiguity implicit in Chapter 15 of *Capital*, relates to the question of the 'neutrality of technology'. Interpreters of Marx are many and varied, and this is not the only point on which they split. At one extreme is the position of *technological determinism*, sometimes attributed to Marx on the basis of such quotations as, 'The windmill gives you society with the feudal lord: the steam-mill, society with the industrial capitalist.'[6] A number of non-Marxist theorists – Sigfried Giedion, Lynn White, Marshall McLuhan – have also adopted a determinist view. Lynn White[7] argues ingeniously that the invention of the stirrup led to the feudal system. Marshall McLuhan bases his theories of print, television and other media on the proposition that:

If a technology is introduced from within or from without a culture, and if it gives new stress or ascendancy to one or another of our senses, the ratio among all of our senses is altered.[8]

The 'technological determinist' view is that a technical invention triggers off a series of social changes (in McLuhan's analysis, via a series of psychological or psycho-physiological changes).

Technological determinism can produce seductive theories and in some specific cases they are probably right. Leaving aside the speculations of McLuhan, which are most useful on a poetic rather than a literal level, it is no doubt possible to point to several inventions which have had direct and traceable effects. The social consequences of the discovery of penicillin by Fleming in 1929, or of Abraham Darby's process developed in 1709 for smelting iron with coke, are fairly easy to analyse – within the very narrow contexts of medical and industrial history respectively. But as soon as we shift the discussion to a wider social context, the analytical equipment of technological determinism becomes inadequate. What social determinants affected the discoveries by Fleming and Darby? Why is 'simultaneous discovery' so frequent in the history of scientific innovation? Why did so many civilizations earlier than our own – Chinese, Indian, Egyptian, Greek – build elaborate automata without applying them to industry?[9] Why were so many important twentieth-century technologies – the computer, nuclear power, radar – originally developed for military applications? Why is the use of most of our sophisticated technology controlled by big institutions (one exception being the telephone, which is at least used for very wide person-to-person communication, even though the hardware and allocation of facilities are controlled by large monopolies)?

These questions can only be answered if we study technologies as social institutions. Thus a complete historical analysis of any technology must study the reciprocal action between technical and social factors – 'social' including economic, political, legal and cultural.

Some advocates of technological determinism put forward more sophisticated arguments. One of these is Jacques Ellul, whose timely and influential book *The Technological Society* argued that *technique* was the chief determinant of the whole twentieth century. By *technique* Ellul meant something very broad, perhaps what Marcuse means by *technological rationality*; and the proposition that this cult pervades modern society is now fairly widely acknowledged. Ellul is right to include, under this heading, such phenomena as modern journalism, propaganda and advertising. He does not fall into crudely determinist traps: for instance, he discusses the two time-lags that occur, first between a given invention and the development of a practical technical application for it, and secondly in the 'diffusion' of this application throughout society. Nevertheless, the model of 'invention, application, diffusion' is still too simple to deal with some of the examples I have given above. Ellul writes, for instance: 'Technique reigns alone, a blind force and more clear-sighted than the best human intelligence.' This is attributing some kind of autonomy to technological rationality, whereas technology consists of nothing but transposed human labour, mental and manual, articulated with the material world. Again, Ellul writes: 'Capitalism did not create our world; the machine did.' In fact, the forms which machinery took during the industrial revolution were adaptations to the needs of the capitalist system (large complexes favoured the interests of factory-owners). And conversely, non-industrial forms of capitalism had already developed – for instance in the organization of farm-land and farm labour – without the necessary intervention of machinery.[10]

It is in reaction against technological determinism that an opposite emphasis has arisen recently in Marxian theory. Here the technology is regarded as itself *determined* – a symptom of particular social processes – rather than determining. For instance, it has been argued that the central metaphors of cybernetics, engineering and computing – the metaphors of 'control', 'communication', 'interaction' and so forth – are products of managerial, post-Keynesian capitalism or bureaucratic socialism.[11] Marcuse writes of the computer in *Negations*:

The formal rationality of capitalism celebrates its triumph in electronic computers, which calculate everything, no matter what the purpose, and which are put to use as mighty instruments of political manipulation, reliably calculating the chances of the annihilation of the whole, with the consent of the likewise calculated and obedient population.[12]

We may expect to hear more of this line of argument over the next few years, particularly as recent neo-Marxist theory from Germany (the tradition to which Marcuse belongs) becomes better known in the Anglo-Saxon world; and it certainly carries considerable persuasion. Marcuse sums it up in the preface to *One Dimensional Man* with what deserves to be a classic statement of this case:

Technology as such cannot be isolated from the use to which it is put; the technological society is a system of domination which operates already in the concept and construction of techniques.

Advocates of this position attack the view that technology is 'neutral', i.e. that it can serve different social and political ends according to how it is used. The critique of technological rationality by Habermas, Marcuse, Robert Young and others is important, and nobody will deny that technology is socially *conditioned*; but the critique is in danger of leading to an extreme and simplistic conclusion that *all* technology is determined by relations of power and class.[13]

The view that technology is 'neutral' has a sound basis in Marx's texts, but some important discriminations need to be made. Soviet Marxists[14] since Lenin have believed that mature capitalism and socialism have the same *technical* base, and the historical decision as to how this base is used is a *political* decision. The techno-economic basis of both is seen to be mechanized industry, and a general cult of productivity and 'technological rationality'. But the objectionable features of capitalism have, in the Soviet system, been eliminated, for the simple (and very inadequate) reason that production has been nationalized.

Soviet Marxists made the mistake of taking over the whole apparatus and ideology of Western industrialism unexamined. The neo-Marxist critique of technocracy is as damning to Soviet Russia as it is to the USA. For example, it is Soviet policy to develop technologies in aerospace and in computers which are almost indistinguishable from those developed by capitalist corporations and government agencies. Yet the Concorde aeroplane and the IBM 360 data-processing system (both of which have Soviet counterparts) clearly carry a socio-political load, even if they are nominally borrowed for the cause of the people: the Concorde is – at least in one influential view – a prestige project designed for the convenience of executive fatcats, and the IBM 360 primarily (though not exclusively) a medium for institutional control. Soviet Russia has found herself in the position of imitating capitalism to a substantial degree, and official Marxist-Leninist intellectuals have ingeniously used the theory of the neutrality of technology to justify this.

Marx is at pains to distinguish possible uses of machinery from its actual use under capitalism. In *Capital* he drives home this distinction by a historical analysis of the revolts by workmen in earlier times against the introduction of machinery. He looks back to seventeenth-century revolts against the introduction of the ribbon-loom and the wind-sawmill, to an eighteenth-century revolt against wool-shearing machinery, and to the more recent phenomenon of Luddism: 'It took both time and experience before the work people learnt to distinguish between machinery and its employment by capital, and to direct their attacks, not against the material instruments of production, but against the mode in which they are used.' Elsewhere, Marx praised the political insight of the Silesian weavers in 1844 for destroying in their revolt not only factory machinery but also account books and title deeds – so that their revolt 'begins precisely where the English and French workers' revolts end'.[15]

The machine had become for the workman the 'material embodiment of capital'.

The character of independence and estrangement which the capitalist mode of production as a whole gives to the instruments of labour and to the product, as against the workman, is developed by means of machinery into a thorough antagonism. Therefore, it is with the advent of machinery, that the workman for the first time brutally revolts against the instruments of labour.

In historical practice, according to this chapter of *Capital*, machinery strengthens the capitalist exploitation of man by man, already reinforced by the growth of factories. Yet this is not a necessary consequence of machines, which could be used for different socio-political ends. Indeed, machines have a revolutionary potential since they can save man from the dehumanizing effects of specialization:

It is [machines] that sweep away the handicraftsman's work as the regulating principle of social production. Thus, on the one hand, the technical reason for the life-long annexation of the workman to a detail function is removed. On the other hand, the fetters that this same principle laid on the domination of capital, fall away.

Capitalism in the machine age acquires a new dynamic, and here how prescient Marx was!

Modern industry never looks upon and treats the existing form of a process as final. The technical basis of that industry is therefore revolutionary, while all earlier modes of production were essentially conservative. . . .[16] All fixed, fast-frozen relations, with their train of ancient and venerable prejudices and opinions, are swept away, all new formed ones become antiquated before they can ossify. All that is solid melts into the air, all that is holy is profaned, and man is at last compelled to face with sober senses his real conditions of life, and his relations with his kind.

Though Marx's texts will bear other emphases, I have no doubt that this is the kernel of his argument on technology. Technology is *in principle* neutral. As a matter of historical fact, it is far from neutral since it comes to embody socio-economic relations, relations of power. But it is historically possible and (in Marx's view) necessary for a liberating technology to supersede an oppressive technology, at the same time as socialism supersedes capitalism, to form a 'higher stage' of human development. True, the machinery we know is the 'material embodiment of capital' and embodies capitalist power relationships; but capitalist technology is volatile, unstable, and thus a possible resource for social revolution.

Of course, the elements in a capitalist technology may have to be reshuffled and subverted to supply a fit technical basis for a socialist society. The current 'alternative technology' movement is perfectly compatible with this reading of Marxism. (Marx nowhere, I think, suggests that the steam-powered industry of Victorian England must be the basis for the future communist society.) There remain enormous problems for any socialist pro- gramme of alternative technology. How much capitalist tech- nology can be taken over unexamined? What are the criteria for regarding a given technology as socially and environmentally sound?[17] Can such a programme restrict itself merely to re- shuffling elements in the existing technological apparatus – for instance, using machine-tools to make sophisticated household tools for handicrafts, or using video and cable TV for local com- munity television? Some thinkers, such as Derrida and Sohn- Rethel, argue that the specific patterns of Western civilization – slavery, property and commerce – are historically inherent in the 'concept and construction of techniques'. Is it therefore necessary to go much further and rethink the whole foundation of Western mathematics and logic?

These questions are not easily answered, but a reading of Marx gives us the best available equipment for considering them. To sum up: he makes us aware of the enormous social importance of technology without forcing us into the fallacy of technological determinism. We also learn of the socio-political load built into historical technology. We preserve the notion that technology is neutral in principle, by seizing the contradiction between its historical reactionary character and its potential revolutionary character.

By leaning on Marx we are able to demystify all the ideologies which describe technology as something outside and beyond man. As we have seen, technology is nothing but the result of man's mixing his labour with nature. Indeed – as I have suggested earlier in this book – advance in technology is simply a process of increasing the *permutability* of resources: adding to the range of things we can do in a constrained world. Marx's texts force us to adopt a *critical* approach to technology, and to science as well, an approach which treats them as social and institutional practices, stripped of the mystification which has caused them to be regarded by some as autonomous forces. As I shall argue in my final chapter, there is one technology – perhaps the only one so far in the history of man – which must correctly be regarded as a kind of autonomous force: this is the nuclear bomb. But to say this is really to say that the structures of power-politics which developed the nuclear bomb gave themselves thereby a permanent justification for their continued existence.

Nothing in Marx's teachings forbids us from vesting the most sanguine hopes in the potential of technology for helping to create a better future. Nevertheless, the dangers that technology may become a nightmare in our imperfect society are underlined by him as enormous. A wrong use of technology is one which cramps the creative development of man's embodied consciousness. Thus Marx provides us with searching insights into the nature of technology and its relations with the body, but his only prospect of escape from the contradiction between the Romance of Technology and the Recoil to the Body lies in a communist society. In such an ideal society, the Romance of Technology and the Recoil to the Body would both be totally satisfied and hence permanently superseded. Marx never ventured to explain in detail how such a society would function, and – in the light of historical experience – there is much justification for setting our sights somewhat lower.

The Evidence of Rousseau

Jean-Jacques Rousseau is still more equivocal than Marx and it is easy to read a range of different views into his work by selective emphasis. Some of his opinions are now merely of historical interest. Here too I shall make no attempt to summarize his social and political theory as a whole, but will examine his contribution to the theory of technology. Rousseau, like Marx, brings his discussion of technology back to the body. In 1753, he wrote as follows in his *Discourse on the Origin of Inequality*:

The body of savage man is the only instrument that he knows, and he employs it for several uses, of which our own are, for want of exercise, incapable; it is our industry that takes away from us the force and agility which necessity obliges him to acquire. . . . Leave civilized man time to gather all his machines around him, and there can be no doubt about his easily overcoming the savage man; but if you want to see a still more unequal combat, place them naked and disarmed face-to-face with each other, and you will soon recognize the advantage of having unceasingly all one's forces at one's disposition, of being always ready for every event, and of carrying oneself, so to speak, always complete in oneself.

In Rousseau's analysis, civilized man has literally *scattered* the faculties of his body through externalizing them in tools and machines. Civilized man is no longer a complete, self-contained, do-it-yourself kit. In fact, 'primitive' man is often crippled by disease or malnutrition, whereas the 'civilized' soldier benefits from a trained body and a scientific diet. Nor is nakedness as common as Rousseau thought among tribal societies. His hypothesis must be taken in a metaphorical way. It surely applies to the recent French and American experience of war in Indo-China, for instance; for though the Vietnamese were neither naked nor unarmed at Dien Bien Phu, they had the advantage of much greater mobility and flexibility against the French military machine. The US Army's reliance on fire-power and computer technology in Vietnam was notorious. Rousseau's idea also ties in with the experience of any businessman who travels by motor-car and elevator, leaving even the exercise of writing to a secretary, but finds that the gardener at his suburban villa, or the crew of his motor-boat, is better able to handle some physical emergency. To compensate for this atrophy of his body, the administrator will no doubt engage at weekends in some kind of bodily relaxation, like golf or shooting game-birds; but here he is studiously preserving some selected faculties of his body in good order, just as our industrial society schedules golf-courses or game-reserves as artificial pleasances dotted among the factories, offices and dormitory suburbs. Finally, Rousseau's idea also makes sense within the context of Marx's description of the worker under capitalism as a 'living appendage of the machine', pumped dry by the dead labour of capital.

As Rousseau suggests, civilized man experiences a nightmare of unarmed confrontation with the barbarian. Our recourse against this nightmare is to build up mighty defences of bombers, publicity and consumer goods (or bombers and state propaganda in the communist countries). Those politicians with the most machinery at their disposal sometimes seem in public appearances to have replaced their bodies by animated puppets – an illusion created by the use of cosmetics for television and coaching in crude techniques of persuasion by gesture and tone of voice.

The truth of Rousseau's idea is of a metaphorical rather than a factual order, having less to do with the actual conditions of 'primitive' life than with the feelings of Western man towards primitive societies. This is a complicated story, for Western primitivism was nourished not only by the discovery of strange societies which defied conventional assumptions about human nature, but also by a translation into secular terms of the theological doctrine of the Fall of Man – and no doubt as well by a guilt about the cruelties of some colonialism, something that had already been expressed grandly by Montaigne some two centuries before Rousseau.[18]

One of the themes in Rousseau's treatise on education, *Emile* (1762),[19] is man's enslavement by machinery and specialization. Here he is describing life on an imaginary island:

> What will [Emile] think when he sees that the arts only perfect themselves by subdividing, by multiplying to an infinite degree the instruments of each? He will say 'All those people are foolishly ingenious'. One would think they are afraid that their arms and legs might be of use to them, so much do they invent instruments to do without them. To exercise a single art they have enslaved themselves to a thousand others; a town is needed for each workman. As for my comrade and me, we put our genius into our dexterity; we make tools for ourselves which we can carry everywhere with us.

Rousseau foresaw the horrors of the assembly line even earlier than Blake did:

> I would not approve of those stupid professions whose workpeople, without skill and almost like automata, only exercise their hands in one and the same task. Weaving, stocking-making, stone-sawing – what is the point of using men of judgment for these jobs?

Rousseau sees a continuum between simple tools and complex machines, all of which he discusses with admirable concreteness as adjuncts to, and products of, the body. Simple objects, such as the map and the globe, he describes as 'machines'. He would like to get rid of some of the most everyday, taken-for-granted, machines, such as the watch – that favourite technology of the age he was born in. Even the bedtime candle, a 'low-level technology' if ever there was one, is unpopular with Rousseau since it atrophies the sense of touch:

> Why are we not trained like blind people to walk in the dark, to get to know bodies that we can reach, to imagine objects that surround us –

to do, in short, at night without light everything that the blind do by day without eyes? . . . We are blind for half of our lives; with the difference that truly blind people always know how to move, and we do not dare to make a step when it is pitch dark. 'We have light' someone will object. So what? Always machines? Who says that machines will always follow you around where you need? As for me, I would rather Emile had eyes at the tips of his fingers than in the candlemaker's shop.

Rousseau's words seem highly topical as I write, at a time when an energy crisis in Britain has made low-level technologies, such as bicycles and candles, desirable and temporarily scarce.

Children's bodies, says Rousseau in *Emile*, should not be too cushioned against physical rough-and-tumble; too much protection is another kind of debilitating mediation between the body and the outside world:

What is to be said about those batteries of machines that are collected around a child to arm him cap-à-pie against pain, so that when he grows big he remains at the mercy of pain without courage or experience, thinking himself dead at the first sting, and fainting when he sees the first drop of his blood?

Again, rich men think they are privileged when they pay to enjoy the products of the warmer months all the year round, but it is at the cost of numbing their bodies to the rhythm of the seasons:

To cover one's mantelpiece in January with forced vegetation, with pale odourless flowers, is less adorning the winter than it is disfiguring the spring. It is depriving oneself of the pleasure of going out to the woods to look for the first violet, spy out the first bud, and cry in a seizure of joy: 'Mortals, you are not abandoned, nature is still alive'.

Rousseau is fundamentally a moralist, if often a perverse one, and his view of the moral implications of technology is thoroughly equivocal. Jean Starobinski, one of his finest interpreters, comments as follows on Rousseau's *Discourse on the Origin of Inequality*:

The power that man acquires over the world is paid for by his loss of the direct contact that made his first happiness. All his relationships become mediated and instrumental. The tool interposes itself between man and a nature submitted to his wishes; equally, as he takes possession of his distinct identity, man sees the perfect sphere of his immediate [i.e. non-mediated] life crack; he loses the closed unity, the coherence of the primordial state which has neither inside nor outside.[20]

For Rousseau, the moral or intellectual development of man and his technical acquisitions are interdependent. He subscribed to no simple causal determinism. And it is wrong to think of him as a dreamy primitivist. Rousseau emphasized man's responsibility, so that even 'human nature' must be seen as man's work rather than as a gift of nature or God. Rousseau's notion of *perfectibilité* means that man is infinitely transformable *in principle*, a view that does not contradict his belief that in historical practice man's natural goodness has been invariably spoilt by his institutions.

Rousseau rejected all facile ideologies of progress (so popular during the age of the Enlightenment) and all wishful thinking about the future of society and technological advance; but his sober affirmation of man's responsibility for his own product, for his own future as product of his product (to shift into Marxian terms), is encouraging today when more ebullient philosophies have been succeeded by a widespread mood of stale disillusion in the great industrial countries.

In short, Rousseau's writings on technology need not be read as contradicting Marx's historical materialism. His ranking of the work of farmers, metalworkers and carpenters over that of, say, jewellers and 'finishers' is not merely an emotional outburst against luxury and the marketing of *objets d'art*. It makes a distinction between, on the one hand, *use value* and the true needs of men (in Marxian terms) and, on the other hand, *exchange value* and false needs. This view may seem perverse or outdated to many people, since our culture rates *objets d'art* so highly. Yet it would be taken totally seriously by a number of radical artists today, who believe that the cult of finely made art-objects is an indecency in a world where widespread starvation and physical misery can be seen, through the television screen, in every living-room, and would endorse William Morris's view that art must be won back to the daily labour of the people.

In sum, the 'dialectical' relationship between man's body and his instrumentation is central to Rousseau's concept of technology, as it is to Marx's. At a deep level, there is a similar ambivalence in Rousseau to that of Marx over the social consequences of man's inventiveness.

As a practical resource for periodically mending the divisions of social life, Rousseau recommends the public open-air festival. Examples which he gives in different works are the ancient Greek theatre (not the bourgeois European theatre, which he criticizes); the athletic contests and regattas of his own Geneva; and a country wine-harvest in France. [21] The great virtue of these occasions is that the spectators become actors themselves: 'Let everyone see himself and love himself in the others, so that all are better united for it.' [22] Rousseau was right that the confluence of joyous bodies, undifferentiated by task or rank, is the most convincing demonstration available to any community that it is not determined by principles of instrumentality and power. Here is the reason why in the mid-twentieth century so many artists, film directors, choreographers, men of the theatre, and anthropologists, have turned their attention to festivals. Festivals are a palpable source of real, if incomplete and temporary, restitution of wholeness for men alienated from themselves and from each other.

The Evidence of Mauss

Rousseau and Marx are two of the greatest intellectual influences on the modern world. The third thinker that we shall be interrogating in this chapter, Marcel Mauss, is not colossal in influence but is well respected in the history of sociology and anthropology. Mauss was a member of the French group associated with the journal *Année sociologique*, and is best known for his work on the anthropology of gifts and of magic. The essay of Mauss's that we are interested in here is a brief one called 'The Techniques of the Body' (1936).

This essay is of interest to sociologists because Mauss emphasizes cultural variation in bodily behaviour, asserting that such behaviour can never be 'natural' (since every action carries the imprint of learning) and that it must be studied within a context of symbolic systems.[23] Its relevance here is that it carries to a logical conclusion our procedure of looking for the roots of technology in the body.

Mauss noted that recent theory (at the time he wrote) considered 'technique' to exist only when there was an instrument. Going back to much older sources, for instance to Plato's ideas on music and dance, Mauss realized that a more penetrating analysis must begin with the techniques of the body. He defined 'technique' as a *traditional efficacious act*, adding that such acts are comparable to the magical, religious or symbolic act.

The body is the first and the most natural instrument of man. Or more exactly, without speaking of instrument, the first and the most natural technical object, and at the same time technical means, of man, is his body. . . . Before techniques with instruments, there are techniques of the body.

This is wholly consistent with Rousseau's notion of technology as man's scattered body, and with Marx's theory of labour. Mauss's analysis leads us to see technology as the sum total of physical manipulations rather than as the sum total of technical objects. How far is this true?

There are some kinds of job – notably, anything to do with chemistry – where focusing on the body's role would seem at first sight to be of limited application, since the key transformations are taking place at a molecular level. But anything *socially meaningful* that you can do with chemistry – cooking a meal for the family, treating a disease, even photocopying a sheet of paper for the boss to read – begins and ends with a human body (or bodies) as 'operator' and 'operand' respectively. The chemical transformations become what cyberneticians call a 'black box', that is to say we use them as we use a camera or motor-car, without necessarily having any idea of their internal mechanics.

Mauss's perspective on technology has been criticized in Ellul's *The Technological Society*, and the latter's objections are worth analysing. According to Ellul, what Mauss developed is a theory useful for the sociologist who deals with the primitive, but not for the sociologist of modern society:

Can it be said that the technique of elaboration of an economic plan (purely a technical operation) is the result of such movements as Mauss describes?[24] No particular motion or physical act is involved. An economic plan is purely an intellectual operation, which nevertheless is a technique.[25]

Moreover, says Ellul, most technical operations today depend not on manual movement but on the 'organization and on the arrangement of machines'. Technique, he claims, is no longer 'traditional' but autonomous and anti-traditional. Finally, techniques such as propaganda operate on a moral, psychic or spiritual level, rather than a physical level. Ellul considers that Mauss's analysis was valid in Western society till the eighteenth century, and is still valid for primitive societies, but is inapplicable to our own times.

To discuss Ellul's objection fully, we would have to get into deep water philosophically. Briefly, Ellul does not engage with the materialist conception of history which locates the chief determinant of the historical process in labour, and in man's material interchange with nature. It is within this general framework that the split between mental and bodily techniques must be considered.

Alfred Sohn-Rethel[26] has provided one of the most useful expansions of Marx's diagnosis of the split between mental and manual labour, a split which (said Marx) must disappear under communism. Science, for Sohn-Rethel, is the paradigm of mental labour divided from manual labour. Pure science, mathematics, logic, and the notion of the pure intellect must be analysed as products of this split. So must the notion of 'spiritual' values and the philosophical tradition known as Idealism. In our society, manual labour has been largely drained of its intellectual or creative ingredients, which have become the monopoly of a managerial or technocratic class. 'Control of social production cannot lie with the workers so long as such control necessitates intellectual work beyond their scope.' In a true communist revolution, such as we may be witnessing the early stages of in China, the workers must gradually re-appropriate the intellectual ingredients of labour. 'In its further stages the process entails the absorption of technology and science by the workers.' Sohn-Rethel goes on to speculate that abstract Western logic, which maintains and even celebrates the split between mental and manual labour, is correlated historically with the emergence of the institutions of commodity exchange and monetary relations in ancient Greece. His analysis of the historical situation seems to me more convincing than his optimistic projections into the future, but this is true of all academic Marxist theory.

Jacques Ellul's position is that science and technology have created a qualitatively new society beyond human control. His mistake is to treat science and technology as autonomous forces rather than as forms of social practice. Let us take the two examples – economic planning and propaganda – that he uses against Mauss to support his own argument that 'techniques' do not necessarily involve bodily movement. I think it is possible to show that they do.

Think of the economic planner sitting in Whitehall or the Kremlin. Does his work involve what Mauss calls efficacious, traditional techniques of the body? I believe so, and surely any good professional actor would agree. Traditional, certainly: there is a clear element of learnt repetitive behaviour (an anthropologist might call it ritual behaviour) in all efficacious practices, and in a large administrative office as much as anywhere. (It is true, but not relevant to my present argument, that the pace of re-training has quickened in industrial society.) Bodily, too, because our administrator is not a disembodied spirit but a human being engaged in material interchange with his environment. Typical features of his work are scanning of inputs for out-of-line conditions (there is perhaps an 'explosion' in the office every few weeks when he is especially discomposed by one of these); assertion of dominance over subordinates and of submission to superiors; public speaking (for which he has probably been trained on a special course); participation in the ritual feasts of business lunches and receptions; and lubrication of sticky situations. Formal meetings, and symbolic acts such as signing of documents or leaving the room in a huff, contain a clear element of theatre or dance ritual. A senior economic planner is paid essentially to make or recommend decisions: decision-making is a 'mental' act but it is expressed physically and certainly has physical results, even though decisions about economic planning only affect individuals at many removes and after a time-lag. 'Faceless' our economic planner may be to the general public, but the power he exerts over other people is real; and we should not forget that it is eventually a physical power exerted by his body over other people's bodies, however mediated this power may be by telephone calls, dictating machines, slide-rules and pocket adders, memoranda, statistics, reports, questionnaires, rubber stamps, paper-clips and staplers and punchers – in short the whole hierarchy of technical apparatus by which administrative power trickles down from top to bottom. Ultimately, it is as a result of this man's acts that an individual stands in a queue for the dole, or migrates to a foreign country. Vernacular expressions like 'manipulation' and 'pulling strings' and 'big noise' confirm that the most calculating acts are performed by *embodied* minds.

It is true, perhaps, that the resources of the body used by high-powered decision-makers are a restricted set: clipped speech, the clenched cigar, the occasional striking of the desk with the fifth metacarpal of one hand, the dismissive flick of the fingers. Kingsley Amis's poem *Masters* sums this up well and, incidentally, adds tellingly that power takes its toll by making its possessors forbidding to other human beings:

> Those whom heredity or guns have made
> Masters, must show it by a common speech;
> Expected words in the same tone from each
>   Will always be obeyed.
>
> Likewise with stance, with gestures, and with face;
> No more than mouth need move when words are said,
> No more than hand to strike, or point ahead;
>   Like slaves, limbs learn their place.

In triumph as in mutiny unmoved,
These make their public act their private good,
Their words in lounge or courtroom understood,
But themselves never loved. . . .

The Masters' bodies have become atrophied into stuffed shirts.

The company executive or the planner specializes in controlling the administrative hierarchy like a finely-tuned musical instrument, whereas the propagandist or commercial advertising expert (Ellul's other example) specializes in short-circuiting hierarchies. These are paid by their minister or sales director to get right through to the individual producer or consumer, sitting at home or on his way to work; to which end they have to be fluent both in perverting all the devices invented by poet and artist, and in modern consumer-oriented technologies such as TV filming and poster printing and distribution. There is nothing immaterial (as Ellul claims) about the work of the copywriter and his technical supporters, nor about the acts – of purchasing, voting, volunteering and so forth – which his 'target population' is intended eventually to commit.

So here are two different kinds of technocrat. The economic planner thinks of the individual person as a mere element in a mathematical model of the economy. The propagandist or advertising man is a kind of inverted artist. But both are ultimately using techniques to manipulate a technological apparatus whose eventual goal is to work on the bodies of others as programmable instruments.

Mauss's reduction of technology to the techniques of the body seems to me more convincing than Ellul's mystification of technology as an autonomous force. Mauss's analysis needs to be refined, however, to take account both of certain bodily techniques which have been specifically potent in the growth of industrial society, such as writing, drawing, enumeration and measurement – all associated with the historical split between mental and manual labour – and the impact of certain inventions – such as printing, photography and electricity – which have made possible a vast apparatus of machines for transmission of information. We should not be misled by the apparent complexity of industrialized society into losing sight of fundamental principles. When Ellul considers the techniques of economic planning or propaganda and concludes, 'This has nothing in common with the primitive techniques studied by Mauss', he is like a visitor to a fully automatic power-station who says, 'So much for Marx's theory that labour is all-important.' In all cases we can trace the operations of a given compound system back to the labour of individual persons – their efficacious, traditional acts, their techniques of the body.

In discussing the 'techniques' of the economic planner and the propagandist, I mentioned that each uses the bodies of others as part of his available instrumentation. This is otherwise known as exploitation or manipulation, which exists in many different forms, but always involves the treatment of other persons or their bodies as instruments. There should be no difficulty in understanding this concept, since in a sense we use a waitress as an instrument every time we ask her to get a cup of coffee. The extent to which we use other people as instruments is indeed frightening, and nothing is harder to live up to than Gabriel Marcel's teaching of a psychology 'in the second person' (*toi*).[27] Most people's consciousness most of the time is conjugated no further than introspection in the first person (*moi*) and objectifying in the third person (*lui*).

We can and do make a thorough job of using other people's bodies as instruments, and we can allow our own bodies to be pretty extensively used by other people as instruments (from their point of view). But we can only to a limited extent use our own body as an instrument, for it will always kick back against this treatment. You will notice how Mauss, in the quotation above, writes, 'The body is the first and the most natural instrument of man', but then has second thoughts about the term 'instrument' and tries to find a more satisfactory term. The body is a kind of philosophical anomaly in nature. It is both *object* – something with a given weight and texture and dimensions, a given horse-power and breaking-strain – and *subject*, for the body is (in Merleau-Ponty's words) 'my point of view on the world', 'that through which there are objects'. Or – more correctly – it is neither object nor subject.

Even the most exploited of men can say 'I am not an object' when his body rebels against being treated as an instrument by others. This is part of his inalienable ability to resist determination. Sometimes (and this pattern is probably common to all societies, though intensified by industrialization) he will spur himself on to get into a position of dominance himself, where other people become his instruments; but this is self-defeating, since he soon discovers that all his human relationships have become instrumental – friendships that last only for the duration of a particular job, a particular contract, a particular connection. If he asks a friend to a meal, the friend will wonder what his ulterior motive is. Only within the cushioned and excluding situation of marriage and the family, or a few close friendships surviving from his youth, can he manage second-person (*toi*) relationships, and not always then.

The refusal to have one's own body used as an instrument can also lead to a reluctance to use other people's bodies as instruments. Indeed, this could fairly be called a 'natural' reaction. Self-respect, in the sense of a recoil to one's own body and its desires as a refuge against the mechanization of experience, can thus stimulate an imaginative questioning of the implications of mechanization, as we saw in Chapter 3. This in turn can lead to an inert primitivism, which in our society is surely an irresponsible evasion. Which brings us back to the impasse we had already run into at the end of the last chapter.

Chapter Five

Towards a Human Technology
—and a Human City

In this final chapter, I try and embark on some resolution of the problem so far exposed. It may be asked what sort of an exercise this is. Certainly no panacea is being offered; what I am trying to do is more like the following. I hope to have been successful in persuading the reader that the Romance of Technology and the Recoil to the Body represent two necessary constituents in any truly modern consciousness, that is in any consciousness that is seriously alive to the peculiar situation of living in the late twentieth century. We have also, in the last chapter, examined social theory which confirms and enriches the earlier conclusions based largely on cultural evidence. I imagine the present reader as someone who has substantial options open to him as to how he spends his energies. He may be a student, with his future un-committed; or a professional writer or artist or teacher at a turning-point in his development; or someone more committed to a pre-determined way of life but with time and energy to spend on activities of his own choosing. I also assume that the reader is interested in the past both for its own sake and as a morality which can teach us to build the future. Also – and at this point perhaps some people will want to split off – I would argue that there are better things to do than making variations on the great work of the past (though I accept that the latter may be better than the childish pursuit of novelty). The problem is to order the past in one's mind and then break away from it. This is fundamentally the same problem whatever medium one works in – whether one is a writer, an exhibition artist, a performing artist, a co-ordinator of other people's talents, a teacher, a student or scholar or critic, or finally if one is simply a citizen whose 'medium' is a particular network of the social and economic system.

Let us look first at the case of the American poet Walt Whitman (1819–92) and see to what extent he can help us in trying to do sufficient justice to both the Romance of Technology and the Recoil to the Body – how far we can go along with him on his Open Road. I have postponed discussion of Whitman to this point because he seems to be something of an odd-man-out.[1]

No other nineteenth-century poet was so audacious as Whitman in introducing the whole landscape of industrial technology, including technical jargon, into his poetry.

> With latest connections, works, the inter-transportation of
>   the world,
> Steam-power, the great express lines, gas, petroleum,
> These triumphs of our time, the Atlantic's delicate cable,
> The Pacific railroad, the Suez canal, the Mont Cenis
>   and Gothard and Hoosac tunnels, the Brooklyn bridge,
> This earth all spann'd with iron rails, with lines of
>   steamships threading every sea,
> Our own rondure, the current globe I bring . . .
>
> (*Song of the Exposition*)

> Thee for my recitative,
> Thee in the driving storm even as now, the snow, the
>   winter-day declining,
> Thee in thy panoply, the measur'd dual throbbing and
>   thy beat convulsive,
> The black cylindric body, golden brass and silvery steel,
> Thy ponderous side-bars, parallel and connecting rods,
>   gyrating, shuttling at thy sides . . .
> Type of the modern – emblem of motion and power –
>   pulse of the continent,
> For once come serve the Muse and merge in verse, even
>   as here I see thee,
> With storm and buffeting gusts of wind and falling snow,
> By day thy warning ringing bell to sound its notes,
> By night thy silent signal lamps to swing . . .
>
> (*To a Locomotive in Winter*)

> The blast-furnace and the puddling-furnace, the loup-lump
>   at the bottom of the melt at last, the rolling-mill, the
>   stumpy bars of pig-iron, the strong, clean-shaped
>   T-rail for railroads . . .
>
> (*A Song for Occupations*)

Nor did Whitman participate in the nineteenth-century critique of industrialization. This was just as much an issue for debate in America as it was in Europe, and, as Leo Marx's *The Machine in the Garden* shows, there was scarcely a major American writer who did not deal with it somehow. Yet industrialization came later to America than to Britain, and many Americans apparently believed that the huge size of their country, as well as its 'manifest destiny', would enable them to extract all the required benefits from machinery while remaining a basically rural civilization. It was a common practice in mid-nineteenth-century America for a young man to earn a little money in a factory as a stepping-stone to settling in the countryside, rather than as the beginning of a career in industry. English capitalists resolved the same dilemma in a different way by purchasing manorial estates with industrial fortunes.

Emerson knew Carlyle and Wordsworth personally, but joined in the American enthusiasm for technology while combining it with a love of nature and contempt for cities. Later in his life he became sceptical, as did many of his distinguished contemporaries (Henry Adams warned of the danger of the whole world being blown up, as early as 1862). But Walt Whitman stood firm. One commentator, A. L. Cooke, observes:[2]

Nor did he change his attitude later in life when some of the leading writers of the day joined with the socialists in decrying a machine age. In reference to a newspaper story on Tennyson's protests against the introduction of a railroad near him in the Isle of Wight, he remarked to [H. L.] Traubel that he 'did not sympathize with such sensitiveness', that he did 'not fear the age of steam'. Then he added 'There is Ruskin: Ruskin seems to think himself constituted to protest against all modern improvements.'

In some of his poems Whitman went so far as to extol the excitements of war with archaic bloodthirstiness:

> Beat! beat! drums! – blow! bugles! blow!
> Make no parley – stop for no expostulation,
> Mind not the timid – mind not the weeper or prayer,
> Mind not the old man beseeching the young man,
> Let not the child's voice be heard, nor the mother's
> entreaties,
> Make even the trestles to shake the dead where they
> lie awaiting the hearses,
> So strong you thump O terrible drums – so loud you
> bugles blow.
>
> (*Beat! beat! drums!*)

This mood soon disappeared after his actual experience of working as a wound-dresser in a hospital during the Civil War:

Arous'd and angry, I'd thought to beat the alarum,
    and urge relentless war,
But soon my fingers fail'd me, my face droop'd and I
    resign'd myself,
To sit by the wounded and soothe them, or silently
    watch the dead . . .

                    (*The Wound-dresser*)

The unique interest of Whitman in the context of my present book
is that though no single poet of his age expressed the Romance of
Technology more abandonedly (compare his industrial Bene-
dicites to the feeble effort of Tennyson to give the International
Exhibition a write-up), no single poet carried liberation of the
body so far either. In his work, that is: for in his life he seems to
have been sexually repressed. Whitman understandably avoided
the stigma that would certainly have resulted from admission of
his homosexual leanings – to the extent of pretending to have had
several illegitimate children, of whom no trace exists.[3] Repression
and frustration in his actual human relations may have been one
of the conditions for writing poems of such *literary* uninhibitedness.
Is it uninhibitedness, such exultation in a diffused, polymorphous
sexuality? The question is one on which psychoanalysts divide.
The more normative wing insists that 'perversions' are invariably
the product of a pathological process in early psychic life, such as
a defective relationship with the mother. A more tolerant school
regards normality simply as part of the cultural code of a given
society at a given time; and on this reading Whitman's poems are
vaticinations of a less repressive sexual code:

This poem drooping shy and unseen that I always carry, and
    that all men carry,
(Know once for all, avow'd on purpose, wherever are men
    like me, are our lusty lurking masculine poems,)
Love-thoughts, love-juice, love odor, love-yielding,
    love-climbers, and the climbing sap,
Arms and hands of love, lips of love, phallic thumb of love,
    breasts of love, bellies press'd and glued together with
    love . . .
The boy's longings, the glow and pressure as he confides to
    me what he was dreaming,
The dead leaf whirling its spiral whirl and falling still and
    content to the ground,
The no-form'd stings that sights, people, objects, sting me
    with,
The hubb'd sting of myself, stinging me as much as it ever
    can any one,

The sensitive, orbic, underlapp'd brothers, that only
  privileged feelers may be intimate where they are,
The curious roamer the hand roaming all over the body,
  the bashful withdrawing of flesh where the fingers soothingly
  pause and edge themselves,
The limpid liquid within the young man,
The vex'd corrosion so pensive and so painful,
The torment, the irritable tide that will not be at rest,
The like of the same I feel, the like of the same in others,
The young man that flushes and flushes, and the young
  woman that flushes and flushes,
The young man that wakes deep at night, the hot hand
  seeking to repress what would master him,
The mystic amorous night, the strange half-welcome pangs,
  visions, sweats,
The pulse pounding through palms and trembling
  encircling fingers, the young man all color'd, red,
  ashamed, angry;
The souse upon me of my lover the sea, as I lie willing
  and naked . . .

(Spontaneous Me)

I have perceiv'd that to be with those I like is enough,
To stop in company with the rest at evening is enough,
To be surrounded by beautiful, curious, breathing,
  laughing flesh is enough,
To pass among them or touch any one, or rest my arm
  ever so lightly round his or her neck for a moment,
  what is this then?
I do not ask any more delight, I swim in it as in a
  sea . . .

(I Sing the Body Electric)

Behold, the body includes and is the meaning, the
  main concern, and includes and is the soul;
Whoever you are, how superb and how divine is
  your body, or any part of it! . . .

(Starting from Paumanok)

Without shame the man I like knows and avows the
  deliciousness of his sex,
Without shame the woman I like knows and avows hers.

(A Woman Waits for Me)

And particularly impressive is Whitman's attempt to create an
embodied and erotic relationship with the reader:

Come closer to me;
Push closer my lovers and take the best I possess,

Yield closer and closer and give me the best you
    possess . . .

            (*A Song for Occupations*, opening in
                 first edition of *Leaves of Grass*)

I do not say these things for a dollar or to fill up
    the time while I wait for a boat,
(It is you talking just as much as myself, I act as
    the tongue of you,
Tied in your mouth, in mine it begins to be
    loosen'd.) . . .

                  (*Song of Myself*)

Here the reader finds himself actually grasping the poet's
shoulders, as it were, instead of a yellowing octavo volume, and
is asked to stand off unless he accepts some rather awesome
conditions:

Whoever you are holding me now in hand,
Without one thing all will be useless,
I give you fair warning before you attempt me further,
I am not what you supposed, but far different.

Who is he that would become my follower?
Who would sign himself a candidate for my affections?

The way is suspicious, the result uncertain, perhaps
    destructive,
You would have to give up all else, I alone would
    expect to be your sole and exclusive standard,
Your novitiate would even then be long and exhausting,
The whole past theory of your life and all your
    conformity to the lives around you would have to
    be abandon'd,
Therefore release me now before troubling yourself
    any further, let go your hand from my shoulders,
Put me down and depart on your way . . .

       (*Whoever you are holding me now in hand*)

Whitman would have found blissful release as a bearded, beaded
guru in the memorable hippy summers of the 1960s:

Stranger, if you passing meet me and desire to
    speak to me, why should you not speak to me?
And why should I not speak to you?

                  (*To You*)

And indeed these lines survive as a pithy challenge to the 'lonely
crowd'.

    Whitman saw the body as making everyone the son or daughter
of God, and as ferrying the seeds of life between generations:

I say that the body of a man or woman, the main matter, is so far quite unexpressed in poems; but that the body is to be expressed, and sex is. Of bards for These States [i.e. the USA], if it come to a question, it is whether they shall be the bards of the fashionable delusion of the inherent nastiness of sex, and of the feeble and querulous modesty of deprivation. This is important in poems, because the whole of the other expressions of a nation are but flanges out of its great poems. To me, henceforth, that theory of any thing, no matter what, stagnates in its vitals, cowardly and rotten, while it cannot publicly accept, and publicly name, with specific words, the things on which all existence, all souls, all realization, all decency, all health, all that is worth being here for, all of woman and of man, all beauty, all purity, all sweetness, all friendship, all strength, all life, all immortality depend. The courageous soul, for a year or two to come, may be proved by faith in sex, and by disdaining concessions.[4]

How are we to account for what seems to be a contradiction in Whitman? We know that contradictions were nothing to him. He wrote in *Song of Myself*:

> Do I contradict myself?
> Very well then I contradict myself,
> (I am large, I contain multitudes.)

And after all, Whitman's work is full of other contradictions. He alternately embraced town and country, American nationalism and internationalism, socialism and capitalism, racialism and humanism, philosophical naturalism and philosophical idealism, love of life and hunger for death. We find that one of his best critics, D. H. Lawrence, was only able to approach Whitman's work in a self-contradictory spirit. Part of his essay on Whitman[5] contains humorous but damaging abuse:

Was he a ghost, with all his physicality? . . .
A certain ghoulish insistency. A certain horrible pottage of human parts. A certain stridency and portentousness. A luridness about his beatitudes.
DEMOCRACY! THESE STATES! EIDOLONS! LOVERS, ENDLESS LOVERS!
ONE IDENTITY!
ONE IDENTITY!
I AM HE THAT ACHES WITH AMOROUS LOVE . . .
. . . The ship of the *soul* is sunk. But the machine-manipulating body works just the same: digests, chews gum, admires Botticelli and aches with amorous love . . .
. . . Walt was really too superhuman. The danger of the superman is that he is mechanical. They talk of his 'splendid animality'. Well, he'd got it on the brain, if that's the place for animality. . . .

Lawrence attacks Whitman's proclamation that his body attracts 'all I meet or know' as if by gravity, and it may be that these words of Lawrence's lie behind Leavis's dictum, 'Discrimination is life, indiscrimination is death':

What can be more mechanical? The difference between life and matter is that life, living things, living creatures, have the instinct of turning right away from *some* matter, and of blissfully ignoring the bulk of most matter, and of turning towards only some certain bits of specially selected matter. . . .

His poems, *Democracy, En Masse, One Identity*, they are long sums in addition and multiplication, of which the answer is invariably MYSELF. . . . He was everything and everything was in him. He drove an automobile with a very fierce headlight, along the track of a fixed idea, through the darkness of this world. And he saw everything that way. Just as a motorist does in the night.

Yet at one point in the essay, Lawrence breaks into heart-felt gratitude to Whitman (not inappropriate since we may be sure that his work is in fact greatly indebted to Whitman's strengths, just as he sinks now and then into a 'mentalism' as mechanical as Whitman's ever was):

Whitman, the great poet, has meant so much to me. Whitman, the one man breaking a way ahead. Whitman, the one pioneer. And only Whitman . . .

Whitman was the first to break the mental allegiance. He was the first to smash the old moral conception that the soul of man is something 'superior' and 'above' the flesh. Even Emerson still maintained this tiresome 'superiority' of the soul. Even Melville could not get over it. Whitman was the first heroic seer to seize the soul by the scruff of her neck and plant her down among the potsherds. 'There!' he said to the soul. 'Stay there!'

Stay there. Stay in the flesh. Stay in the limbs and lips and in the belly. Stay in the breast and womb. Stay there, O Soul, where you belong.

One has to imitate Lawrence's ambivalence in summing up Whitman, though perhaps one can be a little less grudging than Lawrence (on balance) was. Whitman deserves every honour for doing as much justice as he was able to both the claims of technology and the claims of the body. His incompletenesses must surely be forgiven in return for such a generous attempt to embrace all aspects of the life of his time. We must remember that there is a basic simple-heartedness in Whitman, which is not unrelated to a strain in the white American national character that has often been observed. It is not quite the same as the 'classical moment' achieved in the eighteenth century (or exceptionally at a later date by Léger) which results from never so much as questioning the natural continuity between different modes of experience. In Whitman there is also a positive wilfulness at work, a determination to have everything both ways, to have one's cake and eat it – without sitting back to think out quietly the implications of it all. It is one thing to declaim

> Whoever degrades another degrades me,
> And whatever is done or said returns at last to me
> > *(Song of Myself)*

and another to live through the immense moral implications of such cosmic commitment. Lawrence's shrewd diagnosis, that there is a *mechanical* ruthlessness and indiscriminateness at the heart of Whitman's lusty *joie de vivre*, is surely correct.

Thus we may admire Whitman's work, but it is hard to regard him today as a mentor. By contrast, Gerard Manley Hopkins – whose letters reveal a deep fellow-feeling for Whitman – always, as a Jesuit father, kept his erotic leanings firmly under hatches:

> My heart in hiding
> Stirred for a bird, – the achieve of, the mastery
> > of the thing!
> > > *(The Windhover)*

But they come over frankly and purely in many of his poems – not transgressing any sexual taboos but eluding them through theological myth, as religious people have often been able to do. And Hopkins makes us aware, as Whitman never could, exactly what it means to have a respect for the particularity of other selves:

> To man, that needs would worship | block or barren
> > stone,
> Our law says: Love what are | love's worthiest, were
> > all known;
> World's loveliest – men's selves. Self | flashes off frame
> > and face.
> What do then? how meet beauty? | Merely meet it;
> > own,
> Home at heart, heaven's sweet gift; | then leave, let
> > that alone.
> Yea, wish that though, wish all, | God's better beauty,
> > grace.
> > > *(To what serves Mortal Beauty?)*

Hopkins seems to have had little doubt about the negative effects of industrialization:

> Generations have trod, have trod, have trod;
>   And all is seared with trade; bleared, smeared with toil;
>   And wears man's smudge and shares man's smell: the
>   soil
> Is bare now, nor can foot feel, being shod.
>
> And for all this, nature is never spent . . .
>
> *(God's Grandeur)*

Nevertheless, we must say of him, as we do of Blake or Lawrence, that he fails to do justice to a whole aspect of experience: the Romance of Technology.

Whitman certainly reaches a dimension of experience unattained by Verne or H. G. Wells or the Italian Futurists in his glorious verbal unbuttoning of the body. It is only when we go back to the texts of Marx and Rousseau that Whitman seems really incomplete: he is content to extol the body and technology alternately without thinking through the relationship between them.

The determination to have everything both ways, common to us all but perhaps indulged particularly in the United States, goes with a typically American gusto. Similar contradictions may be found in the theories of the great American architect Frank Lloyd Wright, in such statements as: 'We cannot achieve our democratic destiny by mere industrialism, however great. We are by nature gifted as a vast agronomy. In the humane proportion of those two – industrialism and agronomy – we will produce the culture that belongs to Democracy organic.'[6] This is pure Walt Whitman.

The body and technology also coexist, but in a more productive tension, in Saul Bellow's remarkable picaresque novel *The Adventures of Augie March* (1953). Bellow is an uneven writer, but at his best a major novelist – and one of great relevance to our theme, since he makes a move to *integrate* the claims of technology with those of the body.

Let us take as an example of Bellow's abilities one major character from *Augie March*: William Einhorn. The first hundred pages or so of the novel evoke vividly and tenderly a Chicago childhood just before the great Crash. The narrator, Augie, calls Einhorn 'the first superior man I knew'. Einhorn's arms and legs are crippled: he cannot even propel his wheelchair himself, and can only raise his arms to his desk by tugging at each sleeve in turn with his opposite hand. But he is an energetic and inventive businessman.

Many repeated pressures with the same effect as one strong blow, that was his method, he said, and it was his special pride that he knew how to use the means contributed by the age to connive as ably as anyone else; when in a not so advanced time he'd have been mummy-handled in a hut or somebody might have had to help him be a beggar in front of a church, the next thing to a *memento mori* or, more awful, a reminder of what difficulties there were before you could even become dead. Whereas now – well, it was probably no accident that it was the cripple Hephaestus who made ingenious machines; a normal man didn't have to hoist or jack himself over hindrances by means of cranks, chains and metal parts. Then it was in the line of human advance that Einhorn could do so much; especially since the whole race was so hepped-up about appliances, he was not a hell of a lot more dependent than others who couldn't make do without this or that commodity, engine, gizmo, sliding door, public service, and this being relieved of small toils made mind the chief center of trial.[7]

While Lawrence uses the ignoble device of making Sir Clifford Chatterley a war cripple to underline his psychological plight, Bellow makes Einhorn represent triumph over physical constraints. We are reminded that another important character in the novel has a disability: Augie's feeble-minded brother Georgie. He too triumphs over it, in his own way, when he is committed to a special institution for life.

'The spirit I found him in', Augie says of Einhorn at one point in the narrative, 'was the Chanticleer spirit, by which I refer to male piercingness, sharpness, knotted hard muscle and blood in the comb, jerky, flaunty, haughty and bright, with luxurious slither of feathers.' And here is the description of Einhorn's office at home:

He was long and well-nigh perfect of memory, a close and detailed reader of the news, and kept a file on matters of interest to him, for he was highly systematic, and one of my jobs was to keep his files in order in the long steel and wood cases he surrounded himself with, being masterful, often fussy for reasons hard to understand when I placed something before him, proposing to throw it away. The stuff had to be where he could lay his hands on it at once, his clippings and pieces of paper, in folders labeled Commerce, Invention, Major Local Transactions, Crime and Gang, Democrats, Republicans, Archaeology, Literature, League of Nations. Search me, why the League of Nations, but he lived by Baconian ideas of what makes the man this and that, and had a weakness for complete information. Everything was going to be properly done, with Einhorn, and was thoroughly organized on his desk and around it – Shakespeare, Bible, Plutarch, dictionary and thesaurus, *Commercial Law for Laymen*, real-estate and insurance guides, almanacs and directories; then typewriter in black hood, dictaphone, telephones on bracket arms and a little screwdriver to hand for touching off the part of the telephone mechanism that registered the drop of the nickel – for even at his most prosperous Einhorn was not going to pay for every call he made; the company was raking in a fortune from the coinboxes used by the other businessmen who came to the office – wire trays labeled Incoming and Outgoing, molten Aetna weights, notary's seal on a chain, staplers, flap-moistening sponges, keys to money, confidential papers, notes, condoms, personal correspondence and poems and essays. When all this was arranged and in place, all proper, he could begin to operate, back of his polished barrier approached by two office gates, where he was one of the chiefs of life, a white-faced executive, much aware of himself and even of the freakish, willful shrewdness that sometimes spoiled his dignity and proud, plaque-like good looks.[8]

Einhorn is no saint; his enemies might have called him a selfish, if soft-hearted, crook. Yet there is a nobility in his appetite for *bricolage*, his creation of a private, eccentric order out of the jungle of Chicago industrialism. In an ideal communist society everyone would be able to get the same satisfactions as Einhorn from the creative permutation of resources. Under capitalism, it is only the rich who can do this extensively. Einhorn is a real-estate broker, which makes him (in Marxist terms) an expropriator of the people. At the same time he is an independent who 'knows how to use large institutions', and indeed cheats them all. He runs a mimeographed paper called 'The Shut-In', sent to a mailing-list obtained from manufacturers of wheel-chairs, braces and appliances. He loses nearly all of his property in the Crash, and his business is scaled down to a poolroom and small agency, till he builds it up again. Other characters in *Augie March*, such as Augie's other brother Simon, dramatize the corruption of the individual under industrial capitalism. Einhorn is certainly corrupt, but at the same time he is a convincing demonstration of the overriding importance of individual determination and resourcefulness. The resourcefulness of this scheming but generous cripple recapitulates the resourcefulness which long ago made an evolutionary success out of such a physically vulnerable creature as man, amid his fiercely carnivorous competitors.

Augie March is crammed (it is rather an over-written book by most literary standards) with illustrations of the peculiar exhilaration of city life, its variety and richness – what I have called in Chapter 3 its 'combinatory opportunities', which exist in parallel with the combinatory opportunities offered by technology. At the same time all goodness and purity *are* corroded by city life. Einhorn's peculiar nobility, though real, is corroded; and Augie himself swings throughout the book between compromise and alienation.

There is one telling passage when he is taken to a brothel by Einhorn, on the night of his graduation from high school. The whore chosen for him by the madam is kind and sensitive:

Yet when the thrill went off, like lightning smashed and dispersed into the ground, I knew it was basically only a transaction. But that didn't matter so much. Nor did the bed; nor did the room; nor the thought that the woman would have been amused – with as much amusement as could make headway against other considerations – at Einhorn and me, the great sensationalist riding into the place on my back with bloodshot eyes and voracious in heart but looking perfectly calm and superior. Paying didn't matter. Nor using what other people used. That's what city life is. And so it *didn't* have the luster it should have had, and there *wasn't* any epithalamium of gentle lovers.[9]

Living in the city means accepting that everyone is used and uses others as interconnecting functions in an immense machine, wearing each other out; those who know the city accept this fundamental fact and go on to enjoy it.

Against these evocations of the appeal of technology and the city, the same novel gives us many examples of primitivist recoil to the body. Thea Fenchel, a rich sporting woman, is meant to illustrate bodily intuition. ('Thea had one superiority in her ideas. She was one of those people who are so certain of their convictions that they can fight for them in the body. If the threat to them goes against their very flesh and blood, as with people who are examined naked by the police or with martyrs, you soon know which beliefs have strength and which do not. So that you don't speak air.') There is a long – though not wholly successful – episode when she and Augie try and train an eagle to catch iguanas in Mexico. At times, Bellow appears to be suffering from a Whitmanesque romantic euphoria, but taken as a whole this novel does seem to articulate a new kind of awareness.

Augie March seems to confirm that both technological and urban glamour (cut-down and unidimensional though it often is), and the simpler but richer and more rounded mode of experience associated with the body, are essential ingredients of life. And they are compatible in principle, rarely compatible in practice. We get a glimpse of how the two may be integrated: in the person of Einhorn, who uses his resourcefulness and insatiable curiosity about life to 'repair' his physical deficiency – giving him an affinity with all of society's deviant or repressed minorities. This is why he is a character of such mythic dimensions.

In the brothel where Einhorn and Augie go, Augie carries Einhorn into a bedroom and lays him down on his back on the bed. Einhorn tells the whore: 'Just a thing or two more I have to tell you. There's my back; I have to go easy till I'm set right, miss, and take everything step by step.' I have already suggested that the technical programming of love-making, as set out in the sex manuals, must be regarded normally as symptomatic of a society obsessed with synchrony and efficiency. Saul Bellow, by the narrative device of making Einhorn a pitiable cripple, turns 'step-by-step sex' into a resource for Einhorn to triumph over his disability, just as his filing-system and his office enable him to do the same.

Bellow has perhaps never equalled in his later work the complex, spontaneous organization that distinguishes the best parts of *Augie March*. His later novels tend to elaborate on a straight contrast between the dehumanizing machinery of city life, and various possible escapes: a relatively conventional structure of feeling. For instance, *Henderson the Rain King* (1959) is a straight forward case of Recoil to the Body. It is the story of an alienated American millionaire who makes a trip to Africa, where he discovers a kind of bodily liberation. He first attempts to apply Western technology to help one tribe by building a bomb to kill a plague of frogs; the bomb goes off, but it blasts out a retaining wall from a cistern and empties a vital reservoir. He has the 'Midas touch in reverse'. Later he learns to roar and prowl like a lion with a tribal prince called Dahfu. Dahfu says: 'As man is the prince of organisms he is the master of adaptations. He is the artist of suggestions. He himself is his principal work of art, in the body, working in the flesh. . . . We have to develop an underlying similarity which lies within you by connexion with the lion.' Henderson has spent too much of his life with pigs, and must get rid of this model from his brain. Eventually Dahfu is killed fighting a lion; Henderson escapes to avoid succeeding to the Wariri throne, and brings a lion-cub back to the United States with him.

In most of Bellow's novels, there is seldom the subtlety and comprehension that we find in *Augie March*, nor the profound multi-dimensional images that occur occasionally in that novel –

for instance, in the passage where Augie describes how he occasionally went to lectures at the university in Chicago but decided that it was not for him:

I wasn't convinced about the stony solemnity, that you couldn't get into the higher branches of thought without it or had to sit down inside these old-world-imitated walls. I felt they were too idolatrous and monumental. After all, when the breeze turned south and west and blew from the stockyards with dust from the fertilizer plants through the handsome ivy some of the stages from the brute creation to the sublime mind seemed to have been bypassed, and it was too much of a detour.[10]

The university stands for the 'sublime mind' which reputedly branches like a tree from humanity's roots in the animal world. Yet it pretends to have grown organically from nature, shielding its man-made walls with a cover of leaves, isolating itself from the industrial environment which in fact pays for it and absorbs its alumni. So the speculative mind tries to isolate itself from the facts of bodily labour and technical resourcefulness, pretending that it has evolved directly from the state of nature. So too the ruling class, Ivy League America, excludes from its myth the economic production on which it depends.

We should note that Bellow does not deny or belittle the authentic 'sublime mind'. He merely warns that it does not always exist where its outward and visible signs are displayed. We all know that the world of culture, arts and the intellect can be very dirty, just as conversely the human spirit can often triumph over the most deprived and forbidding environment. Bellow speaks for a generation of intellectuals that, having considered the equivocal prospects of a communist revolution, where in theory alienation would be abolished, has opted for a less ambitious programme. (Einhorn says, when picketed by a communist organization, 'As if I don't know more about communism than they do. What do *they* know about it, those ignorant bastards?', and in a later passage in the book Augie March sees Trotsky in exile visiting a cathedral in Mexico.) The problem of revolutionizing society is shelved; for it is difficult enough to avoid being programmed by social and economic forces oneself, a mere victim of circumstance. In such a situation, the personal challenge of eluding determinism must become primary.

In the society we live in (and any other society we can honestly envisage emerging from it) the technological and economic determinants are very strong; they will reduce most people's lives most of the time to a state which inhibits full development of the human potential, that is to an 'alienated' state. Bellow is enough of a historical materialist to insist that we appreciate the force of these determinants, rather than retire to a fantasy world. He also continues to insist on the ever-present possibility of eluding them, if only temporarily and occasionally. Augie, the narrator, comes over in this novel as a romantic adolescent who lives in fantasies picked up from books, but there are some deeper implications in the personal creed that he declares:

I sat and read. I had no eye, ear, or interest for anything else – that is, for usual, second-order, oatmeal, mere-phenomenal, snarled-shoe-lace-carfare-laundry-ticket plainness, unspecified dismalness, unknown captivities; the life of despair-harness, or the life of organization-habits which is meant to supply accidents with calm abiding. Well, now, who can really expect the daily facts to go, toil or prisons to go, oatmeal and laundry tickets and all the rest, and insist that all moments be raised to the greatest importance, demand that everyone breathe the pointy, star-furnished air at its highest difficulty, abolish all brick, vaultlike rooms, all dreariness, and live like prophets or gods? Why, everybody knows this triumphant life can only be periodic. So there's a schism about it, some saying only this triumphant life is real and others that only the daily facts are. For me there was no debate, and I made speed into the former.[11]

Here the underlying image is that of the prophet on the mountain who rises above the trammels of the flesh, the gravity of the earth, communing with the heavens. This might indicate a regression to some facile doctrine of a 'spiritual realm' if it were not accompanied by such a concrete acknowledgment of the force of the 'daily facts', and of the difficulty of transcending them. The novel as a whole expresses no such clear-cut choice as Augie makes in favour of the reality of 'triumphant life', but does equal justice to both sides of this particular 'schism'. The 'daily facts' are specifically the products of urban living, in which the promise and glamour of technology and expanded options have drained away, leaving the individual in an unhappy state, so 'fucked over by the system' (as a later generation than Augie's would say) that he forgets how to find the simple satisfactions of human interaction. Since reading these lines of Augie March's several years ago, I have never been able to present my ticket in a laundry without a sinking feeling.

Attempts to elude determinism may prove to do no such thing, as Bellow suggested in his remarks on the ivy-clad Chicago University – remarks which reflect the standard Marxist critique of the detachment of 'bourgeois' culture from its economic origins. But there is some philosophical authority for suggesting that the faculty of eluding determinism is not only possible for man, but is also his specifically human characteristic. Merleau-Ponty writes in *Phenomenology of Perception*: 'All that we are, we are on the basis of a *de facto* situation which we appropriate to ourselves and which we ceaselessly transform by a sort of *escape* which is never an unconditioned freedom.' He goes on to argue that 'every cultural phenomenon has, among other meanings, an economic meaning; and on principle history never transcends economics, any more than it is reduced to economics.'[12] Again: 'Just as our whole life . . . breathes a sexual atmosphere, without its being possible to identify a single content of consciousness which is "purely sexual" or which is not sexual at all, so the economic and social drama provides each consciousness with a certain background or even a certain *imago*, which it sets about deciphering in its own way; and, in this sense, it is co-extensive with history.'[13]

If there is never complete determination, there is always some freedom; and freedom, Merleau-Ponty says, is whole and indivisible: 'as great in the worst torments as in the peace of one's home'. I have read a similar affirmation of liberty into Bellow's *The Adventures of Augie March*, at the risk of over-schematizing that somewhat rambling book. Merleau-Ponty insists, in the same chapter on liberty in *Phenomenology of Perception*, that self-pity and complaining are invariably insincere responses to any personal ordeal:

It is often a matter of surprise that the cripple or the invalid can put up with himself. The reason is that such people are not for themselves deformed or at death's door. Until the final coma, the dying man is inhabited by a consciousness, he is all that he sees, and enjoys this much of an outlet. Consciousness can never objectify itself into invalid-consciousness or cripple-consciousness, and even if the old man complains of his age or the cripple of his deformity, they can do so only by comparing themselves with others, or seeing themselves through the eyes of others, that is, by taking a statistical and objective view of themselves, so that such complaints are never absolutely genuine: when he is back in the heart of his own consciousness, each one of us feels beyond his limitations and thereupon resigns himself to them. They are the price which we automatically pay for being in the world, a formality which we take for granted. Hence we may speak disparagingly of our looks and still not want to change our face for another.[14]

These tough but inspiring words may be transposed from the level of personal crisis to the social and cultural maladies under scrutiny in this book. Many people today complain incessantly about the age they live in, with its runaway technology, the dehumanization of life, the alienation of work, the decline of culture, the loss of the 'spirit of place', and so on. But the negative characteristics of our time are the price we pay for living in it at all. In the light of Merleau-Ponty's words, even such great men as Lawrence, Yeats and F. R. Leavis seem fundamentally insincere when they rail against modern society. Railing of this kind is like speaking ill of one's own face. *Augie March*, despite its faults of structure and of characterization and its hints of Whitmanesque euphoria, is fundamentally sincere, because it is faithful to the flow of a specific, lived experience.

Let us approach from a different angle the major problem we have set ourselves in this chapter, before coming back in a moment to the evidence already gathered.

Any adequate response to the twentieth-century situation must do justice to the claims of both technology and the body. It seems that something particularly subtle and intelligent would be required to meet this criterion fully. To rely on the old protechnological or anti-technological postures is to 'follow an antique drum'. If I may borrow a notion from Mao Tse-tung's essay 'On Contradiction', the Romance of Technology and the Recoil to the Body constitute a unity of a kind: though sharply opposed to each other, *each sustains the other's existence*. But how to break out of the system? Do we require entirely new strategies, or can we revert to forms of resolution or integration that perhaps were achieved long ago, before the issue of technology and modern industry became paramount in our culture?

One of the perennial methods of art has been to take as startingpoint the human form, with all its latent power to arouse sympathy, desire and emotion, and impose a system of rules or conventions on it like a grid. Many Renaissance artists, such as Leonardo and Dürer, were preoccupied with the question of the proportions of the human form, but Western ideals of 'correct' human proportion originated in ancient Greece. It is now known from anthropological studies that ideals of perfect human beauty vary considerably from one culture to another. The tradition of the Greek nude statue owed its artistic success to its integration of two enthusiasms: an interest in geometry, and a confidence in naked physical beauty as the expression of human wholeness.

(Adrian Stokes[15] has argued that the two enthusiasms were not separate for the Greeks, since Pythagorean mathematics depended on notions of wholeness, temper, figure, form.) According to Kenneth Clark, we have only a vague notion of the exact geometric grids used by Polycleitus and other great Greek sculptors. There are, however, a few canons of which we can be certain: for instance, in a female nude the distance between the breasts was meant to be equal to the distance between the lower breast and the navel, and again to that from the navel to the division of the legs. Clark also makes an illuminating comparison between the antique male nude and the Greek temple (a flat frame supported by columns), in contrast to the Renaissance nude and the corresponding architectural system that produced the central-domed church, in which a number of axes radiate from one centre.

Within the basic conventions, there was ample scope for individual artists to find their own balance between mathematics and spontaneity. Clark speculates as follows on the reasons for the nude's enduring value:

It takes the most sensual and immediately interesting object, the human body, and puts it out of reach of time and desire; it takes the most purely rational concept of which mankind is capable, mathematical order, and makes it a delight to the senses; and it takes the vague fears of the unknown and sweetens them by showing that the gods are like men and may be worshipped for their life-giving beauty rather than their death-dealing powers.[16]

The same applies to paintings of the nude, though with the added complication that a two-dimensional rendering of the human form results in a formal interplay between the proportions of the model's body and the proportions of the flat rectangular canvas. In general the tradition of the nude seems to satisfy the criteria set out for consideration in this chapter, meeting both the demands of the body and the demands of technology: the geometric grid imposed by Polycleitus on his sculptures, or by Poussin on his paintings, is a feat of technique which manages to articulate rather than smother a spontaneous, tender delight in the body of the subject. Where the grid is too rigidly imposed, the artistic result seems frozen and mechanical. When the grid is removed (for instance, in those photographs of the nude that are not precariously imitating 'high art') the result often seems incoherent and messy; our eyes are accustomed to what Clark calls the 'harmonious simplifications of antiquity', compared to which a real naked body seems full of wrinkles and pouches.

There is a close analogy with dance and with acting. Dance training and choreography impose a similar grid on the body. When this is too rigid, the result seems frozen and mechanical (hence classical ballet has to be particularly well performed to avoid the risk of appearing ridiculous); when it is too slack, the result is a mess. Classical ballet, and to a lesser extent modern dance, start to impose a grid even before the student has been taught the basic 'positions' and steps, for only boys and girls endowed with certain proportions are accepted by the ballet schools. Martha Graham in Modern Dance, and Artaud and Grotowski in the theatre, show a full awareness of the importance of discipline and technique on the stage, and it is only occasional short-lived anarchistic movements, such as that led by the Living Theater, which disparage technique. (This no doubt explains why Grotowski, in spite of rejecting the technological gimmicks of 'rich theatre' in favour of the 'poor theatre' concentrating on the actor's body, has called his company a theatre *laboratory*, claiming that it could do for the theatre what the Niels Bohr Institute does for physics.)

We have established in the last chapter that the body is of central importance in all the arts, not merely in those art-forms that either represent the human form (painting and sculpture) or use the body as a performing medium. For instance, the relationship of the artist to his materials is itself an embodied relationship, as is the relationship of the spectator (or audience) to the work. Some animal painting and some landscape painting also owe part of their aesthetic appeal to a visual or psychological analogy with the forms of the human body (it has sometimes been humorously remarked that horse-painting is the English substitute for the nude). Any of these art-forms, when practised with technical discipline, satisfy the demands of technology *and* the body.

Literature, too, especially poetry, is a highly technical art, because of the immense complexity of language. Since the best poetry articulates subtle emotional states, states of the embodied consciousness, it may be argued that it is possible for the poet to satisfy the claims of both technology and the body in his work, simply through the imaginative exercise of poetic skill. Donald Davie[17] has drawn attention to the 'architectural' structure of the poetry of Thomas Hardy, who was trained as an architect. One of Hardy's poems is criticized by Davie for being *too* brilliantly and masterfully engineered. 'Its virtuosity is of a kind impossible before conditions of advanced technology.'

There are many ways in which the special conventions transmitted as part of the history of each art-form can be 'worked' as means of articulating and disciplining the spontaneous surge of the body's desires. My only reservation is that this has *always* been the main way in which art has been practised. It is almost a minimum prerequisite for art. Do we not need new ways of responding to the particular cultural crisis of our own time? Is it enough merely to perform variations on the art of the past, even if the techniques of some of the established arts – such as music – have grown very complicated, as if to match the complexity of industrial technology?

There is still one alternative; and it is the most potentially productive means of resolving the contradiction we have identified. This is to take as one's starting-point the actual historical 'givens' of industrial technology and urban culture, debased and narrowing as they may be in some of their aspects, and not to waste one's time railing against them. We need neither protest against them nor accept them, but examine how they actually function as changing and transformable systems. This involves a task of what may be called *deconstruction*. (The word is borrowed from the French philosopher Jacques Derrida and is more accurate than 'disassembly', for it implies an exact reversal of the order in which parts and sub-assemblies were put together.) Deconstruction seems to be exactly what was achieved, in different contexts and for different purposes, in the work of the three thinkers that we considered in the last chapter, as well as in Saul Bellow's novel.

Rousseau spent a lot of his energy, it is true, railing against technology and civilization, but he gave no encouragement to self-indulgent pessimism. Indeed, some thinkers have found it possible to read an optimistic message into Rousseau, based on the idea that man can achieve by his arts, reason and moral sense a 'second nature' in harmony with the original nature from which he sprang. The main point, which I have already stressed in the last chapter, is that Rousseau believed that man was responsible for all his products, including even what he makes of his own 'nature'. In considering how to evaluate technologies, he offered the useful hint that the most acceptable are those that satisfy man's fundamental needs most and de-nature the body least. I have given some illustrations of various ways in which he thought the worst kinds of de-naturing could happen.

Marx was the classic deconstructor; we owe to him the all-important distinction between the *historical* reactionary character of industrial technology and its *potential* revolutionary character. But what about Marcel Mauss? It was certainly an act of deconstruction to peel the 'techniques of the body' away from external instrumentation (though a comparable idea is implicit in Marx's theory of labour). Mauss was a sociologist of scientific bent, and he was more interested in observing and classifying the techniques of the body than in exploring bold hypotheses. But the mere act of looking at technology as he did subverts the idea that technology is 'out there', alien from man, determining his future.

Walt Whitman's sense of the body was all-pervading, and in his enthusiasm for technology he sometimes extolled the actual work process as well as the commodity produced – for instance, the work of butcher-boys or blacksmiths. Whitman had hardly any analytical abilities, however, and the task of deconstructing was beyond him. On the other hand, Saul Bellow is able, in *Augie March*, to articulate a telling contrast between Augie's brother Simon – who, in learning to 'make it' in industrial Chicago, grows up from a proudly idealistic child with 'English schoolboy notions of honour' into a tough, overbearing wheeler-dealer – and Einhorn, who uses technical resourcefulness (his own and that of institutions) to triumph over disability.

Deconstruction is only a means to an end: the reclaiming of technology for human use.

One way in which this might be done is through a communist revolution such as Marx proposed. Some people still believe that a non-authoritarian world communist or socialist state is a realistic political possibility worth fighting for. In this book, I have placed this solution in parentheses, for reasons already stated. Technology is the product and the responsibility of human beings, but none of us is going to succeed overnight in deconstructing the whole edifice. We know that in practice we are limited to a very great extent by past history and by the supremacy of large political and economic structures. What we have that is inalienable is the ability to *elude* determinism. This is done in an unassuming way as a part of practically everyone's daily living, but there are special opportunities which technology offers in expanding the range of possible options.

Any new technology is the aggregation of various resources that have never been combined before in just such a way. Sets of elements that are combined to form the total assembly of elements may be thought of as sub-assemblies structured principally in a hierarchy, but also interacting with each other in patterns that cut across the hierarchy. Each sub-assembly contains a number of elements which are brought into new relationships with the elements in other sub-assemblies, so that the number of relationships between elements becomes enormous. It is evidently impossible for the inventor of the new combination, or the investor in it, to predict all the repercussions of possible permutations of elements. Indeed, someone else may perceive a new set of permutations which are at first invisible to the inventor or investor (since their mental set is fixed), and actually use the technology for his own purposes undetected.

Instances of this form of transformation range from the epoch-making to the trivial. Factories were originally designed largely for the convenience and profit of capitalism, but they resulted in the growth of proletarian consciousness and the establishment of powerful trade unions. (The English laws against unionism were appropriately called the Combination Acts.) Prisons are designed to deter and to rehabilitate the offender, but also serve as 'universities of crime'. Both the factory and the prison are systems for marshalling human bodies, and it is the richness of relationships between these latter uniquely complex elements which makes such institutions so charged with opportunities for subversion or 'deconstruction'. Other technological systems are used in our time for the very unpleasant kind of subversion practised by political terrorists. The highly organized postal service is ingeniously 'worked' to post letter-bombs with minimal risk of detection. The highly organized international airline network is 'worked' for hijacking. The Munich Olympic Games in 1972 used a massive technological apparatus to publicize an international competition, providing a perfect theatre for a group of ruthless Palestinian guerrillas to publicize their case against the Israelis. These last are deplorable, cruel practices, but they demonstrate how vulnerable technological systems are to being turned inside-out by people who approach them from outside the system's own preconceptions.

Lastly, let us take a more trivial, everyday example. An office that invests in a xerox machine is expanding its horizons with a new level of technology: time is saved, meetings are better documented, customers are better served, and so on. But what of the unofficial copying that goes on? Most photocopying machines are used for copying all manner of unofficial papers, like 'round robins' from the staff to the management, or the manuscript of a romantic novel written by the junior accountant in the evenings.

Deconstruction is practised in all these cases: by the communist trade-unionist who stirs up 'trouble' in the factory, by the political terrorists, by the unofficial users of the xerox machine. Each takes a given technological set-up and adapts it. Clearly the act of deconstruction is neither good nor bad in itself: everything depends on its purpose and its context. We are here only interested in the reclaiming of technology for the body, that is for human desires and needs. This is much easier said than done, but it seems that there can be no effective reclamation without deconstruction of some kind: otherwise we are left with the euphoria of Walt Whitman and the Italian Futurists, who lacked any analytical, discriminatory bent – and could only make grand gestures in the wake of passing express trains.

We have examined the work of three theorists of technology and one novelist. Let us see if we can apply the notions of 'deconstruction' and 'reclamation' to a wider field. This involves a temporary departure from the reassuring certainties of the body, but in the confidence that its sure intuitions will bring us back safe and sound. Many people of humane education are reluctant to do this, preferring the security of the known; and their need for such security deserves respect and protection. The survival of a traditional life-class in an art-school, or of a chamber-music group in a provincial town, or of a philosopher pacing the cloister, is surely something to cherish. None the less, the major work of our time is being done by people who penetrate the keeps of technological rationality, rather than by those who stand aside in studios, salons and academies. Only people who take the trouble to understand some aspect of science or technology in detail are in a position to discover how the process of deconstruction and reclamation can be successfully achieved.

Many of the professions stand in need of deconstruction and reclamation. At one extreme, there is the exceptional case of medicine, which may seem to need conservation rather than deconstruction. Medicine at its best stands as a model of how the combinatory opportunities of technology can be used to strengthen and cure and protect the human body, without violating its special nature. Though some procedures in medicine have to treat the human body as a machine or as an object, it is generally accepted that a good physician has to achieve a sympathetic rapport with his patient, and take account of his total well-being rather than isolated symptoms. At its best, the profession has succeeded satisfactorily in accommodating the status of the patient's body, treating it as more than an object.

All this is not to idealize the medical profession, or to deny that it also has a record of mystification and exclusivism. It does stand as a strong argument against any crudely Marxist theory that all technology is the product of power relationships, and also against primitivists who inertly yearn for the past (how many of them would really like to have their blood let in a barber's shop, or be treated by a witch-doctor?). Nevertheless, the traditions of the medical profession need defending against the inroads of industrialism, which – and here the Marxist analysis is very just – threatens to turn hospitals into factories, patients into raw materials for processing, and doctors into businessmen. And even in a profession whose traditions are generally admired, there is considerable scope for providing a more imaginative service to the people at large.

At the opposite extreme are the army and its allied professions, which at first sight may seem to press as far as is conceivable the principle of reducing persons to instruments. If this were the whole truth, then any attempt to 'reclaim' military technology would be futile. Certainly the orthodox training of soldiers is to make them treat the bodies of the enemy as objects, while entering into a competitive strategic 'game' with the enemy's mind. Obviously this is psychologically harmful, and in addition we need no reminders of the more glaring horrors of war. The military machine depends for its functioning on the suspension of moral inquisitiveness and on the submission to orders; so the classic 'military mind' is loyal, efficient, incurious. The problem of when a war is a 'just war' has been much discussed. Here I will merely note that wars are often *won* by conviction rather than by military principles. If one were ever convinced of the need to participate in a 'just war' oneself – for instance, against a genocidal tyranny – it would immediately become a strategic advantage to subject accepted military theories and practices to critical deconstruction.

Between the two extremes of the life-giving technologies of medicine and the death-dealing technologies of war, lies the middle ground of modern technology, which is in continual need of deconstruction and reclamation. In many different fields, this process is being explored at present.

Many architects and town planners, for instance, are rebelling against the established doctrines of their very technocratic professions, chastened by the evidence that their apartment buildings, office blocks and windy piazzas (too costly, alas, to deconstruct physically) create in general a most inhospitable environment. Jane Jacobs's book *The Death and Life of Great American Cities* has been influential in stimulating this revolt. Jacobs stresses the importance of the street, with its diversity, intimacy and built-in security against crime (the windows from which householders are constantly watching the world go by). Lately, we have come to esteem highly such areas as Soho in London or the Latin Quarter in Paris, where these qualities still survive, as well as markets and arcades in many smaller towns. The richest space of this kind is the Walled City of Old Jerusalem, sacred to three great religions and a teeming Arab market-town too: spirit and flesh, incense and ordures, are condensed into a plenitude which seems to cluster round this palpable centre of the world. Carnivals, pageants and other urban festivities have also received attention. The outcry in Paris against the destruction of Les Halles, and later in London more successfully against the destruction of Covent Garden, were spontaneous assertions of the value of the past, the human scale and bodily certainties, against technocratic impositions. (It was surely of symbolic significance that both Les Halles and Covent Garden were anomalous survivals of country-town food markets in the metropolis, the 'bellies' of their cities, necessary reminders that fruit and vegetables do not come only from cans.) When such protests relate to the conservation of the past, they may be seen simply as manifestations of primitivism or Recoil to the Body (and how much this is needed, given the continuing dominance of the technocracy, allied to real-estate interests, in large Western cities!). It is when the town planner has to take into consideration this new climate of feeling in planning future towns from scratch, that he has to try and reconcile the claims of technology with the claims of the body. In many ways the Jane Jacobs view of the city *is* romantic and conservative. Who can doubt that the typical American pattern of prosperous urban living, with its emphasis on flexibility, mobility and high energy-consumption, has advantages which must be taken into account, as well as its much publicized disadvantages?

The town planner today will invariably be working within rigid technical, financial and political constraints, unless he is a 'utopian architect' of the Archigram school whose work seldom goes further than the drawing-board. Yet his is a necessary job with a huge impact on people's lives. Those who declare that nobody of integrity must collaborate with the technocracy are in fact opting out of the problem. The jobs within the technocracy which they leave vacant will be filled by unimaginative functionaries or worse. The challenge facing the town planner today is to *elude* the determinants that press in on him, dictating what a city should be like, and to give opportunities for its future inhabitants to elude these determinants in their own ways. The idea, entertained by some people, that the form of human settlements should in future be decided by democratic vote seems to me very dubious, though it is an understandable reaction against unquestioning trust in the 'expert'. It is a good beginning for the architect or town planner to conceive of his job rather more modestly than in the past, while respecting the extraordinary felicity of scale and proportion that some classical architecture achieves. 'How few', writes Adrian Stokes,[18] 'are the colonnades, those tunnels with pierced sides, how small the perpetuity of silent flank and orifice, how little by which to recognize our own ideal states. . . . As well as of the rational disposition a good building is the monument to physique.'

Bernard Lassus, the French artist and urbanist, has given some valuable hints about the way in which determinism can be eluded by the individual in his copious documentation of the work of the *habitants-paysagistes* (inhabitant-landscapers) – householders on the outskirts of French towns, who make their own houses and gardens into idiosyncratic works of art. Lassus argues that their work should be taken just as seriously as the work of professional artists, and criticizes the concept of 'naive' or 'primitive' art. The *habitants-paysagistes* show extraordinary visual inventiveness, often defeating the local planning regulations. One of the findings which emerges from Lassus's research is that even when the householder is reduced to a tiny miner's cottage or to an apartment in a block, he will often try to reproduce the essential characteristics of a front garden, though it may consist only of a few pot-plants or window-boxes. And this has the effect of identifying the space as a 'house', rather than a mere hut or shed. If it is true (as seems likely) that everyone in our society has an ingrained notion of what a 'house' ought to look like (as we have an ingrained idea of how a 'family' should be structured), then the containerization of the public in apartment blocks may be outraging some very deep unconscious needs. There is an analogy between the façade of a small house and a human face which comes out in children's drawings (the windows being the eyes, the front door the mouth, the roof a hat). Suburban houses, despised till a few years ago, are now respected again. Gardening is obviously a disalienating activity and a most valuable human resource, since it brings us at once into touch with the elements, the seasons, the cycles and equilibria of nature, the roughness of the soil – though it has been well pointed out, in Wilhelm Worringer's wild but inspired comparison of ancient Egypt and modern America (*Egyptian Art*, 1928), that a taste for flowers and gardens follows from a civilization's triumph over, and detachment from, the rigours displayed by nature.

The problem for the planner of future town and cities is to allow openings for this kind of creativity – on both the ambitious scale of some of the *habitants-paysagistes* and the more modest scale that is normal – while, if he can, discouraging the competitiveness and snobbery that are so widespread in many middle-class suburbs. It would be a sad town-planning policy that confined itself to determining (somehow) 'what people want' and satisfying that alone. The important thing is to leave as many openings as possible for the future whereby people can find genuine creative ways of eluding the determinants that weigh heavily on their lives. This does not mean sacrificing the whole tradition of architectural technology and planning theory; 'deconstruction' is not the same as demolition. Deconstruction in this context means being highly critical of everything that is taught, showing particular sensitivity to the political implications of established technology and established theory, then reassembling these into new combinations, and remembering finally that the planner's job is a limited one. His power to dictate people's lives is roughly comparable to the power of a set-designer to dictate the course of a theatrical production. A set-designer can wreck a play totally but he cannot make a play a success on his own. An architect or town planner should see his role as laden with the risk of making people's lives a misery; at best he can supply a setting for people to work out for themselves the situation in which they find themselves. He has no control over the text of the drama that they are to live out. While it is acceptable for a sculptor to build monuments to his ego, it is indecent for habitable buildings to be so closely identified with their architects' names that their users are reduced to jewels in some architect's crown. Human beings can and do triumph over the most disadvantaged environments, but this is cold comfort to the architect or planner who was educated to believe in a high destiny as a builder of the future. The fallacy has been the failure to take account of the fact that the monoliths of modern architecture would be lived in by bodies.

Architecture and town planning are not the only areas of modern technological practice that are currently under review. The alternative technology movement is also focusing on many other areas, such as food, energy and transport. David Dickson's book[19] on the subject draws attention to the complexity of the issues raised and to their intimate relationship with political issues. This field of enquiry is very new and the debate has hardly begun, but it is clear that what is involved is a programme of deconstruction and reclamation.

The problem is that there are multiple criteria for a 'desirable technology' and these sometimes conflict. Plastics, for instance, are light, cheap and durable, but resource-consuming and relatively difficult to manufacture. How to weigh the advantages against the drawbacks? My own prediction is that the more primitivistic wing of the alternative technology movement – preoccupied with creating small-scale communes in rural environments – will gradually give way to what Jerome Ravetz calls 'critical science', that is to say a systematic – and, if necessary, scientifically sophisticated – deconstruction of our scientific and technological 'givens', a reclamation of knowledge and techniques for essential human purposes. This movement will have a primary commitment to feeding the hungry, sustaining the poor, and preserving ecological balance; and it surely deserves every support. But what are the *values* that will underlie 'critical science'? There is a danger that the new critical approach to science and technology will remain confined within the conceptual horizons of 'technological rationality', unless we ask the question: 'For what are science and technology being reclaimed?' Are the people for whom these efforts are being made simply statistical units of economic production and consumption? Or are they bodies like ourselves? Is there such a thing as 'statistical morality'? If we are really interested in other people rather than in economic trends, surely we must approach human problems through the acceptance of the embodiment which we share with them, and not only through the medium of statistical fact-sheets.

The best-known advocate for the selective deconstruction of existing technology is Ivan Illich. Illich uses the term 'tool' to include not only, say, factories but also 'productive systems for intangible commodities such as those which produce "education", "health", "knowledge" or "decisions" '.[20] He has perceived clearly the intricacy of connections between physical technologies and social and political institutions, and the need to reclaim all of these systematically for human ends. Certainly he exaggerates irresponsibly about, for example, the shortcomings of the existing systems of education and medicine, but there are two more serious criticisms to be made.

First, Illich fails to make clear (possibly for tactical reasons) when he is offering theoretical analyses and when he is offering practical proposals. He is right to remind the inhabitants of large urban settlements and centralized states that there is no reason in principle why these should be necessarily identified with historical progress; and that we might be a lot happier if we lived in smaller communities and travelled by bicycle. But he is brave enough to present his case sometimes as if it were a practical political programme; and while his rhetoric is of great value as a stimulus to thought, it does not take sufficient account of the actual obstinate framework of the world's power structures. To begin with, we must surely admit that there is one monstrous product of technology which is virtually incontestable, the nuclear bomb. Any proposal to tinker subversively with the precarious political and military safeguards which protect us from nuclear war would be too risky to justify. Given this surely inescapable truth, social theoreticians must be careful not to make excessive claims for what their theories can do. The institutions of military technology can regrettably be neither wished away nor deconstructed; to this extent we are all saved from being blown up by hierarchic political structures, and if we are honest we will think out proposals for action within the context of the world strategic power-game. How disastrous it would be if the world's intelligentsia were suddenly to take Illich literally and retire to remote peasant communities! Again, Illich is right to argue that high speed of transportation is in principle unnecessary, and exacerbates economic inequality; but we must not forget that air travel has the beneficial effect of encouraging more and more people to conceive of the world as an economic and political ensemble. This may be more important than the drawbacks noted by Illich, for the various nations' economic and political interests are as interlocked as are their strategic interests.

Second, Illich's writing is full of quasi-mathematical terms applied to aspects of human life which cannot be quantified: terms like *limits, scales, controlled curves, parameters, optimization.* These suggest that Illich is too much a slave of technicist preconceptions. His phrase 'tools for conviviality' is an inspired coinage, but we find that he backs away from the implications of conviviality:

I have chosen 'convivial' as a technical term to designate a modern society of responsible limited tools. . . . I am aware that in English 'convivial' now seeks the company of tipsy jollyness, which is distinct from that indicated by the OED and opposite to the austere meaning of modern *'eutrapelia'* [graceful playfulness], which I intend.[21]

Illich's notion of conviviality is too anaemic. I would suggest that the term should be used with Rousseau's concept of the festival in mind, the means whereby an alienated society rediscovers its wholeness. This wider conviviality must spring from the body, which is constantly reminding us of the inappropriateness of applying technicist, quantitative criteria to human affairs except for very narrow *ad hoc* purposes. I have tried in this book to build on Illich's notion of conviviality by redefining it and opposing it to the technicist mode of ordering the world.

It is here that people who prefer a more intuitive, less systematic approach to reality – creative artists in the broadest sense of the word – have an important role. They have no special competence to judge whether the hazards of nuclear power-plants outweigh their advantages, or whether it is economically desirable to build indoor fish-farms. These are matters of social policy and there is no reason to think that the machinery developed by society for reaching appropriate decisions on such matters – setting risks and drawbacks against rewards and advantages – is seriously inadequate. 'Critical science' means simply a reorientation towards sociology and humanist common sense away from the blind trust in technical experts which has so long prevailed. It is now recognized what a heavy emotional investment nearly all experts have in their own systems of discourse. Creative artists could be invaluable in helping to prevent our culture from remaining caught in a deadlock between the Romance of Technology and the Recoil to the Body.

Among creative writers, Saul Bellow shows how this can be attempted, as I have argued in discussing *Augie March*; otherwise it is hard to think of significant figures in our literature who have done so. This may be because the debate on this subject within the literary world is still very crude. William Empson's attempts to introduce scientific metaphors into poetry in the 1930s, on the model of seventeenth-century Metaphysical poetry, are applauded as a brave effort, but do not seem to have stimulated much determination to follow the experiment further. A few literary critics, such as George Steiner, have the breadth of understanding to do justice to both aspects of the contradiction under study here. For instance, Steiner was able to write in 1962 an essay that saw the strengths in the positions of both C. P. Snow and F. R. Leavis, who in the early 1960s engaged in public debate for and against (respectively) the notion that a scientific culture existed alongside the literary culture. Nevertheless, the terms of Snow's 'two cultures' notion were painfully crude and it has not been very productive in stimulating a new generation of writers, while Leavis – though gifted with an unrivalled appreciation of literary distinction – has retreated from the realities of the present day in disgust.

In the visual arts, the situation is rather more promising. Since the Futurists in Italy, the Constructivists in Russia, the Vorticists in Britain, De Stijl in Holland, the Purists in France and the Bauhaus in Germany, artists have shown a sustained interest in fathoming the central issues of industrial society. In the 1960s, a number of people seem to have come to the conclusion (more or less independently of each other) that the best way for this to happen was for more people educated in the arts to make the effort of learning about the scientific and technological aspects of our culture. In practice, many of them have abandoned the attempt, and have returned as if rebuffed to the security of a more familiar milieu, leaving only the most persevering to carry on. Two organizations – Experiments in Art and Technology (EAT) in New York, and the Artist Placement Group in London – were both founded in the late 1960s to introduce artists into industrial contexts, but they have now for the most part handed over their work to individual initiative.

There has also been traffic the other way, a flow of scientists and engineers taking an interest in the arts and often trying to reclaim the arts for *their* ways of thinking – unaware that art has its own deceptively unobtrusive stringencies, different from those of technological rationality. Artists have themselves sometimes welcomed rather than resisted the opportunity for art to imitate a scientistic or technological model, and have submitted to the dominant ethos of technological rationality. Much art that uses mechanical or electronic techniques, or ideas borrowed from cybernetics or behavioural psychology, falls into this category. There have been some useful side-effects on the practice of art in our time. For instance, it has been valuable for artists to realize the importance of team-work, and to attach more importance to the process of investigation than to the commodity produced. But the *raison d'être* of art has often been forfeited.

The truly impressive development has been that some people trained in the arts have been bold enough to go out into the scientific and technological world, get to understand how part of it works, and try to reclaim what it may have to offer for the practice of art: that is, for the disalienating or liberating articulation of a technical medium. Unfortunately this enterprise has become confused with the enterprise of *modelling* art on science and technology, when really it is quite different (I write as one who has not always grasped this distinction clearly in the past). The test of whether the art in question is genuinely disalienating or liberating – rather than its opposite, a distortion of art which turns the human being into a programmable instrument – can only be whether it appeals to the body – not to the intellect alone – with a sense of intuitive rightness.

Very little art in this vein can be hailed as truly successful, so great are the practical, psychological and aesthetic difficulties that weigh on the artist who makes the experiments. There are some important exceptions. I have discussed elsewhere[22] the work of Tsai, Nicholas Negroponte and Edward Ihnatowicz, and will only say here that in each of these cases some sub-set of modern technology had been taken and creatively subverted. Of Tsai's vibrating rods – lit by stroboscopic lamps and responding electronically to the behaviour of spectators – it may be said they cause technology to dance. Like the bodily skill of a dancer, skill has so perfected itself here as to be unobtrusive. Negroponte and Ihnatowicz both use computer technology with wit, equivocating on the theme of man's relationship to the machine. The computer becomes in their hands a resource to be 'worked', an instrument to be 'played', rather than a forbiddingly alien technology.

Though the work of these men, and a few others like them, is the equal in merit of anything being achieved at the moment in the visual arts, the potential of their undertaking is in a way more important. This point has been grasped and acted on by Gyorgy Kepes more thoroughly than by anyone else. Kepes is a Hungarian artist who worked with Moholy-Nagy. In 1945 he started to give courses in design at the Massachusetts Institute of Technology. The 'culture-shock' that Kepes experienced at MIT is typical of what many people experience when they attempt a cross-over between the crudely called 'two cultures'. Kepes felt himself inferior to scientists like Wiener and McCulloch (this was a heroic period for MIT) but found them for the most part totally innocent or blind about art. The eventual outcome of Kepes's long association with MIT was the Center for Advanced Visual Studies, which he founded in 1967 and from whose directorship he has just retired. This offers visiting fellowships for artists to work at MIT, with a particular emphasis on collaborative projects. As an experiment in education it is even more important than as an opportunity for individual artists. The Center is a kind of benign foreign body planted at the heart of an institution that is dominated by 'technological rationality' and is constantly maintaining and increasing the technological power of the USA. MIT has a liberal tradition and a tradition of supporting high-quality art and architecture; but Kepes's Center is doing something altogether more challenging – tackling the technocracy on its own ground. It is rather like the piece of grit that gets inside the oyster, and irritates it. Inevitably, there have been frustrations as well as successes at the Center, but the pattern set by Kepes will surely be copied, with suitable variations, by other institutions. It should become normal for some of our most gifted artists – and writers too – to spend two- or three-year periods in technological institutions, and indeed in industrial companies where this can be arranged.

It will be objected that this approach is an elitist one, and that it is necessary to think in terms of popular culture rather than minority or avant-garde art. Unfortunately, the resolution of the problem we have identified in this book is one which would call for exceptional gifts. 'Deconstruction' cannot usually be done without some specialist knowledge laboriously acquired; and the willingness to learn methodically is not always found in those people who also possess imagination and bold intuition. We should recognize and encourage exceptional capacities when we find them, without being concerned about charges of 'elitism' which are often voiced by those who would reduce everyone to their own level of mediocrity.

This need not exclude an approach on a more popular front. The eluding of determinism is an inalienable human privilege and does not have to be systematic to be effective. Assembly-line workers, ticket collectors or cost accountants do not have a binary choice between either remaining passive appendages to the machinery of industry or else embracing revolution. Satisfaction is obtained in all sorts of ways, some in line with the bosses' interests, others against it (as we see in the industrial ballads of coal-miners and railwaymen, or in trade-union banners and illuminated addresses to retiring leaders, which are all important testimony on the history of industrial relations). To paraphrase Merleau-Ponty, exploitation is always present but never total.

Some groups of seemingly disadvantaged people go further than finding safety-valves from the dehumanizing pressures of industrialism. They actually seize some aspect of technology and appropriate it. This kind of reclamation is one which armchair sociologists and *littérateurs* are particularly ill-equipped to comment on, since it is usually remote from middle-class standards of verbal coherence, and indeed sometimes has the effect of challenging middle-class standards. None the less, John O'Neill[23] has convincingly described the growth of what he calls a 'gay technology' – on the model of Nietzsche's 'gay science' – among Western youth, especially in North America. This is a joyful, libidinal use of the technology of pop music, as well as of the logistics which make possible a massive outdoor gathering – or temporary city – like Woodstock. The phenomenon can be belittled on the grounds that the pop-music industry is big business; its consumers are passive victims; any genuinely subversive tendencies among the young are quickly co-opted for entertainment or otherwise defused; and finally the silent conservatism of middle America swallows up the whole movement. Yet something seems to have changed in the consciousness of the young which cannot be fully analysed or explained away.

Again, Paul Willis's study of an English motor-bike club (see p. 137) shows how the technology of the motor-bike was appropriated by its users as the focal symbol for a whole complex of aesthetic and ethical values hostile to those of the middle class. The bodily sensation of speed and vibration became central to these boys' lives; the motor-bike was appropriated as an appendage of the body so as to be no longer alien. Bike designs that enhanced the sensation of speed (with high cattlehorn handlebars) were preferred to ones that reduced wind-resistance; clothes were chosen for show and sensation rather than for functional efficiency. Crash-helmets were unpopular. Knowledge of local mythology and motor-bike lore – for instance, of the histories of fatal accidents to club members, which were very common – was esteemed more highly than was an engineering knowledge of motor-bikes.

A cold objective analysis of the motor-bike boys would probably demonstrate that these drop-outs from the economic and educational 'achievement ethic' were pathetic victims of the advertising campaigns of BSA and other motor-bike manufacturers, living out the fantasies of copywriters, and were encouraged by society to form clubs specializing in a useless and self-destructive hobby as an alternative to the crime or revolution for which they might otherwise have opted. There would be partial truth in this analysis, but let us imagine that one was to get to know a 'native informant' of the Double Zero Club well, explaining to him these analytical interpretations, while sympathetically examining his way of experiencing the world. (This exercise would reveal, incidentally, that there are ample problems of ethnographic interpretation or translation posed by the sub-cultures of our own society, without venturing into more exotic parts of the world.) Suppose that we were to suggest to him that perhaps he and his mates were being manipulated when they thought themselves most free, like the elated patrons of fruit-machines and pin-ball machines. Probably we would get him to go half-way with us, but there would come a point when he would shake his head and say, 'No, it was not like that.' And anyone who has experienced the dangerous exhilaration of taking a fast bend on a motor-bike would have to agree that this could indeed be a convincing focus for a sub-culture's collective mystique.[24]

Is this not reminiscent of the Futurists' preoccupation with speed? Undoubtedly, the motor-bike sub-culture can merge into a kind of working-class fascism; this is suggested by the fondness for fighting among the boys Willis describes. Such a view is, indeed, the conventional account given of motor-bike culture by outsiders. What is distinctive about Willis's study is that he demonstrates the boys' more attractive characteristics and the way they make the best of an unpropitious social environment. The Italian Futurists were a privileged elite; the Double Zero Club represents an assertion of self-respect and bodily pride by a section of people who, in terms of the social and economic hierarchy, have been shuffled to the bottom of the pack. Though verbally unsophisticated, their life-style is indisputably a *rational* strategy.

A correspondent in the journal where Paul Willis's study first appeared, John Gosling, took up Willis's ideas with enthusiasm, pointing out that it is the orthodox posture among intellectuals to disparage anything to do with technology (he is thinking of intellectuals with a literary or sociological education). He quotes Blake's poem *The Tyger*:

What the hammer? What the chain?
In what furnace was thy brain?
What the anvil? What dread grasp
Dare its deadily terrors clasp?

. . .

Did he who made the Lamb make thee?

– and concludes that we must learn to 'ride the tiger'. Certainly
Willis's ethnographic study is a valuable corrective against the
contempt for working-class life which many middle-class people
feel (including some of those who have 'raised' themselves by
personal achievement from the working class). Indeed, it may
suffer from the opposite fault: a romantic quest for the Noble
Savage. Few are likely to think of the Double Zero Club as an
exemplary social institution. Yet the case has been made that it
may have resolved some social pressures, eluded some social
determinants, in a manner not perceptible to the middle-class
observer, just as sometimes the youth culture may have too, with
its 'gay technology'. We should not look for new cultural resolutions only among the earnest, the 'socially responsible' or the
artistic.

In Chapter 2, I argued that the city is in a sense coextensive
with technology, and that each phenomenon is essentially an
increase in the permutability of resources. Some of the options
made available by the city, like cinemas or indoor sporting
facilities or employment bureaux, are clearly the direct products
of technology. But I touched also on the less obvious question of
the permutability of human relationships, which is itself a kind
of indirect product of urban technologies.

Opponents of city life often condemn the promiscuity and
shallowness of human relations in the city, by contrast with the
depth of mutual understanding that is held to be easier to achieve
in smaller and more stable social units. City dwellers are held to
be alienated from each other and to have relative difficulty in
developing mature friendships and sexual relationships. Neighbours, for instance, deliberately stand off from each other on
issues more intimate than the watering of each other's geraniums,
to avoid the embarrassment of emotional involvement in each
others' thumping and screaming. The observation is particularly
true of sophisticated professional people united by a 'success
ethic' which cuts them off from their families, their old friends,
and immediate local connections. As Jonathan Raban has
sharply commented,[25] it is now not uncommon for these pro-

fessional people to try and participate in the village friendliness of working-class areas of London, which they are in fact destroying by their very presence as 'colonists'.

Yet we must surely acknowledge that the continuous encounters with strangers which characterize city life have an appeal of their own, often of a nakedly sexual character. Jonathan Raban brings out something of this too in his book *Soft City*. When one returns to the city from the gentler rhythms of country life, one feels a sense of loss, but a loss which is compensated for by the stimulus of these brief random encounters. Perhaps those of us who do not indulge in 'cruising' or the frequentation of 'singles' bars should be less priggish than we are about those who do. No doubt some people who engage in this typically urban life-style carry to an extreme the very widespread fault of treating other people as tools. But others are surely admirably capable of sympathy and openness in their relationships, and delight to extend their range of human relations through the chance encounters of the city, almost as a means of asserting human freedom, or as a kind of research programme into human chemistry. We must surely admire the gift that some people have of striking up friendships or romances with strangers in trains, cafés or parks, without fear of being attacked, solicited or otherwise unpleasantly involved.

Whereas modern imaginative literature is generally weak on the subject of technology, it offers rich documentation on the subject of urban promiscuity, and here it has been followed by the narrative film. Among the stock themes of contemporary fiction and narrative cinema are: the daily lives of prostitutes; chance meetings in bars, hotels or apartment blocks; and the Dionysiac party.

As Walt Whitman contrives to have it both ways with technology, so he does with the city. In a poem called *Give me the Splendid Silent Sun*, he devotes the first twenty lines to praising the 'primal sanities' of the countryside, family life, domesticity. This the poet yearns for when he is in the city, but the city seduces him with the 'faces' which it gives him continuously:

> O I see what I sought to escape, confronting,
>   reversing my cries;
> I see my own soul trampling down what it ask'd for . . .

He continues, 'Keep your splendid, silent sun . . .', and the second half of the poem praises 'faces and streets':

give me these phantoms incessant and endless along
the trottoirs!
Give me interminable eyes! give me women! give me
comrades and lovers by the thousand . . .

There is a hint in this poem of a genuine effort by Whitman to
acknowledge an apparent contradiction between longing for
domesticity and longing for promiscuity. Certainly his appetite
for the swivelling eyeballs of strangers was stronger than his
ability to sustain long-term sexual relationships, for which he was
much too egoistic. But unlike other typical city experiences –
speed, noise, lights, merchandise – the experience that Whitman
describes is essentially innocuous, even tender, definitely 'of the
body'. We find the equivocal fascination of chance urban encounters expressed more delicately by Baudelaire in his sonnet
A une passante (1861)

La rue assourdissante autour de moi hurlait.
Longue, mince, en grand deuil, douleur majestueuse,
Une femme passa, d'une main fastueuse
Soulevant, balançant le feston et l'ourlet;

Agile et noble, avec sa jambe de statue.
Moi, je buvais, crispé comme un extravagant,
Dans son oeil, ciel livide où germe l'ouragan,
La douceur qui fascine et le plaisir qui tue.

Un éclair . . . puis la nuit! – Fugitive beauté
Dont le regard m'a fait soudainement renaître,
Ne te verrai-je plus que dans l'éternité?

Ailleurs, bien loin d'ici! Trop tard! *Jamais* peut-etre!
Car j'ignore où tu fuis, tu ne sais où je vais,
O toi que j'eusse aimée, ô toi qui le savais!

Walter Benjamin commented sensitively on this poem:[26]

The delight of the urban poet is love – not at first sight, but at last
sight. It is a farewell forever which coincides in the poem with the
moment of enchantment. . . . But the nature of the poet's emotions
has been affected as well. What makes his body contract in a tremor –
crispé comme un extravagant, Baudelaire says – is not the rapture of a
man whose every fibre is suffused with *eros*; it is, rather, like the kind
of sexual shock that can beset a lonely man. [These verses] reveal the
stigmata which life in a metropolis inflicts upon love.

There is a lot to be said against the 'stigmata' that industrialization and urban life inflict on our most intimate human relations.
Nevertheless, the specific thrill that Baudelaire describes with such
verisimilitude is worth dwelling on a moment. It is a reminder,

recurrent but never superfluous, that one is not the number on one's bus-ticket or cheque-book, but a flux of appetite and desire. Whitman, in one of his poems, conceives of these encounters as being a kind of flow of money with which the city of Manhattan repays him for making it famous in his songs:

> Not the pageants of you – not your shifting tableaus, your
> spectacles, repay me . . .
> Not those – but as I pass O Manhattan, your frequent
> and swift flash of eyes offering me love,
> Offering response to my own – these repay me,
> Lovers, continual lovers, only repay me.

> (*City of Orgies*)

Alienated, hung-up and fucked-over as the city dweller is, which of us – to be honest – would renounce the transient thrills of suddenly meeting a stranger's eyes on the bus, or engaging in an odd snatch of hurried conversation which suddenly takes on a special, enigmatic meaning? If we seize the experience in this way, it does not seem incompatible with the more solid satisfactions of marriage, the family, domesticity and nature's primal sanities. Both kinds of gratification are necessary to our human completeness.

The great merit of urban promiscuity is that it cuts across cliques and hierarchies. No one who lives in a metropolis has any excuse for taking a blinkered view of the society around him; there are constant opportunities for experiencing its diversity. In practice, social life in cities is usually timidly compartmented and structured by class or income-group. Encouragingly, the influence of the 'counter-culture' has been towards the breaking-down of these structures. The attempt to live without structures – recognizing no special bonds of marriage or family or other propinquity – invariably ends in disillusion, but can lead to the next necessary step, which is to develop new political, social and cultural structures. Thus we see alongside the 'alternative technology' movement an 'alternative cities' movement, in which people attempt to deconstruct and reclaim the structures of the city. Experiments with commune living, co-operative groups, people's control of media and institutions, are being carried on in defiance of the accepted norms of the family and economic life. The practical experiments of nineteenth-century 'utopians' such as Robert Owen and the Oneida Community (the latter attempted to sanction a form of what they called 'complex marriage' involving more than two partners) are being viewed with a new respect.

Some of the new experiments turn out disastrously. They are practised on the whole by sophisticated middle-class minorities rather than by the working class. They have to make headway against a deeply entrenched and defensive *status quo*. All this does not detract from the long-term change taking place.

I have only touched on the problems of the city in this book, not because these problems are unimportant or easily solved, but because – as I have argued in Chapter 2 – the issues of technology are more fundamental than, and in this sense 'precede', the issues of the city. Here I shall merely emphasize that, though the city consists of a mass of people thrust in one another's way by the hazard of complicated economic interdependences, rather than by individual ties of sympathy, the possibility of eluding these determinations always remains. Connections are all the time being made; and above all, the whole milieu of the city carries a kind of diffused erotic charge. The city also carries in continuous exchange myriads of cold and 'flu viruses, the commuter's scourge, a kind of venereal disease of the eyes and nose.

We may try to make these thoughts about the city a little more concrete by considering a recent application of the computer, which is as yet of only trivial importance: computer dating. With the introduction of more sophisticated software and eventually with the help of on-line terminals and picture-telephones in the home and elsewhere, computer dating will surely one day become a standard popular amenity. The computer's unique ability to sort, match and organize coded information will enable subscribers to specify their wants in great detail, and make matches of all kinds with others. We can imagine people playing games with the system. For instance, a beautiful girl who wanted to be admired for her intellect might 'lie' to the system, as might an heiress who wanted to get away from gold-diggers. Something similar already exists embryonically in the service operated by some disc jockeys: on the BBC's Radio One, David Hamilton reads out 'Romantic Messages', against a background of soupy music, from girls who wish to meet the man of their dreams. Again, the small-ad pages of underground and radical papers are used by various people who wish to match their needs with others': often, but not always, people with deviant sexual habits. This may be a valid way of escaping from a desperate personal situation.

At present, people who use computer dating or the small ads in *Time Out* or the *Village Voice* are generally regarded as pathetic 'lonelyhearts'. In fact they are resourcefully 'working' the combinatory potential offered by the city, to get out of an impasse. Employers and employees, buyers and purchasers of everything from houses to budgerigars, have long used a similar system to match specific requirements; and this is considered a thoroughly reputable practice, since it does not transgress any middle-class conventions. Many a life is being lived out in gloom and repression because of ungratified desire; there are thousands of eminently 'matchable' lives in bed-sitters. Technology could be used to relieve the multiple loneliness of urban life, just as the telephone is already used so effectively by organizations like Alcoholics Anonymous and the Samaritans. Everyone experiences this loneliness from time to time, but – by using computer dating – no one need ever languish in a hotel room, longing to shake the dust of a town from off his feet. Of course, there will be abuse of the system by confidence-men (and -women), but we will learn safeguards against them.

We have now considered a number of different ways in which technology can be deconstructed, subverted, reclaimed for the body, and determinism eluded. This can be done – is being done – by artists and intellectuals and teachers, by architects and town planners, by 'critical scientists', by social and civic reformers. I have also been at pains to show that this is not the province of highly educated and sophisticated people only. The most exploited people in society (on any objective economic reading) appear to preserve great resources for resisting alienation, and for transforming a situation of affront to one of dignity. This resourcefulness occasionally 'surfaces' in phenomena such as the youth-movement of the 1960s, whose origins must be traced to such places as Liverpool and the black ghettoes of America. Presumably, as soon as these resolutions of industrial-urban experience reach the surface and become 'legible' to the middle class – when they are quickly appropriated as a middle-class resource – they become less valuable for the repressed section of society that invented them, and are gradually replaced by new combinations of elements whose 'code' cannot be read by the middle class and is in turn dismissed as barbarism. It is therefore worth asking what kind of a service the sociologist is doing by trying to crack these codes.[27]

The strengths of working-class people, and of certain repressed groups such as the blacks, are pretty widely acknowledged, even sometimes over-romanticized. It is perhaps appropriate to have concluded my list of various possible strategies for reclaiming technology with the example of computer dating, which at present is a dubious service used only by 'lonelyhearts'. For these are among the 'rubbish people' of our society – like the old and the mad – who receive little admiration, merely pity. It may be salutary to remember that they too share the innate resourcefulness of human beings for eluding determinism. Excluded from the cosiness of domestic hearths, they may be pioneering a new liberating urban technology.

This may seem a frivolous, far-fetched or decadent suggestion, but in principle it has more cultural potential than any other application of computer technology. Certain practical applications of the computer, such as medical diagnostics or air traffic control, are obviously of unquestionable social utility, but their function is to restore normality or avoid disasters, rather than make life more joyful. Projects for using the computer to introduce a new variety into mass-produced consumer goods (such as chairs or clothes) are still in effect attempts to restore a little (but not very much) of the individuality of manual crafts, which have been sacrificed to mass production. Most other applications are designed for the convenience of large organizations. The principle of computer dating could be used as a foundation for enhancing the individual's options and freeing him or her from inhibition and circumstance. Do we not have here the seeds of the 'liberating technology' about which such commentators as Marcuse have only speculated vaguely?

We are used to being dealt out numbers and codes by institutions. There are blank spaces for these 'personal memoranda', such as one's national insurance number and blood-group, in the front page of one's diary. A totally technocratic society would allocate to every individual a unique string of digits, regularly updated (it would have to be quite long), incorporating all the information about him required by the central data bank (car registration number, credit rating, voting habits, sexual peculiarities etc.). A totally libidinal society would recognize no identifiers of any kind and speak only in verbs. With the kind of technology I am postulating – based on the currently derisory pastime called computer dating – the individual would have continuous control over any 'descriptors' applied to himself, the kind of control we have in everyday conversation, where we can say 'I'm feeling on top of the world' one moment, and 'I'm a rotten swine' five minutes later, without thereby supplying contradictory data.

New liberating technologies will be based on a double insight. The first is that enormous combinatorial potential among man and man, and between man and nature, is lying all the time untapped. The second is that whatever is good in the world issues from the desires, sympathies and common sense of the body: *le corps a ses raisons que la raison ne connaît pas*.[28]

'Man is born free, and everywhere he is in chains.' For an image to close this book I turn to Harry Houdini, the great showman and escapologist. We must get to know as much about the chains and 'mind-forged manacles' as did the people who devised and made them. Only then can we rely on the body's sinuous resourcefulness to cast them off, so that we bob up to the surface, to fight again another day.

Notes on the text

The full title of articles and books referred to by date of publication in these notes will be found in the bibliography.

CHAPTER 1

1 1944.

CHAPTER 2

1 The history of the bridge is discussed in Trachtenberg (1965).
2 'Doc' Smith (1890–1965) was a doughnut-mix specialist when he had his first science-fiction story published in 1928. There is a concordance to his works: Ellik and Evans (1966).
3 Klingender (1968) contains a chapter on the eighteenth-century notion of 'the Sublime'. See also Sussman (1968).
4 Baynes and Robinson (1970) have produced a lively study of work in both 'high' and popular art.
5 Nicolson (1968), vol. 1, p. 40.
6 Wollheim (1968), sections 23, 47, 63.
7 Act 2, scene 3.
8 Stokes (1967) p. 4. The reader who consults the text of *Reflections on the Nude* will see that Adrian Stokes is here using a distinction made by Kleinian psychoanalysts between 'part-object' and 'whole-object' relationships. A 'part-object' is an organ or function that is split off from an object's other organs and functions, on the analogy of the first object that the child perceives, his mother's breast. A 'whole-object' is the whole, separate person.

In this book I have avoided the term favoured by Stokes and Kleinian psychology, 'whole-object', and used instead another phrase borrowed from Stokes, 'whole body'. This is simply to avoid semantic confusion. For though the body of another person is, in a weak sense, always the 'object' of my perception, it is clearly not an object in the sense of 'inanimate entity'.

Stokes seems to imply in this quotation that when our feelings for other human beings are blocked, we will wrongly displace these feelings on to things – which is surely true.
9 Boas (1930), p. 21.
10 Williams (1973), p. 125.
11 Quoted Klingender (1968), Warburg (1958).
12 A short book has been de-

voted to this painting alone: Gage (1972).

13 D. and T. Clifford (1968) argue that Turner succumbed to 'competitive vulgarity'; see also Newton's review of their book (1968). For appreciations of Turner, see Stokes (1963) and Ruskin's *Modern Painters*, vol. I, parts I and II.

14 Ruskin eloquently challenged these judgments in vol. I of *Modern Painters*, arguing that on the contrary Turner was incomparable for 'truth'. 'J. M. W. Turner is the only man who has ever given a transcript of the whole system of nature' (part II, section VI, ch. III). Indeed, Ruskin's appreciation of Turner is also a meditation on the aesthetic concept of 'truth'. Ruskin defends Turner's lack of interest in the human figure on the grounds that the focus of Turner's landscapes is typically on the background and middle distance. Turner unites the foreground to the background and middle distance 'by the most precise and beautiful indication or suggestion of just so much of even the minutest forms as the eye can see when its focus is not adapted to them' (part II, section II, ch. IV.) This is true, but does not explain why 'truth' to the human form is a missing element in Turner's paintings of interiors as well. As Adrian Stokes writes, 'we cannot discover in Turner's art much affirmative relationship to the whole body, to human beings. They tend to be sticks, or fish that bob or flop or are stuffed.'

15 Handley-Read (1958).

16 p. 333.

17 For a note on Dickens, see p. 213.

18 Some interesting examples of Victorian verse glorifying railways and steam will be found in Wyndham Lewis and Lee's anthology of 'bad' verse (1935). A more serious anthology of industrial verse is Warburg (1958). A few examples exist – such as the sonnet called 'The Steam Threshing-Machine' (1868) by Tennyson's elder brother Charles Tennyson Turner – in which the 'innocent' feeling of continuity between nature and machines is maintained.

19 The English translations of Verne's titles are given here. When those vary from the original French title significantly, the French title is cited as well. The English-speaking reader is warned that many English translations of Verne are very bad.

20 Michel Serres (1974) is much more sophisticated and contains brilliant insights, but many readers will not be convinced by his interpretative method.

21 Daniel Bell's *The Coming of Post-Industrial Society* is useful on the rise of the ideology of technocracy, though the slogan which he has chosen for the book's title seems unconvincing to me.

22 Some authorities believe that this and some other posthumous novels attributed to Jules Verne were either rewritten by his son Michel, or indeed written by the latter in the first place; others that Michel Verne had merely an intellectual and political influence on his father.

207

23 Aldiss (1973) gives an account of other early science fiction, for instance Mary Shelley's *Frankenstein*. Interplanetary travel was first conceived of as long ago as the seventeenth century.

24 1973.

25 This tale is well discussed in Sussman (1968).

26 Bk II, ch. 2.

27 Bk I, ch. 16.

28 Bk I, ch. 11.

29 Otto Lilienthal, pioneer of gliding.

30 Bk II, ch. 2.

31 Chs. 23–5.

32 Such as Martin (1968) or Apollonio (1973).

33 1970.

34 Vorticism, the movement led by Percy Wyndham Lewis, was a kind of English wing of Futurism. The Vorticists' artistic practice differed in important respects from that of the Italians; for instance, they emphasized rigidity and stability, as opposed to flux and speed. But their doctrinal enthusiasm for machinery was broadly similar. For a sensitive appreciation of the unique character of Vorticism, see Richard Cork (1974). One artist of the group, Epstein, expressed a complex, ambivalent attitude to machinery, and its relationship to the body, in his haunting sculpture *The Rock Drill* (1913–14). Wyndham Lewis was a well-known writer as well as a painter. His fiction is marked both by persistent machine imagery and by an unsubtle note of dissociation of mind from flesh.

35 Lawrence (1932) to A. W. McLeod, 2 June 1914.

36 1971.

37 See especially J. J. P. Oud's essay 'Art and Machine' in Jaffé (1969).

38 1960.

39 A counter-influence was the agrarian, 'biomorphic' or 'organic' ideology of Frank Lloyd Wright, though Wright did not oppose the machine age. Wright's *The Future of Architecture* expresses his ambivalence of feeling towards machinery and the city, which I shall mention in Chapter 5.

40 See Rudofsky (1965) and Oliver (1975).

41 See Golding and Green (1970).

42 Cooper (1949), p. 20.

43 'Bulletin de l'Effort Moderne', no. 2, February 1924. Trans. Charlotte Green in Golding and Green (1970).

44 Buckminster Fuller's only really serious failure – but it is a major one – is his refusal to consider the political implications of the rise of technology and a technocratic elite. His 'environmental determinism' and lack of interest in sociological issues must also be noted as limitations in a self-styled 'comprehensivist'.

45 See Horvat-Pintarić (1970).

46 For surveys of the field see Reichardt (1968) and Burnham (1968); also my own *Science and Technology in Art Today*, which was, however, intended to serve as a critical reorientation rather than as a historical survey.

47 See Bell (1973).

48 1969.

49 Marx (1973), p. 479.

Chapter 3

1 1964.
2 *Vala*, Night the Seventh 1797.
3 Ibid.
4 Standard Edition (Hogarth Press, London) XIX, p. 26. *The Ego and the Id* was published in 1923.
5 1959, p. 309.
6 1970, ch. 3.
7 See Newton (1967–68).
8 Sartre (1960), vol. I, p. 717.
9 Horkheimer and Adorno (1972), p. 231–33.
10 Ibid., p. 233 f.
11 The term 'displacement' is Freud's; see *The Interpretation of Dreams* (1900) ch. 6. It has been adapted to contexts outside psychoanalysis, for instance by animal ethologists.
12 1973.
13 Raymond Williams (1958) has carefully analysed the development of the notion of the 'organic' in the nineteenth century, and Herbert L. Sussman (1968) provides some further examples.
14 1955.
15 1971.
16 Blake was also the heir to an old tradition of sexual radicalism associated with certain politically radical groups active in the seventeenth century. See Christopher Hill (1972).
17 1964.
18 Roszak (1972), p. 305.
19 It can, however, be persuasively argued, in favour of the orgasm, that its *ecstasis* connects us sanatively with the timeless dream of pre-human forms.
20 Roszak's earlier book (1970) includes valuable critical introductions to the work of Marcuse, Norman Brown and Paul Goodman. It will be clear to anyone who knows Roszak's books that I differ with him not only in being sceptical about mysticism but also in stressing the positive values and potential of technology.
21 These facts and quotations are taken from the Pléiade edition of Rimbaud's complete works. There is also a very readable biography of him by Enid Starkie, in English (1938).
22 Some passages from Nietzsche might have been included in this chapter, particularly *Thus Spoke Zarathustra* 1. 3 'On the Afterworldly' (where Zarathustra criticizes those who deprecate the here-and-now for the greater glory of another world) and 1. 4 'On the Despisers of the Body'. His critique of Christianity for 'throwing filth' on sexuality (*The Twilight of the Idols* x. 4) is also important. 'A dogma of the "immaculate conception"... But with that, conception is maculated' (*The Antichrist* 34). Aphorisms of Nietzsche's clearly anticipate psychoanalysis: 'The degree and kind of the sexuality of a human being reaches up into the ultimate pinnacle of his spirit' (*Beyond Good and Evil* 75). Nietzsche has an important place in both philosophical and literary history, but I have not discussed him in detail in this chapter because as a philosopher he is too inconsistent to be easily summarized, while as a writer his contribution does not add much to the other literary examples I have cited.

23 *Jerusalem*, 10.

24 *Reflections on the Revolution in France*.

25 1957.

26 For an entertaining debunking of *Women in Love* and Lawrence in general see Kate Millett (1969). Somehow it is possible to accept many of her points about Lawrence's vindictiveness towards his characters, and his male chauvinism, without accepting that she has in any way scratched the book's greatness.

27 Ch. 17.

28 1957, p. 231.

29 Ch. 3.

30 I am indebted for this quotation to Alastair Hamilton (1971). The aesthetics of fascism are also discussed by John Fraser (1974).

31 Compare this image from *Dipsychus* (1865), a poem by Arthur Hugh Clough:
The age of instinct has, it seems,
      gone by
And will not be forced back. And
      to live now
I must sluice out myself into canals,
And lose all force in ducts . . .

32 Zamyatin (1970), p. 204.

33 1974. For a sensible critique of Jaulin based on Utilitarian values, see Lucy Mair (1975).

34 1972.

35 The same view is expressed with bawdy wit in George MacBeth's poem 'The Painter's Model'.

36 Symonds (1882), ch. VI, p. 233.

37 1967.

38 Adrian Stokes has written sensitively (1932) on the convention of the *putto* as used by Donatello, which he sees as profoundly liberating.

39 This quotation, and other information on nineteenth- and early twentieth-century sculpture, are borrowed from Albert E. Elsen (1973).

40 1961.

41 1967.

42 Ruskin: '. . . For that daring frankness of the old men, which seldom missed of human grandeur, even when it failed of holy feeling, we have substituted a mean, carpeted, gauze-veiled, mincing sensuality of curls and crisping-pins . . . ' (*Modern Painters*, vol. 2, section III, ch. IV).

43 See Gowing (1966) for some contemporary accounts, and paintings of Turner on Varnishing Days. Ruskin complained bitterly that 'No *picture* of Turner's is seen in perfection a month after it is painted', since some of the colours lost lustre and some of the paint did not always remain firm. 'The fact of his using means so imperfect together with that of his utter neglect of the pictures in his own gallery, are a phenomenon in human mind which appears to me utterly inexplicable; and both are without excuse.' (*Modern Painters*, vol. 1, part II, section I, ch. VII, footnote).

44 1971.

45 Quoted O'Neill (1972), p. 160.

46 Stokes (1934*b*). The reader who is interested in this rewarding but difficult author is recommended to read two introductory essays by Wollheim (1965, 1972).

47 Harrison (January 1973), p. 14.

48 Harrison (February 1973), p. 59.

49 David Toop has collected documentation on new and rediscovered musical instruments into a small book (1974).

50 Alan Trachtenberg has well argued, in a forthcoming book on photography, that this medium is potentially an exemplar of egalitarian, non-repressive technology, since the experiences both of taking photographs and of posing for them are common in almost everyone's life.

51 It is possible that this sequence of photographs may have been 'set up' for some admonitory purpose and does not record a real execution. This would give the tableaux a rather different meaning, but none the less the black central figure, surrounded by the white controllers of the technology, must be aware of the symbolic scene he has been induced to act out.

52 Sachs (1937), p. 11.

53 Kermode (1961), p. 12.

54 Ibid., p. 13.

55 Sachs (1937), p. 26.

56 Rivière (1960), p. 93.

57 Ibid., p. 95 ff.

58 The great tradition of classical ballet should not be dismissed, and anyone who is wearied by the stridency of some Modern Dance propaganda may be refreshed by reading Adrian Stokes's *Tonight the Ballet*, which is an eloquent defence. He contrasts, for instance, the 'real hellenism' of classical ballet with the 'superficial hellenism' of Isadora Duncan, whom he condemns (in 1934!) as suitable for television rather than the theatre; and he attacks the bogusness of European 'Yoga', with its 'hasty mazy mesh of improvised gods and surges'. The positive view of classical ballet is that, like the tradition of 'life painting', it is a precious heritage to be preserved on account of its ritualism (not despite it): the very fact that the ritual is not questioned by its participants, but taken for granted, makes it invaluable. As Stokes observes (in a proposition that is not only true of dance): 'It belongs to the beneficence of all great art that the ideal world it reveals is offered to us, not as something withdrawn or sacrosanct, but as something familiar' (Stokes, 1934a, p. 67).

59 See, for instance, North (1972).

60 Shakespeare's *Venus and Adonis*, verses 229–40, is just one *locus classicus* of this association.

61 See p. 95.

62 Goodman (1968), p. 114 f.

63 The three quotations that follow are all from Artaud (1938).

64 This chapter is indebted to Temkine (1970) and Virmaux (1970).

65 One French commentator, Jean-Loup Rivière (1971), argues that Grotowski's theories still involve repression rather than liberation of the body; I can only leave the question open here.

66 Steiner (1972), p. 98.

67 1973.

68 1972.

69 1972, 1975.

70 See Benthall and Polhemus (1975).

71 See Hinde (1972) and Polhemus (1975).

72 1975.

CHAPTER 4

1 Ollman (1971) gives a stimulating commentary on this and other related texts of Marx's, though his philosophical interpretation is not accepted by all scholars.

2 Marx (1959), p. 108.

3 Ibid., p. 156.

4 Ibid., p. 83.

5 Anyone wishing to pursue this question should consult works by O'Neill, Ollman, Meszaros, Schacht and Althusser listed in the Bibliography. The most extensive study of the concept of alienation is the symposium edited by Frank Johnson (1974). Clayre (1974) criticizes the promoters of such theories as being out of touch with the real feelings of workers.

6 Marx (1900), ch. II, section 1.

7 1962.

8 McLuhan (1962), p. 24.

9 For a lively essay on the history of automata, see Metzger (1969). Stokes (1972*b*) writes of the endless 'man-made proliferation of dead material' by machines as 'very frightening', and 'were it not for kindred fears, at least a few of our machines would have been developed – a prototype of the steam engine was designed and built in classical times – much earlier'.

10 See Williams (1973).

11 S. and H. Rose (1971).

12 Marcuse (1968), p. 224 f.

13 This debate is taken up by Williams (1974) in relation to the technology of television.

14 See Marcuse (1958), ch. 6.

15 'Critical Remarks on the Article: the King of Prussia and Social Reform' (1844). See Marx (1971), p. 216.

16 The passage that follows is a footnote in *Capital* quoted from Engels and Marx's *Manifesto of the Communist Party* (1848).

17 For a consideration of these issues, largely concerned with industrial technologies, see Dickson (1974).

18 Montaigne, *Essays* III. 6.

19 *Emile* has been rightly criticized by Rousseau's commentators – most recently by Charvet (1974) – for the deplorable moral positions into which Rousseau is led in his attempt to build a coherent philosophical system.

20 See Starobinski (1974).

21 The first two examples come from Rousseau's *Lettre a M. d'Alembert sur les Spectacles*, the third from part 5, letter 7, of *La Nouvelle Héloïse*.

22 This notion of Rousseau's, and that of *amour de soi* (or 'love of the human species') as the origin of morality, are criticized by Charvet (1974) as denying the particularity of individuals, and therefore as being morally pernicious. I would argue that the embodied empathy on which Rousseau insists is a *condition* of any appreciation of particularity.

23 These ideas of Mauss's have been developed by Douglas (1970) and Polhemus (1975).

24 Ellul refers to a slightly different quotation of Mauss's. I have tried to be as fair as possible to both sides of the argument

without getting into textual niceties, and suggest that the reader should consult the original texts if he wishes to check. Mauss did not live to reply to Ellul himself.

25 Ellul (1954), ch. 1.

26 1973.

27 'Man exists only in so far as he treats himself as being for others, in relation to others' Marcel (1935), p. 151.

CHAPTER 5

1 The presence in Dickens's novels of some positive symbols of the technological future (Daniel Doyce the inventor in *Little Dorrit*, the railway in *Dombey and Son*), amid the profound and comprehensive critique of industrialism for which he is better known, suggests that Dickens is another author who sometimes eludes or transcends the contradiction I have been pointing out. F. R. Leavis rightly defends Dickens against the charge of 'Luddism', and treats him as the main historical link between Blake and Lawrence. This 'placing' helpfully illuminates the connections established by all these three great writers between economic exploitation and the thwarting or perversion of erotic desire. However, Dickens differs crucially from the other two in being quite unable to come to terms with the positive aspects of sex.

It is noteworthy that when Dickens was looking for a symbol of natural spontaneous vitality to set against Gradgrind and Bounderby in *Hard Times* (they represent, respectively, Benthamite statistical utilitarianism and the more ruthless kind of Victorian capitalism), he chose a troupe of circus performers with their horses, and explicitly stressed their bodily artistry. This novel might have provided a further example for my Chapter 3 on the Recoil to the Body. The symbolism of the circus performers comes out today rather stronger, probably, than Dickens can have consciously intended. (See the chapter on *Hard Times* in the Leavises' book on Dickens, 1970.)

2 1934.

3 See Asselineau's informative two-volume study of Whitman (1962).

4 *Leaves of Grass* (1856), p. 356.

5 See *Studies in Classic American Literature* (1924).

6 Quoted Blake (1963), ch. 14.

7 Ch. V.

8 Ibid.

9 Ch. VIII.

10 Ch. XIII.

11 Ch. X.

12 Merleau-Ponty (1962), p. 171.

13 Ibid., p. 172.

14 Ibid., p. 434.

15 1958.

16 Clark (1956), ch. 1.

17 1973.

18 1961.

19 1974.

20 Illich (1973), ch. 11.

21 Ibid., Introduction.

22 Benthall (1972) and, on Ihnatowicz's recent work, Benthall (1973).

23 1972.

24 The motor-bike is treated as

a symbol of disalienating technology in Robert M. Pirsig's interesting narrative work *Zen and the Art of Motorcycle Maintenance.* Many themes in this text will be found to illustrate or illuminate arguments I have made in my book; for instance, the contrast between the narrator, who derives much aesthetic pleasure from intricate mechanical tasks, and his friends John and Sylvia, who have a deep prejudice against technology.

25 1974.

26 'On some motifs in Baudelaire', section V. Benjamin (1968).

27 There is certainly a hope that research of this kind may eventually help to make the dominant majority less narrow-minded. For a particularly thorough analysis of a 'protected' code, see Anne Sutherland's book on the gypsies in America (1975).

28 The question of how these *raisons du corps* work is one that anthropology may one day answer. To reduce them to archaic, mechanistic behaviour-patterns surviving in civilized man is, as I have argued on p. 93, to underestimate them. More helpful is a recent suggestion by Mary Douglas (1972) that intuition or 'guts reaction', far from being irrational, corresponds to characteristics in a total system of classification. The system once 'set' allows new experience to be judged instantly and self-evidently. Such 'guts reaction', comparable to the 'split-second scanning of animal knowledge', is particularly powerful in detecting anomalies in the classification system. The kind of knowledge Douglas describes may not surface to the conscious mind, and so might properly be called 'of the body'. But far from being 'natural' (in the sense of animal, pre-social or pre-cultural) human classification systems often correspond to particular structures of *social* organization. Douglas's paradoxical implication is that the *more* our knowledge seems instinctive and 'natural', the more purely it may reflect socially-generated systems of classification.

Bibliography

ALDISS, Brian W. 1973: *Billion Year Spree: The History of Science Fiction* (London, Weidenfeld & Nicolson)

ALTHUSSER, Louis 1965: *Pour Marx* (Paris, Maspéro; English transl. *For Marx*, London, Allen Lane, 1970)

AMIS, Kingsley 1956: *A Case of Samples*, poems (London, Gollancz)

1960: *New Maps of Hell: A Survey of Science Fiction* (New York, Harcourt Brace; London,

Gollancz, 1961)

APOLLONIO, U. (ed.) 1973: Futurist Manifestos (London, Thames & Hudson)

ARTAUD, Antonin 1938: *Le Théâtre et son Double* (Paris, Gallimard)

ASSELINEAU, Roger 1962: *The Evolution of Walt Whitman* (Cambridge, Mass., Belknap Press, Harvard)

BANHAM, Reyner 1960: *Theory and Design in the First Machine Age* (London, Architectural Press)

BARTHES, R. 1971: *Sade, Fourier, Loyola* (Paris, Seuil)

BATESON, Gregory and Margaret 1942: *Balinese Character: a photographic analysis* (New York, New York Academy of Science; reissued 1962)

BAYNES, Ken and ROBINSON, Alan 1970: *Work*, Art and Society series (London, Lund Humphries)

BEATTIE, Alan 1972: 'Is Modern Dance a Liberation of the Body? Transformations of the Body Image in the Twentieth Century Arts' (Lecture to London ICA, 7 September 1972, unpublished)

BELL, Daniel 1973: *The Coming of Post-Industrial Society* (New York, Basic; London, Heinemann)

BENJAMIN, Walter (d. 1940) 1968: *Illuminations* (selections in transl., ed. H. Arendt; New York, Harcourt Brace; London, Jonathan Cape)

BENTHALL, Jonathan 1972: *Science and Technology in Art Today* (London, Thames & Hudson; New York, Praeger)

1973: 'Computer arts at Edinburgh', *Studio International*, October 1973

1975: *The Body as a Medium of Expression* (ed., with T. Polhemus; London, Allen Lane; New York, Dutton)

BERGER, John et al. 1972: *Ways of Seeing* (London, Penguin Books and BBC)

BINER, Pierre 1968: *Le Living Theatre* (Paris, La Cité)

BLAKE, Peter 1963: *Frank Lloyd Wright: Architecture and Space* (Harmondsworth, Pelican)

BOAS, George 1930: *A Critical Analysis of the Philosophy of Emile Meyerson* (Baltimore, Johns Hopkins; Oxford University Press)

BROADBENT, John B. 1964: *Poetic Love* (London, Chatto & Windus)

1975: 'The Image of God, or Two Yards of Skin' in *The Body as a Medium of Expression* (ed. J. Benthall and T. Polhemus, q.v.)

BROWN, Norman 1959: *Life Against Death, the Psychoanalytical Meaning of History* (London, Routledge and Kegan Paul)

BURNHAM, Jack 1968: *Beyond Modern Sculpture* (New York, George Braziller; London, Allen Lane)

1971: *The Structure of Art* (New York, George Braziller)

1973: 'A Search for Meaning in Post-Historical Terms', *Arts Magazine*, March 1973

CARLYLE, Thomas 1829: 'Signs of the Times', *Edinburgh Review* no. 98, reprinted in Collected Essays

CHARVET, John 1974: *The Social Problem in the Philosophy of*

Rousseau (London, Cambridge University Press)

CHESNEAUX, Jean 1972: *The Political and Social Ideas of Jules Verne* (London, Thames & Hudson, a transl. of *Une lecture politique de Jules Verne*, Maspéro, Paris)

CLARK, Kenneth 1956: *The Nude* (London, John Murray)

CLAYRE, Alasdair 1974: *Work and Play* (London, Weidenfeld and Nicolson)

CLIFFORD, D. and T. 1968: *John Crome* (London, Faber and Faber)

COOKE, A. L. 1934: 'Whitman's Background in the Industrial Movements of his Time', in *University of Texas Studies in English*, XIV, July 1934

COOPER, Douglas 1949: *Fernand Léger et le nouvel espace* (London, Lund Humphries)

CORK, Richard 1974: Introduction to *Vorticism and its allies*, catalogue (London, Arts Council)

DAVIE, Donald 1973: *Thomas Hardy and British Poetry* (London, Routledge and Kegan Paul)

DERRIDA, Jacques 1967: *De la Grammatologie* (Paris, Minuit)

DICKSON, David 1974: *Alternative Technology, and the Politics of Technical Change* (London, Fontana)

DOUGLAS, Mary 1970: *Natural Symbols: Explorations in Cosmology* (London, Barrie and Rockcliff; New York, Pantheon)
1972: 'Self-evidence', in *Proc. of the Royal Anthropological Inst.*, 1972

ELLIK, Ron and EVANS, Bill 1966: *The Universes of E. E. Smith* (Chicago, Advent)

ELLUL, Jacques 1954: *La Technique ou l'enjeu du siècle* (Paris, Armand Colin; transl. as *The Technological Society*, Alfred A. Knopf, 1964, also Vintage paperback)

ELSEN, Albert E. 1973: *Pioneers of Modern Sculpture*, catalogue essay (London, Arts Council)

ETIEMBLE, R. 1954–61: *Le Mythe de Rimbaud* (Paris, Gallimard, 4 vols)

FRASER, John 1974: *Violence in the Arts* (London, Cambridge University Press)

GAGE, John 1972: *Turner: Rain, Steam and Speed* (London, Allen Lane)

GIEDION, Sigfried 1948: *Mechanization Takes Command* (Oxford and New York, Oxford University Press)

GOLDING, John 1970: 'Léger and the Heroism of Modern Life', in *Léger and Purist Paris*, exhibition catalogue (London, Tate Gallery)

GOODMAN, Nelson 1968: *Languages of Art: An Approach to a Theory of Symbols* (New York, Bobbs-Merrill; London, Oxford University Press)

GOSLING, John 1972: Some Observations on 'Paul Willis, "The motorbike within a subcultural group"', *Working Papers in Cultural Studies*, 3, Autumn 1972 (Birmingham, England)

GOWING, Lawrence 1966: *Turner: Imagination and Reality*, Museum of Modern Art catalogue (New York, Doubleday)

GREEN, Christopher 1970: 'Léger

and L'Esprit Nouveau 1912–28', in *Léger and Purist Paris* (London, Tate Gallery)

GROTOWSKI, Jerzy 1967: 'Towards a Poor Theatre', *Tulane Drama Review*, New Orleans, first published in Polish, 1965

HABERMAS, Jürgen 1971: 'Technology and Science as Ideology' (1968), in *Towards a Rational Society* (London, Heinemann)

HAMILTON, Alastair 1971: *The Appeal of Fascism, A Study of Intellectuals and Fascism 1919–1945* (London, Anthony Blond)

HANDLEY-READ, Charles 1958: 'Aspects of Victorian Architecture', in Pelican Guide to English Literature, *From Dickens to Hardy*, ed. B. Ford (Harmondsworth, Pelican)

HARRISON, Charles 1974: 'Abstract Expressionism', in *Concepts of Modern Art* (ed. A. Richardson and N. Stangos, Harmondsworth, Pelican); also published in *Studio International*, January and February 1973

HIGGENS, Andrew 1970: 'Art and politics in the Russian Revolution', *Studio International*, November and December 1970

HILL, Christopher 1972: *The World Turned Upside Down: Radical Ideas During the English Revolution* (London, Temple Smith)

HINDE, Robert A. (ed.) 1972: *Non-Verbal Communication* (London, Cambridge University Press)

HORKHEIMER, Max and ADORNO, Theodor 1944: *Dialectic of Enlightenment*, first published 1944; transl. 1972 (New York, Herder and Herder; London, Allen Lane)

HORVAT-PINTARIĆ, Vera 1970: *Vjenceslas Richter* (Serbo-Croat and English; Zagreb, Graficki Zavod Hravstke)

HULTÉN, K. G. Pontus 1968: *The machine as seen at the end of the mechanical age* (New York, Museum of Modern Art)

HUSSAIN, Farooq 1970: *Living Underwater* (London, Studio Vista)

ILLICH, Ivan D. 1971: *Celebration of Awareness, A Call for Institutional Revolution* (London, Calder & Boyars) 1973: *Tools for Conviviality* (London, Calder & Boyars)

JACOBS, Jane 1961: *The Death and Life of Great American Cities* (New York, Random; London, Jonathan Cape, 1965) 1969: *The Economy of Cities* (New York, Random; London, Jonathan Cape, 1972)

JAFFÉ, Hans (ed.) 1969: *De Stijl* (London, Thames & Hudson)

JAULIN, Robert 1974: 'Ethnocide and History', Royal Anthropological Institute News no. 3, July 1974, London

JENCKS, Charles 1971: *Architecture 2000: Predictions and Methods* (London, Studio Vista)

JOHNSON, Frank (ed.) 1973: *Alienation: Concept, Term and Meaning* (New York and London, Seminar Press)

KERMODE, Frank 1961: 'Poet and Dancer before Diaghilev', in *Modern Essays* (London, Fontana, 1971)

KLINGENDER, Francis D. 1968: *Art and the Industrial Revolution* (London, Evelyn, Adams & Mackay; posthumous ed. of work published first in 1947, revised by A. Elton; also in Paladin paperback)

LASSUS, Bernard 1974: 'De Plus à Moins' in *Nouvelle Revue de Psychanalyse*, Spring 1974

LAWRENCE, D. H. 1924: *Studies in Classic American Literature*, collected in *Phoenix* (London, Heinemann, 1936)
1932: *The Letters of D. H. Lawrence* (ed. A. Huxley, London, Heinemann)

LEAVIS, F. R. 1932: 'Babbitt Buys the World', *Scrutiny*, vol. I no. 1, May 1932
1944: 'Catholicity or Narrowness?', *Scrutiny*, vol. XII no. 4, Autumn 1944
1957: *D. H. Lawrence, Novelist* (London, Chatto & Windus)
1962: *Two Cultures: the Significance of C. P. Snow* (London, Chatto & Windus)
1970: (with Q. D. Leavis) *Dickens the Novelist* (London, Chatto & Windus)

LOMAX, Alan 1972: 'The Evolutionary Taxonomy of Culture', *Science*, 21 July 1972, vol. 177

McLUHAN, Marshall 1962: *The Gutenberg Galaxy* (Toronto, University of Toronto Press; London, Routledge and Kegan Paul)

MAIR, Lucy 1975: ' "Ethnocide" ', Royal Anthropological Institute News no. 7, March 1975, London

MARCEL, Gabriel 1935: *Etre et avoir* (Paris, Aubier)

MARCUSE, Herbert 1955: *Eros and Civilization* (Boston, Beacon; London, Sphere Books, 1969)
1958: *Soviet Marxism* (New York, Columbia University Press; London, Routledge & Kegan Paul)
1964: *One Dimensional Man* (Boston, Beacon; London, Routledge & Kegan Paul)
1968: *Negations* (London, Allen Lane; Boston, Beacon)

MARTIN, Marianne W. 1968: *Futurist Art and Theory, 1909–1915* (Oxford, Clarendon Press)

MARX, Karl 1900: *The Poverty of Philosophy* (1846–47, transl. H. Quelch, London, Twentieth Century Press)
1959: *Economic and Philosophic Manuscripts of 1844* (transl. M. Milligan, Moscow, Foreign Languages Publishing House)
1970: *Capital* (1867, transl. F. Engels, London, Lawrence & Wishart)
1971: *Early Texts* (transl. and ed. D. McLellan, Oxford, Basil Blackwell)
1973: *Grundrisse: Foundations of the Critique of Political Economy* (1857–58, transl. M. Nicolaus, Harmondsworth, Penguin Books)

MARX, Leo 1967: *The Machine in the Garden* (New York, Oxford University Press)

MAUSS, Marcel 1936: 'Les techniques du corps', *Journal de la Psychologie*, 32, March–April 1936

MERLEAU-PONTY, Maurice 1962: *Phenomenology of Perception* (London, Routledge & Kegan Paul, transl. from the French; first publ. in 1945 by Gallimard, Paris)

MÉSZÁROS, István 1970: *Marx's Theory of Alienation* (London, Merlin Press)

METZGER, Gustav 1970: 'Automata in history' (2 parts), *Studio International*, March and October

MILLETT, Kate 1969: *Sexual Politics* (New York, Doubleday)

MORTENSEN, William 1937: *The Model: A Book on the Problems of Posing* (San Francisco, Camera Craft Publishing)

NAIPAUL, V. S. 1967: *The Mimic Men* (London, André Deutsch)

NEWTON, J. M. 1967/8: 'The Great Art of Fellini?', *Cambridge Quarterly*, Winter 1967/8
1968: 'For the Tate's Crome Exhibition', *Cambridge Quarterly*, Autumn 1968

NICOLSON, Benedict 1968: *Joseph Wright of Derby, Painter of Light* (London, Routledge & Kegan Paul; New York, Pantheon, 2 vols)

NORTH, Marion 1972: *Personality Assessment Through Movement* (London, Macdonald & Evans)

OLIVER, Paul 1975: *English cottages and small farm-houses*, exhibition catalogue (London, Arts Council)

OLLMAN, Bertell 1971: *Alienation: Marx's Conception of Man in Capitalist Society* (London, Cambridge University Press)

O'NEILL, John 1972: *Sociology as a Skin-Trade: Essays towards a reflexive sociology* (London, Heinemann)

PAZ, Octavio 1970: 'The New Analogy: Poetry, Painting and Technology', 3rd Herbert Read Lecture (London, Institute of Contemporary Arts)

PIRSIG, Robert M. 1974: *Zen and the Art of Motorcycle Maintenance* (New York, William Morrow; London, Bodley Head)

POLHEMUS, Ted (ed.) 1975: *Social Aspects of the Body* (London, Allen Lane; New York, Random)

PRINCE, F. T. 1963: *The Doors of Stone*, poems (London, Rupert Hart-Davis)

RABAN, Jonathan 1974: *Soft City* (London, Hamish Hamilton)

RAVETZ, Jerome 1971: *Scientific Knowledge and its Social Problems* (London, Oxford University Press)

REED, Henry 1946: *A Map of Verona*, poems (London, Jonathan Cape)

REICHARDT, Jasia (ed.) 1968: *Cybernetic Serendipity*, ICA exhibition catalogue (London, Studio International)

RIVIÈRE, Jacques (d. 1925) 1960: *The Ideal Reader*, selected essays in transl. (London, Harvill)

RIVIÈRE, Jean-Loup 1971: 'Grotowski, le corps et le signe', *L'Autre Scène*, Cahiers du Groupe de Recherches Théatrales de l'Université de Caen, vol. 3, Spring 1971

ROSE, Steven and Hilary 1971: 'The myth of the neutrality of science', in *The Social Impact of Modern Biology*, ed. W. Fuller, (London, Routledge & Kegan Paul; New York, Doubleday)

ROSZAK, Theodore 1970: *The Making of a Counter Culture: Reflections on the Technocratic Society and its Youthful Opposition* (New York, Doubleday; London, Faber & Faber)
1972: *Where the Wasteland Ends: Politics and Transcendence in Post-industrial Society* (New York, Doubleday; London, Faber & Faber)

RUDOFSKY, Bernard 1965: *Architecture without Architects: A Short Introduction to Non-pedigreed Architecture* (New York, Museum of Modern Art)

SACHS, Curt 1937: *World History of the Dance* (New York, W. W. Norton)

SARTRE, Jean-Paul 1960: *Critique de la Raison Dialectique* (Paris, Gallimard)

SCHACHT, Richard 1970: *Alienation* (New York, Doubleday; London, Allen & Unwin)

SCHÖFFER, Nicolas 1970: *La Ville Cybernétique* (Paris, Tchou)

SERRES, Michel 1974: *Jouvences sur Jules Verne* (Paris, Minuit)

SEWELL, Elizabeth 1961: *The Orphic Voice* (London, Routledge & Kegan Paul)

SNOW, C. P. 1959: *The Two Cultures and the Scientific Revolution* (Cambridge, University Press)

SOHN-RETHEL, Alfred 1973: 'Mental and Manual Labour in Marxism', in *Situating Marx* (ed. P. Walton & S. Hall, London, Human Context Books)

STARKIE, Enid 1938: *Arthur Rimbaud* (London, Faber & Faber; reprinted 1961)

STAROBINSKI, Jean 1964: Introduction to *Discourse on the Origin of Inequality* in Rousseau, *Œuvres complètes*, vol. 3 (Paris, Pléiade)

STEINER, George 1962: 'F. R. Leavis', reprinted 1967 in *Language and Silence* (London, Faber & Faber; New York, Atheneum)

1972: *Extra-Territorial* (London, Faber & Faber; New York, Atheneum)

STOKES, Adrian 1932: *The Quattro Cento* (London, Faber & Faber)

1934*a*: *Tonight the Ballet* (London, Faber & Faber)

1934*b*: *The Stones of Rimini* (London, Faber & Faber)

1958: *Greek Culture and the Ego* (London, Tavistock)

1961: *Three Essays on the Painting of our Time* (London, Tavistock)

1963: *Painting and the Inner World* (London, Tavistock; the essay on Turner is reprinted in *The Image in Form*)

1965: *The Invitation in Art* (London, Tavistock)

1967: *Reflections on the Nude* (London, Tavistock)

1972*a*: *The Image in Form: Selected Writings* (ed. R. Wollheim, Harmondsworth, Penguin)

1972*b*: 'The future and art', *Studio International*, September 1972

SUSSMAN, Herbert L. 1968: *Victorians and the Machine: The Literary Response to Technology* (Cambridge, Mass., Harvard UP)

SUTHERLAND, Anne 1975: *Gypsies, the Hidden Americans* (London, Tavistock)

SYMONDS, John Addington 1882: *Renaissance in Italy: The Fine Arts* (London, Smith, Elder & Co.)

TEMKINE, Raymonde 1970: *Grotowski* (Paris, La Cité)

TOOP, David (ed.) 1974: *New/Rediscovered Musical Instruments*, pamphlet (London, Quartz Publications)

TRACHTENBERG, Alan 1965: *Brooklyn Bridge, Fact and Symbol* (New York, Oxford University

Press)

TUCKER, William 1972–73: 'Rodin: the language of sculpture', *Studio International*, December 1972 and January 1973

VIRMAUX, Alain 1970: *Antonin Artaud et le Théâtre* (Paris, Seghers)

WARBURG, Jeremy (ed.) 1958: *The Industrial Muse: The Industrial Revolution in English Poetry* (London, Oxford University Press)

WHITE, Lynn, Jr. 1962: *Medieval Technology and Social Change* (Oxford, Oxford University Press)

WILLIAMS, Raymond 1958: *Culture and Society* (London, Chatto & Windus)
1961: *The Long Revolution* (London, Chatto & Windus; New York, Columbia University Press)
1971: *Orwell* (London, Fontana Modern Masters)
1973: *The Country and the City* (London, Chatto & Windus)
1974: *Television: Technology and Cultural Form* (London, Fontana Paperbacks)

WILLIS, Paul 1972: 'The motorbike within a subcultural group', *Working Papers in Cultural Studies*, 2, Spring 1972, (Birmingham, England)

1975: 'The expressive style of a motor-bike culture' in *The Body as a Medium of Expression* (ed. J. Benthall & T. Polhemus, q.v.)

WOLLEN, Paul 1971: 'Art in Revolution: Russian art in the twenties', *Studio International*, April 1971

WOLLHEIM, Richard 1965: Introduction to Adrian Stokes, *The Invitation in Art* (q.v.)
1968: *Art and its Objects* (Harmondsworth, Penguin Books; New York, Harper & Row)
1972: Introduction to Adrian Stokes, *The Image in Form* (q.v.)

WORRINGER, Wilhelm 1928: *Egyptian Art* (London, G. P. Putnam's Sons)

WRIGHT, Frank Lloyd 1953: *The Future of Architecture* (New York, Horizon Press; London, Architectural Press, 1955)

WYNDHAM LEWIS, D. B. and LEE, Charles (eds.) 1935: *The Stuffed Owl: An Anthology* (London and Toronto, Dent)

YOUNG, Robert M. 1972: 'The Human Limits of Nature', in *The Limits of Human Nature* (ed. J. Benthall; London, Allen Lane; New York, Dutton)

ZAMYATIN, Evgeny 1920: *We* (1970, new transl. from the Russian, London, Jonathan Cape)

Index

Page numbers in italics indicate illustrations

Adams, Henry 164
Adorno, Theodor 71–2, 92
Althusser, Louis 144
Amis, Kingsley 44, 158–9
Antonioni, Michelangelo 144
Arbus, Diane 108
Artaud, Antonin 130–3, 181
Asselineau, R. 213
Atget, Eugène 59

Balla, Giacomo *120*
Banham, Reyner 58, 61
Barthes, Roland 74
Bateson, Gregory 131
Baudelaire, Charles Pierre 200
Bazalgette, Sir J. 35–6
Beattie, Alan 110, 112
Beck, Julian 132
Bell, Daniel 63, 207
Bellamy, Edward 40
Bellow, Saul 171–9, 182–3, 192
Benjamin, Walter 200
Berger, John 17, 100–1, 103–4
Blake, William 17, 31, 67–79, 83, 85, *120*, 130, 171, 197–8, 209, 213
Boas, George 29
Boccioni, Umberto 55
Bragaglia, Anton 55
Brancusi, Constantin 103, *122*
Broadbent, John B. 67, 76, 138–9
Brown, Norman, 70, 136, 209
Burke, Edmund 15, 85
Burnham, Jack 33, 104, 135, 208
Burnham, James 40
Burns, Robert 69
Burton, Decimus 35–6, *117*
Butler, Samuel 52
Byron, Lord 69

Carlyle, Thomas 88, 143, 164
Charvet, J. 212
Chekhov, Anton 84

Chesneaux, Jean 39
Chomsky, Noam 63
Clark, Kenneth 17, 100–2, 180
Clark, Lygia 134
Clay, Cassius 136
Clayre, A. 212
Cleaver, Eldridge 136
Clough, A. H. 210
Coleridge, S. T. 75
Comte, Auguste 39
Conrad, Joseph 37, 83
Cook, Peter 61
Cooper, Douglas 58
Courbet, Gustave 102, *121*

Darby, Abraham 145
Darré, R. W. 91
Darwin, Erasmus 26, 28–9, 31–2
Davie, Donald 181–2
Degas, Edgar 102
Delacroix, Eugène 102
Derrida, Jacques 149, 182
Dickens, Charles 31, 37, 213
Dickson, David 190, 212
Doesburg, Theo van 58
Douglas, Mary 70, 214
Duchamp, Marcel 105
Duncan, Isadora 111, 211
Dyer, John 31

Eliot, George 37
Eliot, T. S. 61, 95
Ellis, Havelock 69, 84
Ellul, Jacques 145–6, 156–9, 213
Elsen, Albert E. 102–3, 210
Emerson, R. W. 164
Empson, William 192
Epstein, Jacob 208
Etiemble, R. 84

Fanon, Frantz 136
Fellini, Federico 34, 71

Fleming, Alexander 145
Fleming, Ian 23
Forster, E. M. 91
Freud, Sigmund 69, 72, 74, 78, 84, 130
Fuller, Buckminster 61–2, 208
Fuller, Loïe 109

Gabo, Naum 57
Gauguin, Paul 72, 103
George, Stefan 72, 91
Giedion, Sigfried 144
Goethe, Johann Wolfgang von 78
Goodman, Nelson 129–30
Goodman, Paul 63, 209
Gosling, John 197–8
Gowing, L. 210
Graham, Martha 111, *127*, 181
Grotowski, Jerzy 131–3, 181

Hamilton, David 202
Hardy, Thomas 69, 181–2
Harrison, Charles 106–7, 138
Higgens, Andrew 55–6
Hinton, Michael 135
Hopkins, G. M. 170–1
Horkheimer, Max 71–2, 92
Houdini, Harry 205
Hussain, Farooq 62
Huxley, Aldous 95–100, 131

Ihnatowicz, Edward 194
Illich, Ivan 190–2
Ingres, J. A. D. 102, *121*
Inness, George 34, *115*

Jacobs, Jane 64, 187
James, Henry 22
Jaulin, Robert 97, 210
Johns, Jasper 106

Kandinsky, Wassily 106
Keats, John 75
Kepes, Gyorgy 194–5
Kermode, Frank 109–10
Klein, Melanie 206
Klein, Yves 106
Klingender, Francis D. 25–35, 206
Klüver, Billy 62
Kristeva, Julia 80

Laban, Rudolf von 112
Lassus, Bernard 188
Lawrence, D. H. 24, 44, 56, 61, 69, 72, 75, 78, 84, 87–94, 97, 130, 131, 143–4, 168–72, 179, 210
Leavis, F. R. 17, 47, 61, 73, 80, 87, 89–91, 179, 193, 213
Ledoux, Claude Nicolas 31

Léger, Fernand 58–60, 170
Lenin, Nicolai 40, 144, 147
Lévi-Strauss, Claude 27
Living Theater *128*, 132, 181
Lomax, Alan 109
Loyola, Ignatius 69

MacBeth, George 210
McLuhan, Marshall 62, 144
Mair, Lucy 210
Malevich, Kasimir 57, 106
Malina, Judith 132
Malinowski, Bronislaw 97
Mallarmé, Stéphane 109
Malthus, Thomas 31
Manet, Edouard 102
Mao Tse-tung 179
Marcel, Gabriel 160, 213
Marcuse, Herbert 19, 63, 74, 78, 95, 136, 144–6, 204, 209
Marinetti, F. T. 54–6
Marx, Karl (and Marxism) 15, 19, 25, 40, 48, 65, 71, 73, 87, 91, 105, 140–51, 154–5, 159, 171, 173, 177, 183, 186
Marx, Leo 34, 163
Mauss, Marcel 19, 155–61, 183
Mead, Margaret 97, 131
Merleau-Ponty, Maurice 24, 160, 178–9, 196
Metzger, Gustav 212
Michelangelo 104
Millett, Kate 210
Mondrian, Piet 57, 106
Montaigne, Michel de 152
Morris, William 69, 143, 154
Mortensen, William 101

Naipaul, V. S. 74
Negroponte, Nicholas 194
Nicolson, Benedict 27, 30
Nietzsche, Friedrich Wilhelm 69, 72, 78, 84, 209–10
Nijinsky, Vaslav 110–11, *126*, 132

Ollman, B. 212
Oneida Community 201
O'Neill, John 135–6, 196
Orwell, George 95–100, 131
Owen, Robert 201
Ozenfant, Amédée 58–9

Pal, George 50
Paz, Octavio 95, 113
Pirsig, Robert M. 214
Pollock, Jackson 106, 108, *123*
Pope, Alexander 32
Prince, F. T. 94–5

Raban, Jonathan 198–9
Ransom, John Crowe 73
RAT Theatre 133–4
Ravetz, Jerome 190
Reed, Henry 94
Reich, Wilhelm 78, 110
Renoir, Pierre Auguste 102
Richter, Vjenceslas 62
Riefenstahl, Leni 91–2
Rietveld, Gerrit 57
Rimbaud, Arthur 17, 69, 72, 79–84, 130, 209
Rivière, Jacques 110–11, 132
Rochelle, Drieu la 91
Rodin, Auguste 55, 103–5, *122*
Roebling, John 36
Rosso, Medardo 55, 103
Roszak, Theodore 63, 78–9, 209
Rousseau, Jean-Jacques 17, 19, 55, 67, 97, 140, 150–5, 171, 182, 192, 212
Rubin, Jerry 136
Ruskin, John 54, 143, 207, 210
Russell, Bertrand 91

Sachs, Curt 109–10
Sade, Marquis de 74–5
Saint-Point, Valentine de 56
Saint-Simon, Comte de 39–40
Sapien, Darryl 135
Sartre, Jean-Paul 71
Schiller, Friedrich 88
Schöffer, Nicholas 61
Scoglio, Joseph 112
Serres, Michel 46, 207
Seward, Anna 32
Sewell, Elizabeth 32
Shakespeare, William 27, 211
Shaw, G. B. 52
Sleigh, Sylvia 101
Smart, Christopher 76
Smiles, Samuel 35–7
Smith, E. E. 23, 206
Sohn-Rethel, Alfred 149, 156–7
Snow, C. P. 61, 193

Starobinski, Jean 153
Steiner, George 133, 193
Stokes, Adrian 17, 24, 27, 100, 101, 103, 105, 180, 188, 206, 207, 210, 211, 212
Storey, David 102
Stubbs, George 90, 102
Sussman, Herbert L. 208, 209
Sutherland, Anne 214
Sykes, Peter 133–4
Symonds, J. A. 101

Tatlin, Vladimir 57
Tennyson, Alfred, Lord 38, 165, 207
Toop, D. 211
Tsai, W. Y. 194
Trachtenberg, Alan 206, 211
Tucker, William 103
Turner, J. M. W. 33–4, 35, 104, *115*, 207, 210

Veblen, Thorstein 40
Verlaine, Paul 79
Verne, Jules 38–49, 54, 84, *118–19*, 171, 207–8

Wells, H. G. 46–54, 91, 171
Weyde, William van der 108, *124–5*
White, Lynn 144
Whitman, Walt 13, 18, 69, 130, 163–71, 174, 179, 183, 185, 199–201
Wigman, Mary 111
Williams, Raymond 47, 73, 208, 212
Willis, Paul 137–8, 196–8
Wollen, Peter 57
Wollheim, Richard 27, 210
Worringer, Wilhelm 189
Wordsworth, William 37–8, 68, 73, 75–6, 79, 164
Wright, Frank Lloyd 171, 208
Wright, Joseph 26–35, 58, 100, *114*
Wyndham Lewis, Percy 208

Yeats, W. B. 84–7, 91–4, 110, 130, 179
Young, Robert M. 146

Zamyatin, Evgeny 95–9